W9-AGT-728

REIMAGINING
THE CALIFORNIA LAWN

Water-conserving Plants, Practices, and Designs

REIMAGINING THE CALIFORNIA LAWN

Water-conserving Plants, Practices, and Designs

Carol Bornstein, David Fross, Bart O'Brien

Cachuma Press
Los Olivos, California

DEDICATIONS

To Ralph Philbrick, whose encouragement and confidence in me helped launch the California chapter of my life. To my mom for assigning me to the flower beds instead of the lawn and to my dad for letting that be his department.—Carol Bornstein

For the staff of Native Sons Wholesale Nursery.—David Fross

Without you, there is nothing: to the plants of the world (except weeds). And to the memory of my grandparents, Bart and Kate Sullivan whose ranch had a truly Californian mixed lawn of grasses, freesias, English daisies, lippia, clovers, Ipheion, wild onions, and plantains. They, and their garden, will be with me always.—Bart O'Brien

Copyright © Cachuma Press 2011

First edition

All rights reserved. No part of this book may be reproduced in any form or by any electronic or mechanical device without written permission of the publisher. Request for permission to make copies of any part of the work should be mailed to: Cachuma Press, P.O. Box 560, Los Olivos, California, 93441.

All photographs in this book are protected by copyright.

Writers: Carol Bornstein, David Fross, Bart O'Brien
Editors: Marjorie Popper and John Evarts
Proofreaders: Marjorie Lakin Erickson and Sue Irwin
Graphic Design and Production: Katey O'Neill
Photography: All photos are by John Evarts except for those credited to other individuals.
Printed in Singapore

Library of Congress Cataloging-in-Publication Data

Bornstein, Carol, 1953-
 Reimagining the California lawn : water-conserving plants, practices, and designs / Carol Bornstein, David Fross, Bart O'Brien. -- 1st ed.
     p. cm.
 Includes bibliographical references and index.
 ISBN 978-0-9789971-2-0 (pbk. : alk. paper) -- ISBN 978-0-9789971-3-7 (hardcover : alk. paper)
 1. Xeriscaping--California. 2. Gardens--California--Design. 3. Lawns--California. 4. Drought-tolerant plants--California. I. Fross, David, 1946- II. O'Brien, Bart, 1956- III. Title. IV. Title: Water-conserving plants, practices, and designs.

 SB475.83.B67 2011
 635.9'5209794--dc22

                                            2010048136

Front cover, clockwise from upper left: *Artichoke agave and blue fescue.* / *California native meadow.* CHAD SLATTERY / *Blue oat grass, lavender, and bluebeard.* SAXON HOLT / *Blut ice plant.* SAXON HOLT / *UC Verde buffalo grass (background).* • Back cover, from top: *Spanish lavender and deer grass.* / *Hybrid yarrow and autumn sage.* / *Blue chalksticks and thread-leaf agave.* • Page i: clockwise from upper left: *Gold tooth aloe.* / *Blue grama.* / *French lavender.* / *California goldenrod.* STEPHEN INGRAM • Page ii: *Canyon Prince wild rye and autumn moor grass.* SAXON HOLT • Page iii: *Hybrid yarrow.*

CONTENTS

For decades, California horticulturists, nursery owners, and garden designers have been promoting landscape alternatives to water-consumptive lawns. One popular option is a greensward of clustered field sedge (shown). SAXON HOLT

INTRODUCTION

Lawns are the most ubiquitous element in the cultivated American landscape. While the concept of the lawn emerged in England and France as early as the 1500s, it did not gain widespread popularity in the United States until after the Civil War. American landscape designer Andrew Jackson Downing published *Treatise on the Theory and Practice of Landscape Gardening* in 1841, and in this influential book he extolled the idea of an expanse of "grass mown into a softness like velvet." One of Downing's associates, Calvert Vaux, later teamed up with Frederick Law Olmsted in a competition to gain the honor of designing a park in the center of New York City. They won the contest in 1858 with a concept they called the "Greensward Plan," and their pastoral vision for Central Park included flowing swaths of lawn. Olmstead, considered the father of American landscape architecture, saw the lawn as a type of community parkland and championed its use as a unifying element in residential development.

As utilization of turfgrass in urban parks and other public spaces increased, the lawn idea spread to residential landscapes and gardens. Although initially limited to the estates of the wealthy, lawns began to attract the interest of Americans of more modest means, especially with the emergence of suburbs. Affordable new technology, in the form of a hand-pushed lawnmower, likely played a role in our embrace of the lawn as a manageable and attractive feature of the suburban lot. When Englishman Edwin Budding first introduced the lawnmower in 1830, he touted his new invention by claiming, "Country gentlemen will find in using my machine an amusing, useful and healthful exercise." Lawns became a symbol of comfort and social status, and they followed settlers west across the developing American landscape. They were considered so important that Frank J. Scott, in his 1870 book, *The Art of Beautifying Suburban Home Grounds,* states persuasively, "A smooth, closely shaven surface of grass is by far the most essential element of beauty on the grounds of a suburban house."

Lawns appealed to our sense of aesthetics and prestige. As Michael Pollan noted in *Second Nature* (1991), they served "to provide a suitably grand stage for the proud display of one's own house." Lawns also came to fill a practical need with the emergence of "set-backs," which stipulated that new homes be built a minimum distance—often 25 feet or more—from the street. Supported by Olmstead and others, this idea was eventually codified into most of the country's municipal planning codes. The overwhelming landscaping choice for these front yards was turfgrass, often accompanied by a few ornamental plants. Olmsted's design for a residential community outside Chicago deliberately connected each front garden so that the landscape read like a park. Careful maintenance of one's lawn for the good of all would became part of the social contract in suburbs from coast to coast.

A lush green carpet of turfgrass remains the standard landscape feature for most new homes and subdivisions. SAXON HOLT

Deeply associated with leisure, recreation, and communal spaces, the lawn is now entrenched in the national psyche, much like baseball and Thanksgiving. A $40 billion-per-year lawn-care industry encourages homeowners to beautify and connect their neighborhoods with a seamless and comforting green carpet. Today, about 50,000 square miles of manicured turf—an area nearly 1/3 the size of California—cloak the country in a shroud of velvety green. A University of Ohio study found that 600 additional square miles of lawn are added each year as a result of new development. What currently dominates these lawn plantings is a handful of grasses, most of them exotic: Kentucky bluegrass from Europe and northern Asia, Bermuda grass from Africa, and zoysia grass from Asia. Only a few lawn grasses are North American natives, and fewer still are native to California. Installed as monocultures and managed as turf, such plantings unfortunately offer little or no value as habitat for most of our indigenous fauna.

The lawn appears to be an indispensable part of our horticultural heritage and yet this question is now frequently asked: To what extent is our love affair with the lawn sustainable, if at all? The resources necessary to maintain a luxuriant carpet of turfgrass—especially in a private residential setting—have received increasing scrutiny in recent years. The recognition of resource limits and a concern about toxic lawn-care chemicals have helped spawn an "anti-lawn" movement. Critics who describe lawns as "unnatural" or a "wasteful luxury" point out that American lawns are treated with more pesticides and herbicides per acre than any other crop grown in the country. This trend was recognized as early as 1962, with the publication of Rachel Carson's historic work, *Silent Spring*. She called attention to the indiscriminate use of pesticides in our front yards with the observation, "One may get a jar-type attachment for the garden hose, for example, by which such extremely dangerous chemicals as chlordane or dieldrin are applied as one waters the lawn." Although these specific pesticides are no longer available, others have taken their place, and additional chemicals, including herbicides and synthetic fertilizers, are regularly applied to lawns. Some chemical manufacturers suggest up to five applications of their product a year to achieve a healthy, visually satisfactory lawn. Many of these chemicals do not remain stationary and cycle freely into the surrounding environment. In his book, *American Green* (2006), Ted Steinberg suggests that the lawn is "a nationwide chemical experiment with homeowners as guinea pigs."

Our soil and water are not the only unintended recipients of lawn-care pollutants. Until recently, the use of a typical 3.5-horsepower gas mower for one hour released as many volatile organic compounds—which are precursors to smog—as driving a new car for about 350 miles. In the 1990s, California's Air Resources Board established a tiered series of new emissions standards for small-engine products, and the volume of noxious fumes from lawn-mower engines is fortunately now on the decline. When it comes to global warming, lawns have been viewed as carbon "sinks" that remove carbon dioxide from the air and store it as organic carbon in the soil, but a recent study at the University of California at Irvine disputes this notion. The research notes that chemical fertilizers applied to lawns give off nitrous oxide, a greenhouse gas 300 times more powerful than carbon dioxide. The study concluded that when all the typical lawn-grooming inputs and management practices are factored in—ranging from fertilizer production to mowing and re-sodding—turfgrass areas in parks and playing fields are actually net emitters of greenhouse gases.

There are myriad reasons to reconsider the traditional lawn, but in California and other arid Western states, the most compelling argument is quite simple: lawns demand too much water. Five rivers provide the majority of California's water: the Colorado, Sacramento, San Joaquin, Kern, and Owens rivers. Other smaller rivers and their watersheds contribute an additional and critical share, including the Russian, Carmel, Salinas, Santa Ynez, Ventura, Los Angeles, Santa Ana, and San Diego rivers. Dammed, allocated, and shipped through a convoluted system of aqueducts, pipelines, and canals, many of these rivers are used to exhaustion, and their once-abundant fisheries have nearly vanished. About 20% of all the electricity and more than 30% of the natural gas consumed in California are used to pump, convey, and treat our water. This vast water infrastructure has made it possible for the lawn to become a fixture of the California landscape.

Climatologists, ecologists, and hydrologists have warned for some years that the supply of available water is going to fall in western North America. A 2010 study commissioned by California's state legislature called for substantial reductions in pumping from the overtaxed Sacramento-San Joaquin River Delta, a source of water for approximately two out of three state residents. The original 1934 allotment of the Colorado River is based on a 21-million-acre-foot annual flow, but the actual average annual flow since 1934 has been lower by 2 million acre feet. Miscalculations aside, the realities of drought, silting reservoirs, population growth, and climate change present enormous challenges, both today and in the future.

One of the top industries in California is agriculture, and it utilizes the principal share of the state's water resources and infrastructure. Up to 80% of the state's developed water goes to farmers, with the rest directed to urban and suburban consumption, along with a small amount diverted for the conservation of native fauna and flora. As much as 70% of the water flowing to California's cities and suburbs is used to support our gardens and other outdoor features, such as hot tubs and swimming pools. The typical suburban lawn in California consumes approximately 50% of this water, or about 45,000 gallons per year for a modest-sized front and backyard suburban lawn. Official lawn census data is not available, but it is estimated that up to 300,000 acres of California are covered in residential lawn. Collectively, lawns are irrigated with as much as 1.5 million acre-feet of water per year; this amount equals the household water demands of 3 million suburban homes. Considered another way, California's residential lawns take up the entire annual flow of the Owens and Kern rivers. California is the only mediterranean-climate region of the world in which lawns are the landscape norm, from expansive estates to modest suburban homes. The typical California lawn has become an

Above: Like many California rivers, virtually all of the Kaweah River is diverted for agricultural, residential, and industrial use.
Left: About 50% of the water applied to landscapes in California is used for irrigating lawns.

extravagance, and it clearly cannot be sustained on the scale of its current expression.

A number of California water districts now pay their customers to remove lawns and convert them to less water-consumptive landscapes. These districts recognize that reduced demand is a necessity and that conservation promises to be the primary source of additional water. The website of the Metropolitan Water District of Southern California unequivocally states, "Conservation is a basic element of Metropolitan's long-term water strategy." Recycled water also provides significant resources for gardens and landscapes, and its use, as well as research into the long-term results of its application, continues to grow. Some water districts even encourage the use of artificial turf, paying customers a $0.30 premium for every square foot purchased. Although seemingly an easy solution, artificial turf

presents serious environmental problems: it heats the urban and suburban environment, increases storm runoff and flooding potential, decreases groundwater percolation, and can harbor harmful bacteria.

Lawn replacement has taken a number of forms across the country as meadows, kitchen gardens, greenswards, hardscapes, and other alternatives fill the space formerly occupied by lawns. Garden writers have explored and championed a variety of no-lawn landscapes in recent books. Heather Flores, in *Food Not Lawns* (2006), and Fritz Haeg, in *Edible Estates* (2008), suggest removing lawns and filling them with edible plantings. Rick Darke, in *The Encyclopedia of Grasses for Livable Landscapes* (2007), and John Greenlee, in *The American Meadow Garden* (2009), make the case that meadows and other uses of plants in the extensive grass family offer a broad array of graceful options. Debra Lee Baldwin, in *Designing with Succulents* (2007), introduces a rich palette of succulent-plant possibilities, while Beth Chatto championed the gravel garden in *The Dry Garden* (1988). Other writers, like Olivier Filippi, in *The Dry Garden Handbook* (2008) and Heidi Gildemeister, in *Gardening the Mediterranean Way* (2004), point to the inherent beauty of plants from dry climates and urge us to consider our arid climate thoughtfully. California's celebrated flora and natural habitats have inspired a resurging interest in using native plants for lawn-replacement gardens. At least three newer titles focus exclusively on the horticultural virtues and versatility of our state's native species, including: *California Native Plants for the Garden* (2005) by the authors of this book; *Native Treasures: Gardening with the Plants of California* (2006) by M. Nevin Smith; and *Designing California Native Gardens* (2007) by Glenn Keator and Alrie Middlebrook.

In *Reimagining the California Lawn,* we present a variety of alternative designs and describe hundreds of durable species and selections that can be used in place of a traditional lawn. We provide detailed advice on how to take that first step—reducing the size of your lawn or, better yet, removing and replanting it with something entirely new. There is no insistence on hard rules or boundaries, and your garden's style may naturally evolve over time. You might start with a drought-resistant greensward that you later transform into a meadow or rock garden. A groundcover carpet that begins with a single perennial may be converted into a tapestry as more species are added to the mix. A vegetable and cut-flower garden could transition into a meadow of wildflowers and native grasses if your time becomes too constrained for tending your produce. Form and function are a matter of taste, and the choices are intoxicatingly plentiful. We hope this book's exploration of lawn alternatives serves as a catalyst. The guide to a beautiful California landscape with water-conserving plants is at your fingertips.

A diverse palette of plants and virtually unlimited design options are available when creating lawn alternatives. This garden pairs artichoke agave with blue fescue.

CHAPTER ONE

GARDEN DESIGNS FOR LAWN REPLACEMENT

For decades, the lawn has been the common denominator in California gardens. All too often, this is simply because turfgrass is the default choice for covering flat surfaces. The lawn has also remained popular because it performs many functions in our landscapes. It serves as a play area, an outdoor room, or as an additional horizontal surface to handle overflow from hardscapes such as patios. Turf provides a connective tissue between different plantings, materials, pathways, and levels in the garden, and it can be a green "canvas" that surrounds beds, mounds, and other more sculptural features. Larger expanses of grass work as cooling "air conditioners," preserve unobstructed views to and from homes, and add defensible space to properties in regions prone to wildfires.

A turfgrass lawn may be versatile, but its drawbacks—especially in California's mediterranean and desert climates—are multiple and well documented: it offers minimal aesthetic interest, generates substantial green waste, and is virtually useless to wildlife. Foot for foot, it requires more water, labor, fertilizer, pest control, herbicide, and equipment than almost any other type of garden installation. For these and other reasons, many Californians are seeking plants and designs that offer an alternative to the traditional lawn. Fortunately, every function that turfgrass fulfills can be equally satisfied with a different plant or combination of plants.

Whether you envision a garden space that imitates a lawn or want to create an entirely different kind of landscape, you'll find an abundance of design choices. The alternatives presented in this chapter focus on six broad garden styles that can be used to replace a traditional lawn: greenswards, meadow gardens, rock gardens, succulent gardens, carpet and tapestry gardens, and kitchen gardens. We also discuss rooftop gardens, known as green roofs. These design options generally have two things in common: they are low in profile and most fulfill the ground-covering role that lawns traditionally perform in the landscape. Although appropriate for a lawn conversion, designs that produce a higher profile—such as a woodland garden—are not featured.

Some of this chapter's design alternatives, such as greenswards, share many similarities with lawns; others, such as rock gardens and kitchen gardens, represent a more dramatic departure from the lawn in terms of function, form, and maintenance. Each alternative includes suggestions on appropriate usage of that particular style, historical examples within California and from afar, design tips, and installation and maintenance recommendations. In addition, there is a list of recommended plants to use with each design alternative. All of the selected plants for the lists are drawn from species and cultivars featured in the Plant Profiles section of the book.

Spreading lantana has been used as a lawn alternative in California for decades.

PLANNING THE LAWN-REPLACEMENT GARDEN

Lawns often account for a significant portion of a property's landscape, and when you remove or reduce an area of turfgrass, you may be surprised how much space you have to work with. Before making any decisions, start by itemizing your short- and long-term goals for the site. It's a good idea to ask yourself: "What do I want to do with the space now occupied by the lawn?" Your answer to that question should drive the planning process. For example, if your goal is to create a relatively simple, grass-dominated garden that is more sustainable than a traditional lawn, a greensward or a meadow may be the perfect solution. If you are seeking a landscape that is perhaps more visually complex and features some specimen plants, a succulent or tapestry garden could be the answer. If you are interested in food production and your lawn occupies a sunny area, a kitchen garden may be an enticing option. Some spaces contain ample room for more than one composition; you might design a carpet of perennials that backs up to a rock garden or create a greensward that is tucked into a meadow.

A vital step in designing any garden is to conduct a thorough inventory of the site, including its microclimate, soil type, patterns of light and shadow over the course of the year, air movement, and other features such as dry spots or poorly draining wet zones. Consider having your soil tested if you are unsure of its pH, texture, chemical composition, potential contaminants, compaction level, and drainage. Assess all existing plants and decide which ones you wish to keep or remove along with the lawn. Make note of any views that could be enhanced by judicious screening or framing.

As part of the initial design process, it's a good idea to find out if there are landscape regulations in your community with which you must comply. Many municipalities and homeowners associations have strict guidelines about the heights of walls, setbacks for trees, and use of vegetation in yards or parkways that front on a public right-of-way. In addition, some cities have planning codes that require homeowners to landscape these areas with a certain percentage of live vegetative cover. For example, replacing a large front lawn with only a handful of small plants or leaving the site bare for an extended period could be a violation of local ordinances.

For both budgeting and planning, you will need to decide whether your vision for the new garden includes hardscape features, such as a patio, stepping stones, or retaining walls. With the exception of greenswards and some meadows, which can handle multi-directional foot traffic, most garden plans need to give some consideration to circulation—how best to move among or around the plantings. Like other hardscape elements, the cost of pathways will greatly vary, depending on the materials used and the craftsmanship required for their installation. Beyond pathways, the need for hardscape elements in your garden will largely depend on how you want to use the space and the limits of your budget. A hardscape installation can be basic, such as wood-framed beds in a kitchen garden, or quite fancy, such as a sandstone terrace, outdoor fireplace, and fountain in a succulent garden. Designs and plants that can replace your lawn are the focus of this book, but more details about the materials that you might consider for any hardscape features are discussed under "The Hardscape Option," beginning on page 49.

Most lawns occupy a flat plane, but once the turf is removed, you are free to shape the soil into beds or mounds. Such raised areas add visual interest to a design, and equally important, they can offer improved drainage on sites with soils that drain poorly. Your new garden area will usually have enough topsoil to gather and shape into low mounds; other designs, however, may require more significant additions of soil. If you want a set of deep beds for a kitchen garden or are planning a series of high mounds for a rock garden, it may be necessary to purchase additional soil from a landscape contractor, nursery, or other outside source. As with hardscape features, your garden budget should take

Top: A new landscape features blue fescue. STEPHEN INGRAM
Bottom: Two low-growing cultivars of coyote brush, Pigeon Point and Twin Peaks #2, cover a gentle slope. STEPHEN INGRAM

Steps of native sandstone and a pathway of silver carpet are key elements in this lawn-replacement design.

Above: A low mound, planted with Cedros Island verbena and other mediterranean-climate species, offers visual interest and improved drainage.
Left: A carpet planting of gazania can be a relatively low-maintenance alternative to a lawn.

Top: Silver Carpet California aster, maritime ceanothus, and Point Sal Spreader sage create a tapestry of California natives. CAROL BORNSTEIN
Bottom: Blue chalksticks, Agave franzosinii, *and Zwartkop aeonium thrive in a succulent garden.* STEPHEN INGRAM

into account the expense of importing soil (if necessary) as well as other materials, such as boulders for a rock garden, soil amendments for a kitchen garden, or commercial mulches to top off the surface of a new tapestry planting. Gardeners who are contemplating a green roof should be especially cognizant of material costs and logistics, since they are essentially creating an entire living landscape from scratch.

The style of garden you choose should reflect how much time you personally want to spend maintaining the landscape, or how much money you are willing to pay to have someone else perform this task. If you need to hire an outside gardening service, the cost of maintenance can add up. Plus, there is really no such thing as a maintenance-free landscape; if you aren't spending some time tending the plants on your property, then by definition it is not truly a garden—a cultivated plot of land. Your investment in labor and maintenance will vary with the design you favor and the degree of its complexity. A basic greensward of red fescue or a carpet of woodland strawberry will require different care than a diverse tapestry with shrubs, perennials, and grasses that need pruning, shearing, and deadheading.

The location of the lawn you are converting may help determine the design you select for its replacement. For example, when considering a garden for an unfenced front yard that faces a busy street, you may want to ask yourself: "How much time do I want to spend maintaining a landscape in this very public location?" If your answer is "not much time," then a groundcover of succulents that needs infrequent weeding will be preferable to a high-yield kitchen garden that needs to be tended several times per week. Some gardeners are delighted to "make a statement" with their highly visible front-lawn conversions. A vibrant meadow of California natives may signal your embrace of a different landscaping ethic—one that reflects the region's botanical heritage, acknowledges its seasonal drought, and provides sustenance to its indigenous fauna. A succulent garden on a suburban street flanked by turfgrass yards might boldly declare your affinity for the world's mediterranean plant life and the long history of this horticultural

Yankee Point ceanothus forms a front-yard groundcover that looks good year-round.

tradition in California. When the lawn replacement is in a tranquil back yard, a rock garden designed for quiet contemplation may be ideal. In a narrow side yard, you might replace the grass with a tapestry of fragrant shrubs and perennials that soften the effect of enclosing walls.

Once you have settled upon a design and prepared the site, get your new garden off to the best possible start by planting in autumn. Although you can certainly plant during any season, nearly all planting in California is best done in fall, when the air temperatures cool, rainstorms begin to arrive, and soils are still relatively warm. The actual timing varies from year to year and from place to place. "Fall" sometimes comes much earlier in northern California, often in September, while in inland southern California the fall planting season may not start until late October or even November. Keep in mind that dry spells are quite common during the rainy season, and vulnerable new plants will need supplemental irrigation to prevent them from drying out.

If water conservation is a high priority in your decision to replace the lawn, be prepared to retrofit your existing irrigation system so that it suits whatever new planting scheme you design. The initial cost will pay for itself in water savings over time. Seek advice from your local water purveyor or a landscape professional if you need assistance planning and installing a new system. If you select plants that are well matched to your climate zone, garden site, and soil, you may not need to install permanent irrigation at all; instead, you might opt to provide temporary irrigation during the all-important establishment period and then let plants "sink or swim" on rainfall alone. Watering cans and garden hoses can actually be the most practical method for watering young plants, particularly if you eventually intend to rely almost entirely on natural precipitation. Even the most drought-tolerant plants will likely need some supplemental water after planting. This establishment period will vary, depending upon soil type, watering

Top: This California cottage garden combines the flowers of society garlic, Spanish lavender, and Mexican sage.
Bottom: A few boulders provide accents in this large-scale planting of rosemary.

regime, age of the plant at installation, and time of year when planting. In general, consider a plant to be established when it has doubled or tripled in size and/or after it has been in the ground for two or three summers.

Regardless of your watering system, mulching offers an easy and cost-effective way to help retain soil moisture. Mulch also minimizes extremes in soil temperatures, controls weeds, and conceals drip irrigation tubing. When you spread a layer of organic mulch over the bare surfaces of a landscape, the material mimics the layer of leaves, twigs, and other debris that

A layer of mulch retains moisture in a young landscape with Canyon Prince wild rye, penstemon, and other plants.
STEPHEN INGRAM

Top: Herbs, vegetables, and flowers are companions in this attractive kitchen garden. SAXON HOLT
Bottom: Many nurseries now carry alternatives to turfgrass, such as water-conserving grasses and sedges.

accumulates on the ground in a wide variety of natural habitats. As it breaks down, organic mulch changes soil chemistry, texture, and fertility in ways that are beneficial to many plants. However, gardens with species that originate from drier habitats where there is minimal organic debris—such as deserts and some scrublands and grasslands—are often better served by an inorganic mulch of gravel or pebbles since these materials more closely simulate the soil-surface conditions in such environments. A nutrient-rich organic mulch can favor soil fungi that are pathogenic to plants accustomed to lean soils, particularly succulents. When using mulch, leave space around the plant crowns, and in high fire-danger areas, limit the depth of organic materials to 4 inches or less. Whenever possible, use mulches obtained from local sources, such as the chipped wood generated by tree trimmers working in your neighborhood or the mulch that municipalities or recycling companies create from green waste.

Like many gardeners, you may prefer to replace your lawn by primarily using California native plants. This preference may stem from a desire to create a garden that reminds you of a favorite wild landscape or blends into the surrounding natural area. You may also want a landscape with plants that have evolved in California and have a well-deserved reputation for drought tolerance and hardiness when properly sited. In addition, native plants are the best choices for habitat gardens, which can help sustain native fauna. Although pollinators will take advantage of the nectar and pollen from a wide variety of flowers, for example, many indigenous insect species depend exclusively on native plants for larval food. All of the design options featured in this book can be implemented with California natives. The "Selected Plant Palette" lists that accompany each of this chapter's design alternatives include a number of California native

species and cultivars. (For further information on growing California native plants, see our book, *California Native Plants for the Garden.*)

In the pages that follow, we offer up a variety of garden styles and techniques for reimagining your lawn. Let these examples spark your imagination and help you capitalize upon the unique features of your site to plan a composition that is right for you. Whether you live along the immediate coast or reside high up in the mountains, you can use any one of the following design alternatives to create a water-conserving, low-maintenance California garden. Think of losing your lawn as the first step along the garden path of horticultural discovery and delight.

Dune sedge and Berkeley sedge are blended together in this inviting greensward. SAXON HOLT

A greensward is generally defined as a sweep of grass, sedge, or other grasslike plants that provides a surface accessible to varying degrees of foot traffic. It can fulfill most of the same functions as a traditional lawn and, when mowed or trimmed into a short, dense mat, it is in fact a type of lawn. A managed greensward takes on a formal appearance similar to turfgrass yet may require less water, fertilizer, and other chemicals. A greensward can also be an informal, naturalistic, and low-maintenance feature in a landscape, evoking one of California's native grassland habitats.

Due to their great versatility, greenswards are a widespread element in residential, commercial, and even industrial landscapes. They are utilized in settings as diverse as front and back yards, slopes, banks, drainage basins, dog runs, parks, parkways, and median strips in roads. In the home garden they serve in much the same fashion as a lawn, providing textural and visual contrast to formal beds of color, lines of shrubs, and perennial borders. They also function as a cooling transition from the reflective surfaces of sidewalks, walls, and parking areas. One of the underappreciated aspects of greenswards is their capacity to collect and absorb water that runs off from impermeable surfaces, such as roofs, driveways,

A greensward of California native grasses borders a meadow at the Santa Barbara Botanic Garden.

and roads. During rainstorms, greenswards can serve as bioswales, slowing, guiding, and filtering runoff before it moves into local watercourses.

HISTORY AND EXAMPLES

The lawns that characterize much of California's urban and suburban landscapes were born of greenswards and meadows. In many ways, the original greenswards were

A front-yard planting of blue fescue makes effective use of the tufted appearance of this popular grass.

This well-manicured greensward demonstrates how tufted hair grass can be managed like a traditional lawn. DAVID FROSS

pastures, farmyards, village greens, and similarly utilitarian spaces. These grass-dominated swards were kept low by livestock grazing and hand scythes, and later, by mowing machines. In most areas of the country, rainfall was the sole source of moisture for early greenswards. In more arid regions, supplemental water was supplied with the assistance of hand pumps, windmills, and irrigation ditches. These technologies were eventually replaced by powerful electric pumping stations, massive canals, and an array of other sophisticated water storage and delivery systems—essential infrastructure for sustaining greenswards in California's mediterranean climate, with its long, dry summers.

The relatively casual approach to greenswards in the 19th century evolved into something quite different by the mid-20th century. With the development of new grass selections and intensive management practices, a perfectly cultivated expanse of turf became the centerpiece of many iconic cultural landscapes, such as the infield of Dodger Stadium, the greens of Pebble Beach Golf Course, the verdant slope of Forest Lawn Cemetery, and the multipurpose lawns in countless municipal parks. These lush, manicured surfaces became part of our horticultural identity, and millions have tried to emulate them in their own yards. This love affair with turf has placed inordinate demands on residential water supplies, and for years water purveyors have been suggesting that we reconsider the concept of a lawn; some even pay homeowners to replace them with other alternatives.

There are some greensward alternatives to the traditional lawn that have emerged in the 21st century, and good public examples are scattered around the state. The Leaning Pine Arboretum on the campus of California Polytechnic State University, San Luis Obispo has an outstanding lawnlike greensward of clustered field sedge. The University of California, Santa Barbara has installed a buffalo-grass commons at the northeast side

of its Manzanita Village residential area. At Castaways Park in Newport Beach, the city's Parks and Recreation Department has replaced turfgrass with dune sedge and reduced its water use on the site by more than 30%.

Cherished by naturalists and plant enthusiasts alike, California's wild greenswards are an intriguing source of possible species for reimagining the lawn. Some sites are little more than surviving pockets of natural populations that were once abundant. Others are more extensive, and are even expanding with assistance from restoration ecologists. In cooler areas of the state, you might see a drift of Idaho fescue in the Siskiyou Mountains or a dune swale filled with clustered field sedge near Point Sal State Park. Warmer climate zones claim some of the state's larger native grass-dominated remnants, such as at the Santa Rosa Plateau Ecological Reserve where visitors can see various sedges, three species of needlegrass, deer grass, and dune bent grass.

DESIGN AND INSTALLATION

Embracing the concept of a greensward is just the starting point when working with this elastic design alternative. A greensward can consist of a single species, such as an entire surface of blue grama grass, buffalo grass, or blue sedge, or it can be a combination of compatible species, such as a blend of Patrick's Point red fescue, Pacific hair grass, and clustered field sedge (these three would create a California native-plant interpretation of the concept). Depending on the species, the foliage colors may vary from the traditional lawn's emerald green or blue-green to silver-blue and yellow-green, or even a seasonal brown to blond.

When selecting plants for a greensward, take into consideration its intended uses, the local climate, and the desired level of maintenance. Plant texture, form, and size will determine the grasses or sedges that are most suitable for various uses. Some present a flat plane

Top: Buffalo grass can be closely mowed or left uncut for a tousled look. STEPHEN INGRAM
Bottom: Creeping red fescue creates a lush greensward in this backyard. STEPHANIE CURTIS

The seasonal appearance of grasses and sedges may shape your plant selections as well. For a backyard that sees frequent winter or cool-season use, clustered field sedge might make a better candidate than buffalo grass, since the latter is fully dormant in winter. However, for a lawn located in a hot climate zone, buffalo grass would be better looking in summer than the sedge.

A desire to reduce resource consumption is a guiding principle behind contemporary greensward designs. Your success with this goal will depend on your chosen plant palette and the degree of maintenance that you deem necessary. For example, a small lawn converted from a water-consumptive grass, such as Kentucky bluegrass, to a greensward of blue grama grass, would offer substantial water savings. In addition, a blue grama grass greensward needs only an annual trimming, so this substitution would result in less labor and lower energy inputs. Switching from one species of grass to another does not always achieve a significant reduction in water use, but it may result in less mowing and fewer chemicals. This would happen when a fescue lawn, which often requires weekly mowing, is replaced with an autumn moor grass greensward that only needs to be trimmed every four to six weeks. Another example would be to replace a lawn of dune bent grass with one of clustered field sedge; this might end the need for fertilization or other chemical applications.

A number of variables will collectively determine how long it will take to establish a greensward. It can range from a few months to a year or more, depending on the season of planting, site preparation, size of plants, plant spacing, and irrigation schedule. Placing plants closer initially can shorten the establishment period. You can use plugs or liners or 4-inch and even 1-gallon container plants. Young plants from 4-inch containers may be more vigorous than older ones in 1-gallon pots, and they might fill in more rapidly. The smaller plugs and liner sizes are more vulnerable to desiccation when first installed if irrigation is not monitored carefully. The roots of plugs and some

when mowed or string-line trimmed, while others, although still walkable, have a wavy or tufted surface. Dune bent grass is fine textured with a low spreading habit, and when mowed it is suitable for lawn games and picnics. Blue moor grass has a tufted habit with a coarse texture, and although it is appropriate as a greensward choice, playing croquet on a blue moor grass greensward would prove difficult, even if it were mowed regularly. Blue sedge can withstand regular mowing to retain a low profile, but it has a cleaner appearance if left untrimmed. When cut, the blade tips of blue sedge turn brown, and their rough texture creates a less appealing surface for sitting. Buffalo grass has a running habit; it can be mowed and treated as a traditional lawn, or it can be left uncut for a handsome tousled appearance. Idaho fescue will form an attractive grassland greensward in dry, hot interior valleys, and while you could walk on or through it, this tufted bunchgrass would be a poor choice for an area dedicated to lawn activities, even if trimmed regularly.

Blue grama grass, seen here at the Santa Barbara Botanic Garden, requires less water than most turfgrasses. SAXON HOLT

liners are tightly woven into the container, and these roots should be teased apart with your fingertips before planting to encourage them to move into the surrounding soil. Well-grown plants from 4-inch containers can offer quicker coverage and be as economical as plugs if you cut each one into four pieces with a sharp knife before installation. Until the plants are well rooted and actively spreading, you may need to use a barrier to protect them from gophers, moles, rabbits, deer, pets, and other animals.

MAINTENANCE AND SPECIAL ISSUES

Weeding and watering a new greensward are critical tasks. To rein in future weed infestations, inspect the containers holding your new plants to ensure they are weed free. Your greensward plants will need more frequent applications of water when they are first installed, and unfortunately, a combination of regular moisture and open ground during this establishment period allows weeds to flourish. Although many of the grasses and sedges we recommend for a greensward are effective competitors, vigilant observation and weed removal during this period are essential to prevent weed infestations and to reduce long-term maintenance requirements. Once your greensward has filled in, weeds will be less problematic.

Greensward maintenance—especially mowing and watering frequency—is use driven. A greensward of blue grama grass could be mowed with the regularity of a traditional lawn, particularly if lawn games and picnics are prime uses; but if it serves mostly as a low-growing and walkable groundcover, it will do equally well with only a seasonal trimming to remove aging flower stalks. Clustered field sedge can be enjoyed for its tousled appearance when left untrimmed or it can be manicured into a fine green plane. Water requirements vary with plant choice and the gardener's tolerance of plant dormancy. Some species, like clustered field sedge and blue grama grass, will become infused with varying colors of blond, amber, and brown without summer water and, once established, they can be cultivated without irrigation. Modest summer water might maintain plants with green hues and brown tips while more frequent watering might produce little or no summer dormancy. Most existing irrigation systems will handle the water requirements of lower-growing greensward plant choices, but you will need to adjust sprinkler heads to deliver water efficiently to a taller species, especially if it is left untrimmed. Retrofitting the heads is typically the only fix necessary to accommodate a taller greensward.

SELECTED PLANT PALETTE FOR GREENSWARDS

Used in combination or alone, the following choices offer exciting possibilities for California greenswards. For those who wish to maintain a turflike surface that will be used for frequent foot traffic or outdoor lawn

This recently mowed swath of Catlin sedge displays the informal look of many greenswards. SAXON HOLT

activities, some of the best choices are: dune bent grass, blue grama, buffalo grass, dune sedge, clustered field sedge, tufted hair grass, and red fescue and its cultivars. The optimal California climate zones for growing each plant appear in brackets after the plant name and are abbreviated as follows: c = coastal; i = inland; cv = Central Valley; ld = low desert; hd = high desert; m = mountain; all = all zones. (For more information on the zones, see page 57.) The + indicates plants that need more water than others on this list. California native plants appear in **green type**.

Agrostis pallens, **dune bent grass** [c, i, cv]
Bouteloua curtipendula, **side-oats grama** [all]
B. gracilis, **blue grama** [all]
Buchloe dactyloides **and cultivars, buffalo grass** [all]
Carex divulsa, **Berkeley sedge** [c, i, cv, m]
C. flacca, **blue sedge** [c, i, cv, m]
C. pansa, **dune sedge** [c, i, cv]
C. praegracilis, **clustered field sedge** [all]
C. subfusca, **mountain sedge** [all]
C. texensis+, Catlin sedge [c, i, cv]
Deschampsia cespitosa, **tufted hair grass** [c, i, cv, m]
D. c. var. *holciformis,* **Pacific hair grass** [c, i, cv, m]
Festuca glauca **and cultivars, blue fescue** [all except ld]
F. idahoensis, **Idaho fescue** [all except ld]
F. mairei, **Maire's fescue** [all except ld]
F. rubra+ **and cultivars, red fescue** [all except ld]
Leymus triticoides **and cultivars, creeping wild rye**
    [all except ld]
Sesleria autumnalis+, **autumn moor grass** [all]
S. caerulea+, **blue moor grass** [all except m]
S. 'Greenlee's Hybrid'+, **Greenlee's Hybrid moor grass** [all]

MEADOWS

This meadow features native grasses and perennials grown from seed collected in the homeowner's local watershed. SAXON HOLT

Imagine a landscape ablaze with wildflowers, graced by swaying grasses, and filled with butterflies, birds, and beneficial insects. Who wouldn't want such a lively, colorful scene in their own garden? No wonder such meadow gardens continue to grow in popularity. They appeal to that streak of independence and wildness within us and remind us of the beauty of wide-open spaces.

Botanically speaking, the word "meadow" is sometimes used interchangeably with "grassland" or "prairie," and a meadow is in fact a kind of grassland. Typically devoid of trees and shrubs, grasslands are characterized by an open expanse of grasses, sedges, annual and perennial wildflowers, and bulbs. In California, many botanists restrict the term "meadow" to high-elevation plant communities that stay fairly moist throughout the summer growing season, but in this book, meadows are more broadly defined to encompass grasslands in general.

For the gardener, an important feature of a meadow garden—unlike a greensward—is that it includes herbaceous perennials, annuals, or bulbs along with the grasses and sedges. Since many meadow plants will not tolerate regular foot traffic, a greensward is a better choice for spaces that will see more intensive activities, such as outdoor play. But if you do not need a garden

The California native plant meadow at San Francisco Botanical Garden provides inspiration for residential meadow gardens.

with the resilience of turf, a meadow offers one of the most alluring options for lawn replacement.

HISTORY AND EXAMPLES

Similar to greenswards, the earliest meadow gardens were precursors to today's lawns. These flowery meads included grasses and other plants and were created by transplanting patches of sod from natural meadows into

Above: This backyard meadow of grasses, sedges, and flowering perennials was designed to create habitat for local fauna.
Left: Sulfur buckwheat, elegant clarkia, and common yarrow add seasonal color to this front yard meadow planting.

Yarrow and lupines enliven a meadow planting of Berkeley sedge that surrounds an outdoor fire pit. SAXON HOLT

the private gardens of wealthy landowners. Grazing sheep and manual scything were used to help keep the mead about six inches tall. Over time, the loosely maintained style of meadow lost favor, and the meadow garden was replaced by the more manicured greens that we know today as lawns.

By the early 1900s some landscape designers began to rebel against the formal treatment of gardens. Prominent among them was Jens Jensen, a Danish immigrant who became a respected landscape designer in the United States. Jensen advocated a return to a naturalistic approach in landscape and became a vocal proponent of preserving and protecting Midwestern prairies. His efforts, and those of other conservationists, awakened an interest in the use of grasses as ornamentals. It was not until the 1960s, however, that grasses began to enjoy widespread appreciation for their ornamental value. Nurserymen Karl Foerster in Germany and Kurt Bluemel in the United States championed the use of grasses; their advocacy helped inspire the designs of James van Sweden and Wolfgang Oehme, who pioneered the "New American Garden," a visionary approach that embraced our vanishing grasslands. This style brought undulating drifts of bunchgrasses and herbaceous perennials into public spaces. Finally, grasses were "in," at least on the East Coast and in the Midwest. It took several more years for this idea to catch on out West. Today, grasses are now commonplace in California's landscapes, but their use in naturalistic meadows or grasslands in public spaces is still relatively scarce compared to residential installations.

A few excellent public examples of native meadow gardens are well worth visiting. Perhaps the most renowned is the meadow at the Santa Barbara Botanic Garden. Today, this constantly evolving one-acre tableau features a rich tapestry of native grasses and wildflowers. The award-winning native garden in the Strybing Arboretum at the San Francisco Botanic Garden is a lovely assemblage of both wet and dry meadows framed by a shrubby border. In Berkeley, the Regional Parks Botanic Garden offers several displays that replicate native grasslands from around the state.

Native grasslands and meadows once covered huge swaths of the state but are now greatly diminished due to encroachment by agriculture, grazing, urbanization, and the invasion of exotic species. However, gardeners seeking to create their own personal meadow can still find numerous examples on public lands from which to draw ideas and inspiration. The UC Davis Jepson Prairie Reserve in Solano County offers spring wildflower displays and a large variety of native grasses. For moist montane meadows, Tuolumne Meadows in Yosemite National Park is a much-loved site known for its array of sedges and delicate wildflowers. Point Reyes National Seashore is home to coastal prairies that include plants such as tufted hair grass and Douglas iris. Extensive serpentine grasslands at the Blue Ridge Lake Berryessa Natural Area in the North Coast ranges provide intriguing examples of grasses and wildflowers that thrive in harsh, dry situations.

DESIGN AND INSTALLATION

From a design standpoint, meadows are by definition naturalistic and informal. The commingling of grasses and wildflowers—the very essence of a meadow—does not lend itself to routine mowing, shearing, and dead-heading. Indeed, a major appeal of the meadow garden is vibrant change throughout the seasons—from young green or silvery shoots to elongating wandlike stems and unfolding blossoms and finally to ripening seed heads and subtle autumnal colors. The buzz and hum of wildlife and the motion of wind-tossed grasses are other dynamic elements of the meadow that make this type of landscape so enticing.

In nature, meadows are incredibly complex ecosystems; their assemblages of wildflowers and grasses are often tightly knitted together, and individuals are hard to discern. Similarly, the composition of the meadow garden is best treated as a whole, in contrast to the way you would maintain the distinct plantings of a perennial border. If you are comfortable with the aesthetic of some plants in bloom while others are dormant, you can enjoy these seasonal changes and plan to cut everything back all at once. Keep in mind that a meadow garden with greater plant diversity is usually more complicated to maintain. If one of your goals is to have a lower-maintenance landscape, avoid the temptation to use too many species in your meadow garden.

Whether complex or simple, meadows offer a more visually interesting composition than traditional lawns. Their seemingly random patterns and naturalistic appearance are well suited to rural or informal settings. For properties that border native habitats, meadows make an excellent bridge between formal gardens and adjacent wild areas. Meadows are equally striking when partnered with modern architecture, providing contrast to the bold lines and dramatic forms typical of contemporary structures. In fact, a well-designed meadow will complement any architectural style.

The first step in planning a meadow garden is deciding whether you want a meadow with both tall and short plants or one that is more lawnlike and composed of lower-stature plants. Next, decide whether you want the meadow to be green or brown in summer. If you wish to replicate the natural cycle of our mediterranean climate's moist winters and dry summers, choose cool-season grasses, such as nodding needlegrass or tufted hair grass; these grow during the cooler months and enter dormancy when the soil begins to dry out in summer. Although you can stretch their growth period with some judicious supplemental irrigation, most cool-season grasses perform best when allowed to rest during the hot summer months. A few summer-blooming wildflowers, such as California fuchsias, buckwheats, or goldenrod, will add vibrant color and complement the silvers and tans of the drying grasses. If your meadow is going to feature warm-season grasses, several good choices include grama grass, deer grass, and dropseed. As with any kind of garden, settling upon a color scheme will help to further refine your plant palette.

Spend time thinking about the overall shape of your meadow garden and how it will be viewed. The fine

Canyon Prince wild rye (foreground), autumn moor grass, and blue oat grass grow together in a meadow garden. SAXON HOLT

In spring, colorful wildflowers almost overwhelm this meadow of creeping red fescue on the left. SAXON HOLT

The arching inflorescences of deer grass lend vertical interest to a seasonally dry meadow of deer grass and dune sedge. SAXON HOLT

Above: Douglas iris blooms with California fescue at the Regional Parks Botanic Garden in Tilden Park. SAXON HOLT
Left: California poppies brighten a needlegrass meadow.

textures of many grasses and wildflowers are enhanced when framed by a backdrop of bolder woody plants, a fence, or a wall. Also consider how you will move through the garden, since meadows are meant to be walked through, rather than walked upon. Paths can be constructed of non-living materials such as gravel, flagstone pavers, mulch, or bare earth. For a softer effect, and where foot traffic will be minimal, consider planting the pathways with tough, low-growing species that need little to no mowing, such as grasses, sedges, common yarrow, or silver carpet. Your meadow garden will benefit from the careful placement of a focal point such as a favorite shrub, a bench, or a piece of sculpture to bring visual weight to the composition year-round.

Meadow gardens can be installed in one of several ways: by seeds, plugs, larger container-grown plants, or a combination of all three. Your budget and time frame will influence which method to select. Starting a meadow exclusively from seed eliminates the labor of planting individual pots but will require more vigilant weed control and watering during the germination phase. Planting from plugs is less expensive than using plants from 4-inch or 1-gallon containers, but the smaller root systems of plugs dry out more quickly during the days and weeks immediately after transplanting. Using larger plants initially costs more, but this strategy also produces a more instant landscape. Seeding rates, spacing of container-grown plants, and irrigation methods are all dependent upon the species used. With seeds and plugs, avoid the inclination to sow or transplant annual wildflowers in the first year as the latter can quickly out-compete young grasses. Regardless of method, cool-season grasses and wildflowers are best seeded or planted in fall or early winter, whereas warm-season species perform better when set out in spring.

MAINTENANCE AND SPECIAL ISSUES

Even with thoughtful planning, implementation, and initial care, the maintenance demands of a meadow garden can be considerable. Weed management is crucial during the early development stages, even if the site was previously landscaped with a relatively weed-free lawn. Nearby gardens, seed packets, and container-grown plants may harbor weedy grasses and forbs that will invariably find their way into your new meadow. Learning to distinguish between desirable seedlings versus weedy ones will be critical to the successful establishment of your meadow.

A meadow garden can be designed to thrive on natural rainfall. Supplemental irrigation should only be necessary when dry spells occur during the rainy season. In most climate zones of California, an occasional deep watering of your meadow during dry summer months may prolong its flowering and extend the growing season beyond the normal cycle.

Annual mowing or pruning of the meadow in late summer or fall accomplishes several tasks at once: it removes dead flower stalks and dried leaves; rejuvenates grasses, sedges, and perennial herbs; and reduces the fire hazard posed by seasonally dry vegetation. Be sure to wait until some seeds have ripened before cutting plants back if you want to encourage a new crop of seedlings next year and visits from the many songbirds and small mammals that feast on these seeds.

SELECTED PLANT PALETTE FOR MEADOW GARDENS

The list of possibilities for a meadow garden is practically limitless. In addition to the grasses and herbaceous perennials listed here, consider adding bulbs and annual wildflowers for seasonal color, preferably after the grasses have become established. California poppies, lupines, and clarkias are just a few of the many easy-to-grow native annuals from which to choose. The optimal California climate zones for growing each plant appear in brackets after the plant name and are abbreviated as follows: c = coastal; i = inland; cv = Central Valley; ld = low desert; hd = high desert; m = mountain; all = all zones. (For more information on the zones, see page 57.) California native plants appear in green type.

Achillea filipendulina and cultivars, fernleaf yarrow [all]
A. millefolium and cultivars (not all are native), **common yarrow** [all]
A. 'Moonshine', Moonshine yarrow [all]
A. 'Salmon Beauty', Salmon Beauty yarrow [all]
A. 'Taygetea', Taygetea yarrow [all]
A. 'Terracotta', Terracotta yarrow [all]
Agrostis pallens, **dune bent grass** [c, i, cv]
Aristida purpurea, **purple three-awn** [all]
Artemisia ludoviciana, **western mugwort** [all]
Aster chilensis and cultivars, **coast aster** [c, i, cv]
Bellis perennis, English daisy [all except ld]
Bothriochloa barbinodis, **silver beardgrass** [c, i, cv]
Bouteloua curtipendula, **side-oats grama** [all]
B. gracilis, **blue grama** [all]
Buchloe dactyloides and cultivars, **buffalo grass** [all]
Carex divulsa, **Berkeley sedge** [c, i, cv, m]
C. flacca, blue sedge [c, i, cv, m]
C. pansa, **dune sedge** [c, i, cv]
C. praegracilis, **clustered field sedge** [all]
C. subfusca, **mountain sedge** [all]
C. texensis, Catlin sedge [c, i, cv]
Deschampsia cespitosa, **tufted hair grass** [c, i, cv, m]
D. cespitosa var. *holciformis,* **Pacific hair grass** [c, i, cv, m]
Dierama pendulum, fairy wand [c, i, cv, m]
D. pulcherrimum, fairy wand [c, i, cv, m]
Erigeron glaucus and cultivars, **seaside daisy** [c, i, cv]
E. karvinskianus and cultivars, Santa Barbara daisy [c, i, cv, ld]
Eriogonum umbellatum, **sulfur buckwheat** [all except ld]
Festuca californica and cultivars, **California fescue** [c, i, cv, m]
F. glauca and cultivars, blue fescue [all except ld]
F. idahoensis and cultivars, **Idaho fescue** [all except ld]
F. mairei, Maire's fescue [all except ld]
F. rubra and cultivars, **creeping red fescue** [all except ld]
Fragaria chiloensis and cultivars (not all are native), **beach strawberry** [c, i, cv]
F. vesca ssp. *californica* and cultivar, **woodland strawberry** [c, i, cv, m]
F. vesca ssp. *vesca* and cultivars, woodland strawberry [c, i, cv, m]
Gaura lindheimeri, gaura [all]
Helictotrichon sempervirens, blue oat grass [c, i, cv, m]
Iris arilbred hybrids, arilbred iris [all]
I. douglasiana, **Douglas iris** [c, i, cv, m]
I. germanica hybrids, bearded iris [all]
I. Pacific Coast hybrids, **Pacific Coast hybrid iris** [c, i, cv, m]
I. spuria, butterfly iris [all]
I. unguicularis, winter iris [c, i, cv]
Lessingia filaginifolia and cultivars, **California aster** [c, i, cv]
Leymus cinereus, **Great Basin wild rye** [all]
L. condensatus and cultivar, **giant wild rye** [c, i, cv]
L. triticoides and cultivar, **creeping wild rye** [all except ld]
Muhlenbergia capillaris and cultivars, pink muhly [all]
M. dumosa, bamboo muhly [all except m]
M. emersleyi, bull grass [all]
M. lindheimeri, Lindheimer's muhly [all except m]
M. pubescens, soft blue Mexican muhly [all except m]
M. rigens, **deer grass** [all]
Nassella cernua, **nodding needlegrass** [c, i, cv]
N. lepida, **foothill needlegrass** [c, i, cv]
N. pulchra, **purple needlegrass** [c, i, cv]
Oenothera californica, **California evening primrose** [all except coastal]
O. missouriensis, Ozark suncups [all]
O. speciosa and cultivars, Mexican evening primrose [all]
Pennisetum orientale, oriental fountain grass [all except ld]
Sesleria autumnalis, autumn moor grass [all]
S. caerulea, blue moor grass [all except m]
S. 'Greenlee's Hybrid', Greenlee's Hybrid moor grass [all]
Solidago californica, **California goldenrod** [all]
S. canadensis ssp. *elongata,* **Canada goldenrod** [all]
Sphaeralcea ambigua and cultivars, **apricot mallow** [all]
S. philippiana, trailing mallow [c, i, cv, ld]
Sporobolus airoides, **alkali sacaton** [all]
S. heterolepis, **prairie dropseed** [all]
S. wrightii, **giant sacaton** [all]
Stipa gigantea, giant feather grass [c, i, cv]
Verbena bonariensis and cultivar, purple top [all except m]
V. gooddingii, **Goodding's verbena** [all except m]
V. lilacina and cultivars, **Cedros Island verbena** [c, i, cv, ld]
V. rigida, vervain [all]
Zauschneria californica and cultivars, **California fuchsia** [all]
Z. septentrionalis, **Humboldt County fuchsia** [all]

ROCK GARDENS

Agaves and other succulents are mainstays of this modernistic rock and gravel garden. JENNIFER CHEUNG

Boulders. Rocks. Stones. Cobbles. Gravels. Pebbles. Sands. These natural materials are found throughout California and, in both their wild and man-made constructs, have provided inspiration to many a gardener seeking a well-grounded aesthetic for their plants and landscapes. The contemporary California rock garden has embraced both classic European and traditional Asian styles of rock gardening and has melded them into a broader concept comprising a considerably wider array of plants and settings.

HISTORY AND EXAMPLES
The first uses of rocks in gardens were strictly utilitarian and were incidental to the garden itself. Rocks formed the walls that surrounded ancient gardens, and various rock materials were often employed as the surface of paths or as edging for garden beds.

The earliest-known appearances of rocks as decorative components in gardens occurred in both Europe and Asia, and each of these regions developed distinct styles of rock gardens. Grotto or cavelike structures built from rocks were often seen in early Roman gardens of southern Europe. Over time, these structures evolved into ferneries and re-creations of specific mountain

French lavender adds an accent to the river cobbles covering this bank.

scenes. Eventually, this led to the development of rock gardens for growing alpine plants. In Asia, rocks and boulders were used in gardens to evoke both paradise and wild landscapes. Probably the most famous Asian rock garden is Ryoanji in Kyoto, Japan. This Zen Buddhist masterpiece is composed of fifteen stones set in a large rectangle of carefully pattern-raked sand. At the Huntington Botanical Garden in San Marino, the

Karesansui portion of the Japanese Garden is directly inspired by Ryoanji and is one of the best public examples of a dry Zen garden in California.

There are California gardens that show nearly every phase of rock garden history, though most modern rock gardens in the state reflect a blending of historical precedent as informed by the natural landscape. The University of California Botanical Garden in Berkeley provides several impressive rock gardens. Among the most notable are two composed of California native species; one features plants that are adapted to serpentine soils and another exhibits alpine plants. The nearby East Bay Regional Parks Botanic Garden has a number of rock-centric garden displays; its long-established sea-bluff garden is particularly effective, and the southern California desert collection is exemplary. Portions of the California Channel Islands garden at the Fullerton Arboretum function as a rock garden at a grand scale. Californian-Asian heritage gardens demonstrating extensive use of rocks and stone can be seen in the Japanese Tea Garden in Golden Gate Park in San Francisco, Hakone Gardens in Saratoga, the UCLA Hannah Carter Japanese Garden in Los Angeles, and in The Huntington's Chinese Garden, *Liu Fang Yuan,* or the Garden of Flowing Fragrance.

Some of our most famous California rock gardens are also succulent gardens. The Desert Garden at The Huntington Botanical Gardens in San Marino, the New World Desert Collection at the University of California Botanical Garden in Berkeley, the Cactus Garden at Lotusland in Montecito, and the desert gardens at The Living Desert in Palm Desert are exemplary rock gardens that feature succulents.

Due to its extraordinary geologic diversity, California offers a wide variety of natural rock gardens. Whether you live along the coast or in the hills or mountains,

local wildland parks and natural areas will usually have interesting rock outcrops to study and observe. And wherever you travel, there are rock gardens at the grandest of scale. Draped across the lofty spine of the Sierra Nevada, a chain of wilderness areas encompass alpine fell-fields where hikers are treated to summer-blooming carpets of buckwheats and other low-growing perennials. Wind-shorn ceanothus add to the picturesque beauty of Big Sur's coastal bluffs and cliffs. Agaves and yuccas are juxtaposed among the jumbled monoliths of Joshua Tree National Park.

DESIGN AND INSTALLATION

The most important consideration when designing a rock garden is the interplay between plant and mineral elements. The plants should look good with the rocks—regardless of whether the rocks are native or were imported to the site. In general, rock-garden plants tend to be small or moderate in size. Many successful rock gardens have featured herbaceous perennials, small succulents, and subshrubs that do not overpower their rock partners in the garden. Due to their diminutive stature and showy flowers, alpine plants have long been favored for use in European-style rock gardens. Other than size, there are few restrictions to heed when choosing your

Lavender cotton's blue-gray foliage wraps around boulders edging a flagstone pathway. SAXON HOLT

Shrubby monkeyflower and Cedros Island verbena accentuate the natural contours of these boulders. STEPHEN INGRAM

A variety of California native plants, including sages and California poppies, flourish in a backyard rock garden.

plant palette, but be sure to consider your local climate. Some succulents and herbaceous perennials, for example, will perform best in coastal rock gardens, while heat-tolerant plants, such as cacti and agaves, make good choices for interior and desert rock gardens.

Successful rock gardens can be among the most expensive gardens to construct, as they demand a significant investment in time, labor, equipment rental, and materials. Most properties do not have a ready supply of large rocks or boulders, which makes it necessary to arrange for the purchase, delivery, and placement of rocks for the new garden. The topography of a rock garden is central to its design, and your plan may call for mounds, berms, or similar features. In addition, you may need to incorporate a specialized soil mixture in some areas, depending on the plants you want to grow.

The rock structure of the garden is a permanent feature, and even though a rock garden may have a rather raw initial appearance, the growth of foliage and flowers will soften the overall presentation with each passing year. The decision whether to feature mass plantings of few types of plants or to choose a wide range of different plants will greatly influence the garden's design and will determine future maintenance requirements.

The arrangement of the rocks in a rock garden demands careful consideration. The most renown and celebrated rock gardens have been fashioned by skilled and experienced artisans, but you can succeed if you take the time to do a little advance research. (Our bibliography features several books that cover the construction of natural-looking rock outcrops and gardens.) A good rule of thumb for the placement of large rocks and boulders dictates that they should be roughly one-half to one-third buried. Rocks that have been "planted" in this manner appear to be firmly grounded in the garden and give the landscape a feeling of permanence and age.

This front yard rock garden utilizes a plant palette of aloes, dudleyas, sedums, lavender, and sage.

In addition to judicious citing of boulders, the rock garden design should embrace a long-term vision of how the plantings will fill in as they mature. Without careful selection and positioning, some plants will quickly obscure the very rock features that make this kind of design alternative so visually appealing.

The placement of rocks and boulders creates a variety of microhabitats tailored to suit a wide array of plants. This diversity presents you with many opportunities: you could tuck small plants requiring exceptionally fast drainage into the crevices between rocks; display heat-loving plants against south-facing boulders; locate plants that prefer cool, shady sites at the base of north-facing rocks; or place specimens that favor heavier soils and more water at the bottom of a slope. All these possibilities make rock gardens especially attractive to avid plant collectors.

The insertion of a rock garden into an existing garden requires that you pay particular attention to the location of current and future plantings of large shrubs and trees. In general, these larger plants should be grown far away from rock gardens, because their roots are typically much more invasive, grow more rapidly, and usually out-compete the smaller rock garden perennials and

Bright sandstone boulders offset the rough texture of clustered field sedge, seen here during the dry season.

subshrubs. Their roots may also undermine and disrupt rock outcrops and the overall arrangement of the rocks. The structure and foliage of trees and large shrubs can adversely affect the growth and survival of rock garden plants as well, by producing too much shade and excessive organic debris.

MAINTENANCE AND SPECIAL ISSUES

The more diverse the garden, the more care and attention it will require. A complex rock garden with many species is frequently challenging to water, weed, and groom, but one with a simplified plant palette will be far easier to care for. Much like a succulent garden, a durable rock garden will likely require a period of experimentation in order to determine the best set of plants for your particular site and your maintenance skills. Ongoing weeding and clean up of organic debris are two of the tasks that will keep a rock gardener busy.

After a number of years, some plants may inevitably begin to dominate the view and cover the rock "bones" of the garden. When the garden reaches this stage, you will have to decide whether to prune and/or remove plants to reveal once again the underlying rock structure or to allow unfettered plant growth.

GRAVEL GARDENS

Gravel gardens are a distinct subcategory of rock gardens. The predecessors of contemporary gravel gardens have their origins in Asian, Islamic, and French pattern/parterre gardens in which different colors and sizes of gravels were used to make patterns on the ground or where a single gravel or sandy material was raked into patterns. Today's California gravel gardens have evolved greatly since then and have been influenced by Beth Chatto's gravel garden in the United Kingdom and Roberto Burle Marx's landscape-scale "mosaics" of colored rock and massed carpet plantings in Brazil. The current popularity of gravel gardens has been enhanced by the observations of gardeners who found that many

Kiwi aeonium, thyme, blue fescue, and Christmas cheer are some of the plants in this eclectic backyard rock garden.

drought-tolerant plants, such as succulents and various California natives from chaparral and coastal-sage communities, tend to germinate and grow much better in gravel mulch. The Chaff Garden at Rancho Santa Ana Botanic Garden in Claremont is a gravel garden where seeds of native annuals and perennials are sown in a 4- to 6-inch-deep mulch of local river-washed pea gravel. The Menzies Garden at the San Francisco Botanical Garden contains a small but notable gravel garden of California natives.

Your site may determine the type of gravel you use. Sharp gravels, when placed on a slope to imitate a mountain scree, have a more natural appearance than similarly placed river-washed gravels. Conversely,

Planting beds topped with gray gravel edge a beige-colored gravel courtyard that can double as extra parking space.

Artichoke agave and elegant hen and chicks mix well here with boulders and multi-colored gravels. JENNIFER CHEUNG

rounded river-washed gravels are more visually appropriate for flat areas or in depressions where they may be used to suggest the seasonal presence of water. Sharp gravels tend to compact more quickly than river-washed gravels and can require frequent renovation to maintain their appearance.

When using gravels primarily to make decorative patterns, it is helpful to place a weed mat (do not use impermeable plastic sheeting) on top of the soil before you lay down the gravel. This barrier will smother existing weeds and subsequent weed seedlings, and it will also help keep the gravel clean and prevent it from sinking into the soil. Maintenance includes removing fallen leaves, flowers, twigs, etc. from the gravel surface, and this task can be quite time consuming.

SELECTED PLANT PALETTE FOR ROCK GARDENS

The following list is composed of highly recommended plants that look great with rocks. Before you make your selections, check the Plant Profiles to determine the ultimate size of the plants you are interested in using in your rock garden. Generally, the larger and/or more vigorously growing plants combine well with larger rocks and boulders, while the smaller and less vigorous plants

are best complemented by smaller rocks, pebbles, and gravels. Rock garden sites can be among the most open and exposed parts of a landscape, and in warmer climate zones it is a good idea to select plants that tolerate the maximum summer temperatures and durations of high heat. The optimal California climate zones for growing each plant appear in brackets after the plant name and are abbreviated as follows: c = coastal; i = inland; cv = Central Valley; ld = low desert; hd = high desert; m = mountain; all = all zones. (For more information on the zones, see page 57.) California native plants appear in green type.

Achnatherum hymenoides, **Indian rice grass** [c, i, cv, hd]
A. speciosum, **desert needlegrass** [c, i, cv, hd]
Aeonium sedifolium, dwarf aeonium [c, i]
Agave attenuata and cultivars, foxtail agave [c, i]
A. bracteosa, candelabrum agave [c, i, cv, ld]
A. parryi, artichoke agave [all]
A. victoria-reginae, Queen Victoria agave [c, i, ld, hd]
Aloe aristata, torch plant [c, i, cv, ld]
A. plicatilis, fan aloe [c, i]
A. striata, coral aloe [c, i, cv, ld]
Arctostaphylos edmundsii **and cultivars, Edmunds manzanita** [c, i, cv]
A. hookeri **and cultivars, Hooker manzanita** [c, i, cv]
A. **'John Dourley', John Dourley manzanita** [c, i, cv]
A. pumila, **dune manzanita** [c, i, cv]
Arctotis, African daisy [c, i, cv]
Aristida purpurea, **purple three-awn** [all]
Artemisia pycnocephala **and cultivar, sandhill sagebrush** [c, i]
Berberis repens, **creeping barberry** [all except ld]
Bergenia, bergenia [all except ld]
Carex testacea, orange New Zealand sedge [c, i, cv]
Ceanothus gloriosus **and cultivars, Point Reyes ceanothus** [c, i, cv]
C. **'Joyce Coulter', Joyce Coulter ceanothus** [c, i, cv]
C. maritimus **and cultivars, maritime ceanothus** [c, i, cv]

Ground morning glory's bright green foliage and lavender flowers make a fine contrast with this granite boulder.

Cistus × *hybridus,* white rockrose [c, i, cv]

C. salviifolius, sageleaf rockrose [c, i, cv]

Convolvulus cneorum and cultivar, bush morning glory [c, i, cv, ld]

Cotoneaster dammeri and cultivars, bearberry cotoneaster [c, i, cv, hd]

C. microphyllus and varieties, rockspray cotoneaster [c, i, cv]

Cotyledon orbiculata, pig's ear [c, i, ld]

Dalea greggii, trailing indigo bush [c, i, ld, hd]

Delosperma astonii 'Blut', Blut ice plant [c, i, cv, hd]

D. 'Mesa Verde', Mesa Verde ice plant [all]

Dudleya brittonii, Britton dudleya [c, i]

D. virens ssp. *hassei,* Catalina Island dudleya [c, i]

Dymondia margaretae, silver carpet [c, i, cv]

Echeveria elegans, elegant hen and chicks [c, i, cv]

E. × *imbricata,* hen and chicks [c, i, cv]

Erigeron scopulinus, mat daisy [all]

E. 'W.R.', W.R. daisy [c, i, cv]

Eriogonum arborescens, Santa Cruz Island buckwheat [c, i, cv]

E. cinereum, ashyleaf buckwheat [c, i, cv]

E. crocatum, saffron buckwheat [c, i, cv]

E. grande var. *rubescens,* red-flowered buckwheat [c, i, cv]

E. latifolium, coast buckwheat [c, i]

E. umbellatum, sulfur buckwheat [all except ld]

E. wrightii, Wright's buckwheat [all except ld]

Gazania, gazania [all except m]

Helleborus argutifolius, Corsican hellebore [c, i, cv, m]

Hesperoyucca whipplei, chaparral yucca [all]

Heuchera elegans, elegant coral bells [c, i, cv, m]

Hypericum reptans, Himalayan Saint John's wort [c]

Iris douglasiana and cultivar, Douglas iris [c, i, cv, m]

I. unguicularis, winter iris [c, i, cv]

Juniperus conferta and cultivar, shore juniper [all]

J. procumbens 'Nana', Nana Japanese garden juniper [all]

Lessingia filaginifolia and cultivars, California aster [c, i, cv]

Muhlenbergia dumosa, bamboo muhly [all except m]

Nandina domestica 'Harbour Dwarf', Harbour Dwarf heavenly bamboo [all]

Oenothera caespitosa, fragrant evening primrose [all except c]

Opuntia basilaris, beaver tail cactus [all except c]

O. polyacantha var. *erinacea,* Mojave prickly-pear [all except c]

Origanum dictamnus, dittany of Crete [c, i, cv, ld]

O. rotundifolium and cultivar, round-leaved oregano [all]

Rosmarinus officinalis 'Lockwood de Forest', Lockwood de Forest rosemary [all except m]

R. o. 'Prostratus', Prostratus rosemary [all except m]

R. o. 'Renzels', Renzels rosemary [all except m]

Salvia 'Bee's Bliss', Bee's Bliss sage [c, i, cv]

S. chamaedryoides, germander sage [c, i, cv]

Top: A light sandstone boulder serves as a good foil for the delicate pink flowers of Canyon Delight coral bells. Bottom: Catalina Island dudleya blooms in front of a mortarless sandstone wall.

Santolina chamaecyparissus, lavender cotton [all]

S. rosmarinifolius, green santolina [c, i, cv, m]

Sedum adolphii, coppertone stonecrop [c, i, cv]

S. palmeri, Palmer's sedum [all except ld]

S. spathulifolium and cultivars, Pacific stonecrop [c, i, cv, m]

Sempervivum arachnoideum, cobweb houseleeks [all except ld]

S. montanum, montane houseleeks [all except ld]

S. tectorum, hen-and-chickens [all except ld]

Senecio mandraliscae, blue chalksticks [c, i, ld]

Sphaeralcea ambigua and cultivars, apricot mallow [all]

Sporobolus airoides, alkali sacaton [all]

Stipa gigantea, giant feather grass [c, i, cv]

Teucrium majoricum, fruity germander [c, i, cv]

Thymus vulgaris and cultivars, common thyme [all except ld]

Verbena lilacina and cultivars, Cedros Island verbena [c, i, cv, ld]

Zauschneria californica, California fuchsia [all]

Z. 'Everett's Choice', Everett's Choice California fuchsia [all]

Z. 'Select Mattole', Select Mattole California fuchsia [all]

SUCCULENT GARDENS

Foxtail agave's pointed leaves and dinner-plate aeonium's rounded rosettes provide visual diversity in a succulent garden.

The distinctive shapes and symmetry of succulent plants tempt many gardeners, landscape professionals, and collectors—and for good reason: a well-designed succulent garden is visually striking, whether planted in a formal or naturalistic style. Depending upon which suite of plants you choose to work with, there are dozens of exciting succulents for every climate zone in California—from the immediate coast to the high mountains and across the deserts. For those who live nearer to the coast or farther south in the state, the range of choices is even larger, since many garden-worthy succulents can only grow where freezing temperatures are uncommon.

Succulents are plants characterized by their thick-ened, fleshy or leathery leaves and/or stems. Many have a formal rosette growth habit that inspires their use in pattern plantings. Succulents are typically found in seasonally dry environments such as deserts and mediterranean-climate areas of the world. Cacti are a unique subset of succulent plants, and all but the most primitive cacti are notable for their symmetrical form and structure. Regardless of whether it includes cacti, a succulent garden is almost guaranteed to be an eye-catching alternative to the lawn.

Blue chalksticks can be effectively combined with many other succulents (seen here with thread-leaf agave).

HISTORY AND EXAMPLES

Dating back to the Mission Era, Californians have recognized the beauty and utility of succulent plants in their gardens and landscapes. Among the earliest successful species were Indian-fig cactus, American agave, foxtail agave, jade plant, Spanish dagger, soap aloe, and Pacific stonecrop. The 1950s Modernist movement saw the first widespread plantings of succulents in California

Above: Elegant hen and chicks spreads vigorously and makes an excellent groundcover in sun or partial shade. Left: Aeonium, rosemary, and ice plant are neatly folded into the landscape of this narrow entryway.

This intriguing lawn alternative includes sedum, blue chalk-sticks, aeonium, and other succulents. SAXON HOLT

residential gardens. At that time, succulents were especially valued for their strong shapes and the theatrical drama they created amid the era's Modernist architecture, which often featured austere forms, cleanly delineated walls, and large expanses of glass. These plants literally became living sculptures in an otherwise stark physical environment.

California's most widely recognized garden of succulent plants is the Desert Garden at The Huntington Botanical Gardens in San Marino, which turned 100 years old in 2008. The so-called Arizona Garden at Stanford University in Palo Alto dates back to about 1880. It was originally planted with saguaros that were collected in Arizona and brought to Stanford by train. Many of these first plantings did not thrive in California's mediterranean climate, but, beginning in 1997, this historic garden was brought back to prominence after many years of neglect. At the University of California Botanical Garden at Berkeley, The New World Desert Collection, which started in 1932, and the more recent Southern African Collection, display a wealth of succulent plants and their companions. Lotusland, a public garden in Montecito, is justly famous for its succulent gardens that were developed by Madame Ganna Walska

beginning in the 1940s. In 1971, Ruth Bancroft initiated one of northern California's best succulent gardens; located in Walnut Creek, the Bancroft Dry Garden is particularly notable for its design, as well as its success in a colder climate area of the state. The widely visited J. Paul Getty Museum in Los Angeles, which opened to the public in 1997, includes an often-photographed garden of succulents on its south promontory. The Succulents Under the Sea garden at the San Diego Botanic Garden in Encinitas, which made its public debut in 2004, delights viewers by using succulent plants to evoke the beauty, diversity, and forms of a tropical coral reef.

A wide variety of native California succulents are found in the collections of public gardens, including Rancho Santa Ana Botanic Garden in Claremont, Santa Barbara Botanic Garden, The Living Desert in Palm Desert, and the East Bay Regional Parks Botanic Garden in Tilden Regional Park in Berkeley. San Diego Zoo's Wild Animal Park in Escondido has an impressive array of succulent plants from Baja California, Mexico, as well as native species.

California's native landscapes offer visually impressive displays of succulent plants—particularly in the deserts. Anza-Borrego Desert State Park and the "Palms to Pines" Scenic Byway—which bisects the Santa Rosa and San Jacinto Mountains National Monument—provide access to spectacular examples of native succulents, such as desert agave and beavertail cactus. In the high desert, the Mojave National Preserve claims at least 23 succulent species, including Mojave prickly-pear and banana yucca. Outside the desert, Cabrillo National Monument and Torrey Pines State Reserve harbor remnants of coastal southern California's succulent diversity; both parks contain yuccas and prickly-pears and also have dudleyas. Farther north, in locations such as Pinnacles National Monument and Point Reyes

National Seashore, you'll find nice examples of the succulent Pacific stonecrop.

DESIGN AND INSTALLATION

There are many possible plant choices for a succulent garden, but designers generally recommend using fewer different kinds of succulents and more of each type. If you are unfamiliar with succulent plants, experiment with them for a year or two before deciding to install hundreds of a single type. This test period will help you make sure that your plant selections are a good match to your site. Generally speaking, succulent plants prefer well-drained soils. However, many are adaptable to clay soils if your garden site is sloped, bermed, or mounded (as one might find in a rock garden) to allow water to drain away quickly from the base of the plants. It also helps if the soil rarely stays saturated, especially when the plants are dormant. Keep in mind that many succulents grow best in partial shade rather than in full sunlight, particularly in interior locations of California.

The colors, forms, and textures of succulents lead many designers to use them in dramatic fashion. Gardens featuring mass plantings of succulents are a memorable sight. For example, the spectacle of hundreds of golden barrel cacti in gardens at both the J. Paul Getty Museum and The Huntington have become attractions all their own. Succulent plants also lend themselves to pattern plantings due to the regularity of their growth habits and forms. Low-growing succulents are especially useful as groundcovers, where their unique colors, shapes, and textures may be enjoyed as uniform carpets or in mixed-planting tapestries. For those seeking to replace their lawn with a landscape that is still dense and low profile, these kinds of succulents present an attractive alternative.

Single specimens of succulents can become major focal points in a garden, and their sparing use in a sea of gravel or sand evokes the Zen spirit of a Japanese garden. Due to their sculptural qualities, succulents are readily combined with the hardscape elements of a garden, such as rocks and boulders, concrete, brick, and tile. Most are well adapted to growing for long periods in containers. You can incorporate potted succulents into your garden for added impact or to showcase a prized specimen, especially where the symmetry of their rosettes or intriguing growth forms can be appreciated closer to eye level. Spineless succulent plants are a natural for use near pools or ponds, as most produce little debris and many are adapted to the extreme heat and reflected light found in these environments. Just be sure that these plantings are safe from chlorinated and/or excess water.

When purchasing larger specimens, be certain to note the plant's orientation to the sun and be sure to maintain that orientation in the plant's new location. If the shaded north side of a large specimen succulent is suddenly subjected to the full sun of a south exposure, the plant's flesh will burn; this may leave a long-term unsightly scar or even result in the death of the plant from subsequent rot. Some seemingly innocuous small young succulents may grow phenomenally large and

Top: Zwartkop aeonium (upper right), foxtail agave, and pig's ear (front) offer eye-catching foliage in a garden. SAXON HOLT
Bottom: A vibrant mix of succulents is interspersed with rocks in this well-drained site. SAXON HOLT

Top: At this California bungalow, a fanciful blend of succulents fills a space that is typically covered by lawn. Bottom: Blue chalksticks planted between concrete pavers creates a pleasing geometric pattern. JENNIFER CHEUNG

heavy rather quickly in the right garden conditions, so plan accordingly, because such plants can be quite expensive to remove from your garden.

Succulents can be effectively combined with other drought-adapted plants. Since many non-succulent plants look awkward when inter-planted with succulents, careful consideration should be given to these companions. Some effective non-succulent partners are mediterranean and xeric grasses, such as giant feather grass, desert needlegrass, and Indian rice grass. To extend this planting palette beyond succulents and grasslike plants, consider adding Powis Castle wormwood, Starn coyote brush, fragrant evening primrose, autumn sage, apricot mallow, or lilac verbena.

Among the many choices for a California succulent garden are plants that come with potential hazards. Cacti can be covered with spines, agaves and yuccas may be armed with spine-tipped leaves, and most euphorbias have poisonous sap. These plants are a danger to

children and pets. In addition, weeding around spiny, thorny, and brittle succulent plants is a challenge. Advance planning to minimize weeds in the new succulent garden will be well worth the gardener's time and effort.

MAINTENANCE AND SPECIAL ISSUES

While it is often unwise to categorize the horticultural needs of such a diverse group of plants, nearly all succulents fall into one of two broad categories: those that require warm-season irrigation (summer growers) and those that require cool-season irrigation (winter growers). There are plants in each of these categories that are adaptable to both types of watering regimes, and these are generally the easiest succulent plants to grow in California gardens. Regardless of the plant palette, most succulent gardens require some well-timed irrigation to thrive. Mulches of coarse sand, gravel, or rock will help conserve soil moisture, but they may become problematic when you are adding new plants or if you need to rework the soil. In some inland or drier gardens, a light organic mulch may be a better choice as it will nourish the plants as it decomposes.

Most succulents readily produce pups, which are young plants that form at the base of the parent plant. Pups can be separated from the original plant and replanted elsewhere in the garden. Large succulents growing in containers can present several challenges. As the plants grow, the containers can become top heavy and tip over. This is especially true for tall narrow pots containing weighty aloes or agaves. Container-grown succulents often become rootbound, causing plant health to decline from a lack of sufficient water and nutrients. Always remember to check your succulents and repot them in fresh, well-drained soil as needed. Another problem that can occur is that the dense roots of some succulents may, eventually, clog the drainage holes of their containers. This can result in crown rot and/or root rot, either of which can kill the plant.

SELECTED PLANT PALETTE FOR SUCCULENT GARDENS

The following list is composed of all of the succulent plants described and recommended in this book. For interest and contrast, many gardeners incorporate other equally drought-tolerant perennials and grasses into their compositions for more effective displays. The optimal California climate zones for growing each plant appear in brackets after the plant name and are abbreviated as follows: c = coastal; i = inland; cv = Central Valley; ld = low desert; hd = high desert; m = mountain; all = all zones. (For more information on the zones, see page 57.) California native plants appear in **green type**.

Aeonium arboreum 'Zwartkop', Zwartkop aeonium [c, i]
A. canariensis, dinner-plate aeonium [c, i]
A. haworthii, pinwheel aeonium [c, i]

A. sedifolium, dwarf aeonium [c, i]
A. simsii, aeonium [c, i]
A. 'Tricolor', kiwi aeonium [c, i]
A. undulatum, stalked aeonium [c, i]
Agave americana 'Medio Picta Alba', Medio Picta Alba agave [all except m]
A. attenuata and cultivars, foxtail agave [c, i]
A. bracteosa, candelabrum agave [c, i, cv, ld]
A. deserti, **desert agave** [c, i, cv, ld]
A. desmettiana, smooth agave [c, i]
A. geminiflora, twin-flowered agave [c, i, cv, ld]
A. 'Joe Hoak', Joe Hoak agave [c, i]
A. parryi, artichoke agave [all]
A. victoria-reginae, Queen Victoria agave [c, i, ld, hd]
A. vilmoriniana, octopus agave [c, i, cv, ld]
Aloe aristata, torch plant [c, i, cv, ld]
A. ciliaris, climbing aloe [c, i, cv, ld]
A. maculata, soap aloe [c, i, cv, ld]
A. × *nobilis,* gold tooth aloe [c, i, cv, ld]
A. plicatilis, fan aloe [c, i]
A. 'Rooikappie', Red Riding Hood aloe [c, i, cv, ld]
A. sinkatana, reblooming aloe [c, i, cv, ld]
A. striata, coral aloe [c, i, cv, ld]
A. vera, aloe vera [c, i, cv, ld]
Cistanthe grandiflora, rock purslane [c, i, cv, ld]
Cotyledon orbiculata, pig's ear [c, i, ld]
Crassula arborescens, silver jade plant [c, i, cv, ld]
C. capitella 'Campfire', Campfire crassula [c, i, cv]
C. multicava, fairy crassula [c, i, cv, ld]
C. ovata and cultivars, jade plant [c, i, cv]
C. perfoliata var. *falcata,* airplane plant [c, i, cv]
C. schmidtii, crassula [c, i, cv]
Delosperma astonii 'Blut', Blut ice plant [c, i, cv, hd]
D. congestum 'Gold Nugget', Gold Nugget ice plant [c, i, cv, hd]
D. 'Mesa Verde', Mesa Verde ice plant [all]
D. 'Oberg', Oberg ice plant [c, i, cv, hd]
D. sphalmanthoides, tufted ice plant [all except ld]
Dudleya anthonyi, Anthony dudleya [c, i]
D. brittonii, Britton dudleya [c, i]
D. densiflora, Fish Canyon dudleya [c, i]
D. edulis, ladies' fingers dudleya [c, i]
D. farinosa, coast dudleya [c, i]
D. pulverulenta, chalk dudleya [c, i]
D. virens ssp. *hassei,* Catalina Island dudleya [c, i]
Echeveria agavoides, agave echeveria [c, i, cv]
E. derenbergii, painted lady echeveria [c, i]
E. elegans, elegant hen and chicks [c, i, cv]
E. × *imbricata,* hen and chicks [c, i, cv]
Echinocactus grusonii, golden barrel cactus [c, i, ld]
Graptopetalum amethystinum, graptopetalum [c, i, ld]
G. paraguayense, ghost plant [c, i, ld]
G. pentandrum ssp. *superbum,* graptopetalum [c, i, ld]
Hesperaloe parviflora, red yucca [all]
Hesperoyucca whipplei, **chaparral yucca** [all]

Succulents and silver carpet form the core of a blue-foliaged plant palette that lines this courtyard entrance.

Kalanchoe beharensis and cultivar, feltbush [c, i, ld]
K. fedtschenkoi, rainbow scallops [c, i]
K. grandiflora, kalanchoe [c, i]
K. luciae, paddle plant [c, i]
K. orgyalis, copper spoons [c, i]
K. pumila, flour dust plant [c, i]
K. thyrsiflora, kalanchoe [c, i]
K. tomentosa, panda plant [c, ld]
Opuntia basilaris, **beavertail cactus** [all except c]
O. polyacantha var. *erinacea,* **Mojave prickly-pear** [all except c]
O. santa-rita, Santa Rita cactus [all except c]
Portulacaria afra and cultivars, elephant's food [c, i, cv]
Sedum acre and cultivar, common stonecrop [all except ld]
S. adolphii, coppertone stonecrop [c, i, cv]
S. album and cultivars, white stonecrop [all except ld]
S. dasyphyllum, Corsican stonecrop [all except ld]
S. palmeri, Palmer's sedum [all except ld]
S. rupestre 'Angelina', Angelina stonecrop [all except ld]
S. × *rubrotinctum* and cultivar, Christmas cheer [c, i, cv]
S. spathulifolium and cultivars, **Pacific stonecrop** [c, i, cv, m]
S. spurium and cultivars, two-row stonecrop [all except ld]
S. stefco, stonecrop [all except ld]
Sempervivum arachnoideum, cobweb houseleeks [all except ld]
S. montanum, montane houseleeks [all except ld]
S. tectorum, hen-and-chickens [all except ld]
Senecio cylindricus, narrow-leaf chalksticks [c, i]
S. mandraliscae, blue chalksticks [c, i, ld]
S. serpens, little blue chalksticks [c, i]
Yucca baccata var. *baccata,* **banana yucca** [all]
Y. filamentosa and cultivars, Adam's needle [all]
Y. nana, dwarf yucca [all]
Y. recurvifolia and cultivars, soft-leaf yucca [all except m]

CARPET AND TAPESTRY GARDENS

Silver carpet, beach strawberry, ceanothus, and rockrose each contribute distinct foliage textures to this tapestry.

Carpets and tapestries encompass a vast array of garden styles and present many exciting possibilities for alternatives to the lawn. This flexible category will appeal to gardeners with diverse goals for their landscapes, whether they want to install a colorful carpet of gazanias or wish to emulate the latest California interpretation of the English cottage garden. The feature that unites carpet and tapestry plantings is their use of low-profile, water-conserving plants, many of which are traditionally referred to as groundcovers.

For our purposes, "carpets" refer to broad sweeping drifts of one or a few types of plants that give a fairly uniform carpetlike appearance, such as carpet geranium, Silver Carpet California aster, or Palmer's sedum. The term "carpet" is used here to refer to the cohesive appearance of a planting and does not imply that the landscaped surface is suitable for heavy foot traffic. There are, however, a small number of groundcovers that will tolerate some degree of foot traffic and will perform well in a carpet-style planting. These "walk-on" plants are not intended to withstand daily pedestrian travel or the periodically intense use of a playing field. They need to be carefully selected to match your garden conditions and will require site-specific maintenance.

This casual tapestry blends annuals with perennials such as carpet geranium, California fuchsia, and verbena.

The rather short list of walk-ons includes: African daisy, beach strawberry, common yarrow, lippia, Point Saint George aster, silver carpet, woodland strawberry, and some species of thyme.

"Tapestries" cover the widest variety of planting combinations. In general, think of tapestry plantings as a rich assemblage of different types of plants that, when placed together, are both aesthetically pleasing and ecologically compatible. A classic example of a mediterranean-style tapestry might include a hillside planting of rosemaries, lavenders, rockroses, California native buckwheats, and drought-tolerant sages.

HISTORY AND EXAMPLES

Carpets and tapestries have been central components in gardens from the time humans first began cultivating plants. Whether they were uniform plantings of food crops or mixtures of edible plants, herbs, and flowers, carpets and tapestries have remained a constant theme in our horticultural endeavors. An early example is the combined cultivation of sunflowers, maize, beans, and squashes by indigenous cultures of the American Southwest—a tapestry planting that pre-dates European colonization of North America and continues to this day. The utilitarian herb gardens of the Middle Ages, and the cottage gardens that emerged in England by the 17th century, are other early examples of this approach to garden design.

Since the 1950s, there have been innumerable plantings of carpets and tapestries in California. State, county, and municipal governments—driven by a need to cut water and maintenance costs—were among the first to install them. Some of the earliest carpet-style mass plantings of lily-of-the-Nile, daylilies, and deer grass appeared in road medians and freeway interchanges. Tapestries of native buckwheats and ceanothus have been employed on a large scale to cover embankments along Highways 1 and 101. At the Los Angeles Arboretum, the Grace Kallam Perennial Garden contains excellent tapestry plantings. Many species appropriate for mediterranean climates form tapestries in the City of Santa Barbara's Alice Keck Park Memorial Gardens. The UC Davis Arboretum's Ruth Risdon Storer Garden and adjacent Carolee Shields White Flower Garden offer great examples of tapestries. The UC Santa Cruz Arboretum's entry garden of low-growing and/or smaller California natives is especially effective, and its Australian collection is a tapestry on a grand scale.

From the deserts to the sea, some of California's most beloved native landscapes are essentially wildland carpets and tapestries. The Borrego Valley's spring-blooming carpets of dune evening primrose and other wildflowers attract photographers from around the world. Many of the trails that climb into the wilderness areas of the eastern Sierra Nevada begin among tapestries of drought-tolerant species, such as Great Basin sagebrush and Great Basin wild rye. From San Diego to San Francisco, most Californians live near parklands that feature stands of coastal sage scrub—a natural community known for its multitextured tapestries of often-aromatic plants, such as California sagebrush, black sage, coyote brush, and various buckwheats. North of the Bay Area, dozens of parks protect coastal headlands, terraces, and dunes where visitors can find carpets and tapestries with beach strawberry, coast aster, and other garden-worthy plants.

DESIGN AND INSTALLATION

The key to making carpet and tapestry plantings work for the long term is careful and realistic planning, planting, and maintenance. It is important to make sure that the new plants you choose are well adapted to your garden's microclimate and soils. Some plants are slower growing or more difficult to cultivate. They may be overrun by other plants that are equally well adapted to your garden conditions, but are much more vigorous. Choose your plants carefully and monitor how they compete with one another. If you are a beginning gardener, you may want to ask for species that are considered very durable and virtually carefree; in the horticulture trade, these are often referred to as "bullet-proof" plants.

For ideas about commonly available plants for a carpet or tapestry garden, take a drive or stroll through

Above: Coral Carpet cotoneaster (foreground) and Yankee Point ceanothus can be maintained as low-profile groundcovers. Left: Common yarrow is a hardy lawn alternative that helps sustain insect pollinators.
STEPHEN INGRAM

Top: The feathery foliage and muted colors of Powis Castle wormwood fill this front yard.
Bottom: The whorled blossoms of hummingbird sage add highlights to a tapestry of California natives. SAXON HOLT

together. For example, a combination of junipers, with deer grass as an accent, would be a low-maintenance design suitable for most climate zones in California. As your new landscape fills in, you can add and delete plants or replant as needed or desired. One of the key benefits of most tapestry plantings is that, over time, the plants in your initial palette will compete with, and adapt to, one another, allowing you to discover which plants are best suited to different parts of your yard. Every garden site is different, and a certain amount of trial and error is usually unavoidable.

When combining plants in a carpet or tapestry, chose species that look good together and have similar horticultural needs. In a pairing of gazania and carpet geranium, for example, the fine-textured green leaves of the geranium provide a pleasing contrast to the coarser grey leaves of the gazania—and both species in this carpet planting have low-water requirements. A tapestry composed of creeping barberry, island alum root, Douglas iris, and woodland strawberry would feature California natives with an appealing spectrum of foliage colors and textures for a partially shaded garden. Imitating natural aggregations of plants is another good way to insure their compatibility. For instance, coastal gardeners in California would do well with a tapestry using Carmel creeper ceanothus interspersed with wild buckwheats from maritime climates and a few strategically placed clumps of giant feather grass or Canyon Prince wild rye. An aesthetic and appropriate quartet for an inland valley tapestry might consist of Edmunds manzanita, chaparral yucca, California buckwheat, and California fuchsia.

The possible choices are almost limitless when you are considering a carpet or tapestry planting, but it is important to resist the temptation to include too many different plant species. Pick your favorites and find ways to use them as repeating elements in the landscape.

your neighborhood or a nearby business park and examine those landscapes that do not focus on turf. Due to water-conservation mandates, many newer plantings use groundcovers in lieu of grass, and they often contain species that can be appropriate for carpets and tapestries. Some sites will showcase plants that are both water-thrifty and well adapted to your local soils. When you find a particularly appealing landscape, observe how the individual plants perform over time. Do they seem to require lots of care and water? Do they only catch your attention briefly, but later impress you as being not especially attractive? Are they easily pruned and kept in proper scale for your situation? It is helpful to consider these and similar questions before you invest time, energy, and money to remove and replace your lawn with a new set of plants.

Many gardeners find that it is easier to use fewer different species when installing the basic structure, or "bones," of the garden. Even a tapestry can be simple, using from two to five different types of plants woven

This drought-tolerant tapestry contains lavender cotton, rosemary, Spanish lavender, and other ornamentals. WYNNE WILSON

Carmel Sur manzanita (foreground) is a robust, low-growing cultivar that excels in a variety of garden situations.

Consider the way different foliage types contrast or blend together, and be aware of a species' natural height and space requirements. For some gardeners, an attractive tapestry design will mean highlighting plants with especially ornamental flowers and fruits; for others, it could be creating a visual framework in which to set a specimen plant.

MAINTENANCE AND SPECIAL ISSUES

For such a broad selection of plants, planting combinations, and design possibilities, it is not practical or particularly helpful to prescribe specific or detailed care and maintenance protocols. Weed removal will probably be one of the major tasks during the establishment period, especially if your new groundcovers are slow growing. Once a carpet or tapestry planting matures, it may need only occasional weeding or pruning to keep it looking good. For a more complex tapestry composition, some pruning may be needed throughout the seasons. Any good gardening reference that is California-centric should provide the general sorts of information that you will need in order to care for your carpet and tapestry plantings. Refer to the Plant Profiles in this book for specific plant care and maintenance information.

Tapestry plantings embrace a variety of different plants, and this diversity helps to protect them from pest problems. A carpet planting composed of a single plant species, is, by definition, a monoculture. Similar to other monoculture installations, like many lawns and greenswards, such plantings are potentially more susceptible to pests and diseases. This is primarily because insect pests and diseases have an easier time finding and exploiting a particular type of plant when there is an abundance of it in one place. Inevitably, there will be stronger and weaker individuals within the planting, even though they may all be genetically identical clones or cultivars. The weakest or most stressed plants are usually the first ones to be attacked. Sometimes the cause can be attributed to a clogged drip emitter, a gopher, or even root damage at planting time. When plants in a carpet or walk-on planting die, there will be a period of time when the planting does not look uniform while the new plants fill in the gaps. During their first year, replacement plants within a carpet or tapestry will often require more frequent watering than their established neighbors.

Above, from left to right: Blue moor grass, blue fescue, and blue oat grass are paired with succulents in a flowing design. Left: A simple combination of daylily and catmint can be eye-catching.

SELECTED PLANT PALETTE FOR CARPET AND TAPESTRY GARDENS

The following plants are useful in creating carpetlike plantings. They are all low-growing in stature, although some have flowers and flower stalks that make them appear much taller. Many of our sedges and grasses can also be effectively massed and grown as carpets, but as these plants are the focus of other design alternatives (especially for greenswards), they are not repeated here. The optimal California climate zones for growing each plant appear in brackets after the plant name and are abbreviated as follows: c = coastal; i = inland; cv = Central Valley; ld = low desert; hd = high desert; m = mountain; all = all zones. (For more information on the zones, see page 57.) The † indicates plants that may tolerate limited foot traffic. California native plants appear in **green type**.

Carpets

Achillea clavennae, Greek yarrow [all]
A. millefolium† **and cultivars** (not all are native), **common yarrow** [all]
A. 'Moonshine', Moonshine yarrow [all]
A. 'Taygetea', Taygetea yarrow [all]
A. tomentosa, woolly yarrow [all]
Agapanthus 'Peter Pan', Peter Pan lily-of-the-Nile [c, i, cv]
Arctotis (some forms)†, African daisy [c, i, cv]
Artemisia californica 'Canyon Gray', Canyon Gray **California sagebrush** [c, i, cv]
Aster chilensis 'Point Saint George'†, Point Saint **George coast aster** [c, i, cv]
Bergenia, bergenia [all except ld]
Cotoneaster dammeri and cultivars, bearberry cotoneaster [c, i, cv, hd]
C. salicifolius 'Repens', willowleaf cotoneaster [c, i, cv]
Dalea greggii, trailing indigo bush [c, i, ld, hd]
Dudleya virens ssp. **hassei, Catalina Island dudleya** [c, i]
Dymondia margaretae†, silver carpet [c, i, cv]
Echeveria elegans, elegant hen and chicks [c, i, cv]
E. × *imbricata,* hen and chicks [c, i, cv]
Fragaria chiloensis† **and cultivars** (not all are native), **beach strawberry** [c, i, cv]
F. vesca ssp. **californica** 'Montana de Oro'†, **Montana de Oro woodland strawberry** [c, i, cv, m]
F. vesca ssp. *vesca*† and cultivars, woodland strawberry [c, i, cv, m]
Gazania (some), gazania [all except m]
Geranium incanum, carpet geranium [c, i, cv]
Juniperus horizontalis and cultivars, creeping juniper [all]
J. procumbens 'Nana', Nana Japanese garden juniper [all]
Lantana montevidensis and cultivars, spreading lantana [c, i, cv, ld]
Lessingia filaginifolia 'Silver Carpet', Silver Carpet **California aster** [c, i, cv]
Myoporum parvifolium and cultivars, creeping myoporum [c, i, cv, ld]

This planting of thyme and silver carpet can tolerate moderate foot traffic. STEPHEN INGRAM

Oenothera californica, California evening primrose [all except c]
Phyla nodiflora†, lippia [all except m]
Sedum acre and cultivar, common stonecrop [all except ld]
S. album and cultivars, white stonecrop [all except ld]
S. palmeri, Palmer's sedum [all except ld]
S. × *rubrotinctum* and cultivar, Christmas cheer [c, i, cv]
S. spurium and cultivars, two-row stonecrop [all except ld]
Senecio mandraliscae, blue chalksticks [c, i, ld]
S. serpens, little blue chalksticks [c, i]
Solidago californica, California goldenrod [all]
Sphaeralcea philippiana, trailing mallow [c, i, cv, ld]
Teucrium majoricum, fruity germander [c, i, cv]
Thymus praecox var. *arcticus*† and cultivars, creeping thyme [all except ld]
T. pseudolanuginosus†, woolly thyme [all except ld]
Zauschneria 'Everett's Choice', Everett's Choice **California fuchsia** [all]
Z. septentrionalis 'Select Mattole', Select Mattole **Humboldt County fuchsia** [all]

Tapestries

Virtually all of the plants listed in this book can be used in tapestry plantings. Check the Plant Profiles to make sure your selections are aesthetically compatible and suited to your climate and soils. Then unleash your imagination to create a unique and satisfying composition.

KITCHEN GARDENS

This suburban yard features a kitchen garden that is both bountiful and beautiful. SAXON HOLT

I t is no coincidence that the burgeoning interest in homegrown produce is often intertwined with the movement to replace conventional lawns. When gardeners contemplate a more productive use for that sunny patch of turfgrass in their yard, they frequently turn to a concept that dates to ancient civilizations: the kitchen garden. Some are spurred into action by the prospects of picking perfectly ripened fruits or harvesting fresh vegetables and herbs just steps from the house. Others share the sentiment of wine and garden writer Hugh Johnson, who stated, "A well done kitchen garden is more expressive of the harmony of man and nature than anything else a gardener can do."

Vegetables, fruits, and herbs grown for home consumption form the core of most kitchen gardens. Ornamental plants that offer purely aesthetic values are also a traditional component of this style of garden. Your objective may be a relatively simple affair, perhaps comprising a series of beds for the cultivation of leafy greens and colorful flowers. Or you may envision a kitchen garden that is more elaborate—one that features a blend of edible and ornamental annuals, perennials, shrubs, and trees complemented by hardscape features, such as stone pathways, wooden planting beds, or trel-

Fresh-off-the-vine produce is one of the primary rewards for a kitchen gardener. SAXON HOLT

lises. Either way, the kitchen garden can be elegant and utilitarian.

Unlike other design alternatives in this book, a kitchen garden managed for high yields can sometimes demand as much water and fertilizer as a traditional lawn. But the investment in this enterprise yields tangible dividends: the satisfaction of providing some of your own food, a chance to raise flavorful and unusual

Much of California enjoys a long, mild growing season that is ideal for kitchen gardening. SAXON HOLT

Top: An expansive kitchen garden can supply a surplus for canning, freezing, drying, or sharing. SAXON HOLT
Bottom: This garden design includes a nook for a bench that is tucked in among the edibles. SAXON HOLT

varieties that are absent from most grocery produce sections, and the health benefits of regular exercise as you tend your crops. Depending on what you grow, the amount of space you cultivate, and the techniques you use, there is also a chance to reduce your food bills.

HISTORY AND EXAMPLES

While the term "kitchen" garden can be traced to the late 16th century, the concept has its origins in the early Egyptian gardens and the "paradise" gardens of Persia. Kitchen gardens were also part of the decadent villa gardens of ancient Rome and, later, the monastery gardens of the Middle Ages. Often called herb gardens, they consisted of all manner of utilitarian plants, from annuals to woody species, that were harvested for use in cooking, medicines, cosmetics, or religious and magical ceremonies. Durable and drought-tolerant ornamentals such as rosemary, oregano, thyme, and lavender, were integral to these gardens, and these plants continue to be valued in today's landscapes. It wasn't until the rise

of pleasure gardens during the Renaissance that food plants were separated from ornamentals and relegated to a garden of purely edible plants. We have the French and Scots to thank for bringing edibles and ornamentals back together during the 18th century. Their kitchen gardens had a formal layout with clipped hedges, espaliered fruit trees, and geometrically patterned beds, all softened by commingled flowers and vegetables. Later, during the Victorian Era—when plant collecting was the rage and eclecticism reigned—exotic edibles were introduced and became equally prized constituents of the kitchen garden.

In early American settlements, the kitchen garden was essential to the nutritional needs of pioneers, and a family's ability to grow and preserve fruits and vegetables often meant the difference between a purely meat-based diet and one supplemented by the minerals and vitamins packed into home-grown produce. As American society became more urbanized and commercial agriculture began to provide a consistent and economical source of fruits and vegetables, kitchen gardens were no longer deemed a critical part of a family's well being.

Economic conditions have periodically stirred the nation's interest in kitchen gardens. The financial "Panic of 1893" inspired the mayor of Detroit to open 430 acres of vacant land to urban gardeners; four decades later, during the Great Depression, that city's vegetable plots were called "Thrift Gardens." Wars also brought crop shortages, rising food prices, and the re-emergence of the kitchen garden. The entry of the United States into WWI was the impetus for the first wave of Victory Gardens, and people from all walks of life engaged in growing food in their backyards or on vacant land. Two decades later, during WWII, the Secretary of Agriculture again encouraged U.S. citizens to plant Victory Gardens, and an estimated four million new gardeners complied. The surge in Victory Gardens during WWII even precipitated a run on seeds, temporarily causing a buyer's panic. The number of such gardens declined, however, as wartime food rationing ended.

The "Back to the Land" movement of the 1970s set off a new wave of interest in cultivating kitchen gardens, both in the backyard and on plots of public urban land, now referred to as community gardens. The majority of home gardeners, however, still limited food-producing plants to a minor role and did not weave them into their landscape designs. For many American families, time that was once devoted to a kitchen garden was shifted to other horticultural pursuits, including maintaining a perfectly groomed lawn. Adventurous gardeners experimented with the steady stream of new ornamental plants released by retail nurseries. Others filled the space that might have included a kitchen garden with features more associated with leisure, such as outdoor kitchens, hot tubs, and swimming pools.

Kitchen gardens have long been a part California's rich agricultural heritage. A number of these small-scale food production sites have been preserved or replicated throughout the state. The earliest kitchen gardens were installed at the Spanish missions before California became a state, and these gardens contained the first plantings of olives, figs, grapes, pomegranates, and citrus in California. The restored grounds at La Purisima Mission State Historic Park, near Lompoc, provide a realistic replica of an early mission garden, where roses, angel's trumpets, and Matilija poppies are scattered among the fruits and vegetables. Ardenwood Historic Farm in Fremont exhibits agricultural practices from the 1870s to the present and displays a fine example of a Victorian Era garden. Several public gardens feature impressive herb collections, including Huntington Botanical Garden and the Getty Villa in Malibu. The Elizabeth Gamble Garden Center in Palo Alto exhibits espaliered

fruit trees, and Filoli—a country estate preserved as a historic site near Woodside—has a large collection of heirloom fruit trees. The more contemporary test garden of Sunset magazine in Menlo Park demonstrates new varieties of edible plants along with suitable gardening techniques. Many California wineries feature extensive edible gardens that provide fresh produce for their on-site kitchens. The extensive grounds of Descanso Gardens in La Cañada now include "Nature's Table Garden," a permanent display that combines seasonal vegetables, fruit trees, edible flowers, and herbs.

DESIGN AND INSTALLATION

A few fundamental guidelines will help you design a kitchen garden that is both productive and aesthetically appealing. Before you begin, you will want to consider what kind of structure to incorporate into your plan, how best to arrange garden pathways, and what kind of plant palette to choose. By thoughtfully employing a variety of forms, colors, and textures, the kitchen garden can be a visually stunning composition.

A certain amount of structure, whether from hardscape materials or long-lived plants, will help to create a semblance of permanence—an important consideration in a garden filled with seasonal crops. Kitchen gardens were traditionally enclosed within walls that afforded protection from wind and foraging animals, screened out unsightly views, provided support for espaliered fruits or vines, and captured warmth. If you want to include walls as part of your garden's structure, you may find that you already have a combination of existing elements that can be put to work. For example, you might extend an existing fence or hedge or use the side of a garage or house as a wall. Many water-conserving plants can become a living fence: consider a clipped hedge of olives, which would lend formality and a soft gray-green

Set amid gravel pathways, these raised-bed boxes lend a formal look to this garden. SAXON HOLT

Ornamental plants that are prized for their flowers are integral to many kitchen gardens. SAXON HOLT

Rabbits and poultry are housed next to this garden, and their manure helps to fertilize the crops. SAXON HOLT

backdrop, or a line of upright unclipped rosemary, which offers a deeper green, more relaxed border. Hedging plants that are naturally dense and compact or that have thorns—such as gooseberries or barberries—can help exclude uninvited guests, such as stray pets. Since vegetables, berries, and fruit trees thrive in full sun, try to locate any hedge, screen, or wall where they will cast minimal shade on your plants. If possible, do not site tall plantings or fences on the immediate south side of any food-producing areas within the kitchen garden.

After the edges of the garden are defined, you are ready to consider circulation and the layout of your planting beds. Paths are a critical design element; they not only frame the beds but also provide essential access points. Construct them with a surface that is firm and dry underfoot and easy to maintain. A spacious kitchen garden does not need to be entirely utilitarian; along with paths, consider adding an intimate area for relaxing or dining *al fresco.*

Raised planting beds are a key structural feature in many kitchen gardens. There are three common techniques for creating beds: shape them by digging, raking, and mounding the soil; build them by laying down multiple layers of organic material (known as the "lasagna method," see page 54); or construct them using stone, wood, or other materials to create a more permanent planter. If you use enclosed planters, you may need to bring in additional topsoil to fill them to the desired height. The great advantage of a raised bed is that it allows for improved drainage. In locations where the frost-free season is short, the elevated surface of a raised bed also increases the soil temperature and speeds up growth and harvest dates, especially in conjunction with the use of row covers. With a raised-bed planter box, the bottom can be lined with heavy gauge aviary

wire to deter gophers. Square or rectangular beds are most commonly used, but hexagons and other configurations are certainly possible. Regardless of their design or shape, make the beds narrow enough (usually not more than 3 feet wide) so that you can easily reach into the middle for planting, weeding, and harvesting. If the beds are contained in planter boxes, you might want to build them to include an edge you can sit on.

Trellises, teepees, or hoops are other structural elements that can enhance your kitchen garden design and provide support for vining fruits and vegetables. They add height to the garden composition and can also serve as attractive focal points. These structures are often installed on a temporary basis; this allows them to be introduced or removed from the garden in response to changes in crops and temperatures.

Establishing a plant palette for the kitchen garden is similar to that for ornamental gardening. Envision the kitchen garden as a room and select plants for each level: floor, walls, and ceiling. In place of your old lawn, plant groundcovers such as strawberry, thyme, oregano, or a prostrate rosemary for the "floor." For the garden "walls," consider water-conserving plants such as barberry, currant, pineapple guava, lemonade berry, or upright forms of rosemary. A fence covered with passion vine or a trellis of table grapes are two other edible choices for this function. Many fruit trees, especially dwarf apples and pears, can be espaliered along existing fences or walls or pruned into hedgelike shapes on low trellises. Trees are the garden's "ceiling" and can frame views, create focal points, and shade areas of the kitchen garden not devoted to sun-loving crops. Fruit-bearing trees offer a wide range of ornamental values: citrus has handsome evergreen foliage and fragrant flowers; plums and peaches bring a profusion of spring blossoms; and persimmons produce vivid displays of fall color. Figs, pomegranates, and olives are good choices if you are seeking water-conserving trees.

In a kitchen garden where food production is the paramount concern, design with edible plants first and then add ornamentals that will be compatible. Beds that are dedicated to food crops provide an opportunity to create ever-changing patterns of color and texture. Depending on the size of your beds, each one can have its own theme, such as salad greens, herbs, berries, or heirloom varieties. Some gardeners restrict each bed to one or two kinds of plants; this makes them easier to manage during cultivation and harvest and creates a stronger visual impact. Whether you arrange the beds by themes or not, the occasional flowery "volunteer" will add a welcome dose of serendipity.

MAINTENANCE AND SPECIAL ISSUES

For practical and health reasons, consider planting a cover crop the first year after removing your lawn, especially if toxic chemicals were used to maintain it. A cover crop will help rebuild the soil, and if you use a nitrogen-fixing legume such as clover, it will boost nitrogen levels as well. If you suspect chemical contamination, have the soil tested by a reputable lab and follow the prescribed recommendations.

Kitchen gardens can lend themselves to sustainable landscape practices if you adapt your use of resources. You can save on water by installing drip or other low-use irrigation systems and by maintaining a layer of organic mulch on your planting beds. A 2- to 4-inch-deep layer of organic mulch supplies nutrients as it breaks down. It also minimizes moisture loss from the soil, moderates soil temperatures, and improves the soil's structure over time. Instead of applying chemical fertilizers or synthetic pesticides, use organic fertilizers to supply nutrients, and rely on integrated pest management techniques to control pest infestations. Fruit trees and annual vegetables in particular have high nutrient requirements. Satisfy them with appropriate but not excessive applications of compost or organic fertilizers. Too much fertilizer, even from organic sources, can pollute groundwater and streams. Ideally, make your own compost from kitchen scraps and green waste.

A few other techniques will help you achieve success in your kitchen garden. Start by following the time-honored tradition of rotating your crops. This practice helps to keep soil-borne pathogens and other disease organisms from proliferating and provides an opportunity to plant nitrogen-fixing crops that increase soil fertility. Include flowering plants, such as yarrow, buckwheat, and ceanothus, to attract bees, ladybugs, lacewings, predatory wasps, and other beneficial insects. Strive for diversity, and mass your ornamental plants for the greatest impact. Their blossoms will add beauty and supply a steady source of nectar and pollen for pollinators. Make it a routine to clean up rotting fruits and diseased vegetation to eliminate host material for pests.

You can supply some of the irrigation needs for a thirsty kitchen garden with careful applications of graywater. Since 2009, California has permitted the use of residential graywater that originates from showers, tubs, bathroom sinks, and washing machines (with the exception of water used to wash diapers) for irrigating landscapes. Graywater cannot be applied through sprinklers and is not suitable for root crops or edible parts of food crops that touch the soil, but it is ideal for irrigating shrubs, fruit trees, corn, and other plants in your kitchen garden.

SELECTED PLANT PALETTE FOR KITCHEN GARDENS

Providing a list of food-producing annuals, perennials, vines, shrubs, and trees suitable for a kitchen garden is outside the scope of this book. However, many plants have edible parts, and adventurous gardeners may want

A well-tended kitchen garden is as visually compelling as any ornamental landscape. SAXON HOLT

to include some of them in their design. For example, one can eat the flowers of daylilies, the plump fruits of prickly-pears, and the succulent leaves of ladies' fingers dudleya.

The following plants are good choices for an edible garden. With the exception of the strawberries, which also make a good garden groundcover, most are grown in the kitchen garden for culinary purposes. The optimal California climate zones for growing each plant appear in brackets after the plant name and are abbreviated as follows: c = coastal; i = inland; cv = Central Valley; ld = low desert; hd = high desert; m = mountain; all = all zones. (For more information on the zones, see page 57.) California native plants appear in **green type**.

Fragaria chiloensis **and cultivars** (not all are native), **beach strawberry** [c, i, cv]

F. vesca **ssp.** *californica* **'Montana de Oro', Montana de Oro woodland strawberry** [c, i, cv, m]

F. vesca **ssp.** *vesca* **and cultivars, woodland strawberry** [c, i, cv, m]

Origanum majorana, sweet marjoram [all except m]

O. vulgare, wild marjoram [all]

Rosmarinus officinalis and cultivars, rosemary [all except m]

Salvia leucophylla **'Point Sal Spreader', Point Sal Spreader sage** [c, i, cv]

S. mellifera **'Terra Seca', Terra Seca black sage** [c, i, cv]

S. spathacea, **hummingbird sage** [c, i, cv]

Thymus × *citriodorus* and cultivars, lemon thyme [all except ld]

T. praecox arcticus and cultivars, creeping thyme [all except ld]

T. vulgaris and cultivars, common thyme [all except ld]

GREEN ROOFS

The roof on this home is planted with rosemary, succulents, Maire's fescue, and other grasses. SAXON HOLT

Most of us tend to view landscaping as something that occurs only on the ground. As part of this book's re-examination of the role of the lawn, this design alternative explores the growing interest in literally taking gardens to another level by placing them on roofs and terraces of buildings. Known as green roofs, these types of installations are an exciting trend in horticulture that can transform vast areas of unused horizontal surfaces. With their ability to sustain living mantles of vegetation, green roofs add biodiversity and offer the potential to address several ecological issues associated with urban environments.

The benefits of vegetated roofs and terraces range from the practical to the intangible. Some of the documented advantages of roof gardens are reductions in storm-water surge and urban heating, improved water and air quality, and increased insulation values in buildings. Other research suggests that green roofs dampen noise inside structures and that workers within such buildings are more productive. No longer mere curiosities, green roofs are becoming part of the new urban and suburban landscape of California. Today, they can be found on top of practically every type of structure, from low-slung carports to tall office buildings.

Clustered field sedge and Sonoma Coast yarrow are the main components of this San Francisco green roof. DAVID FROSS

HISTORY AND EXAMPLES

Gardens on rooftops and terraces have a long and detailed history dating back over 2500 years to the famed hanging gardens of Babylon. Excavations in the Roman city of Pompeii have revealed villas with ornate roof and terrace gardens. Mont-Saint-Michel, the stunning French Benedictine abbey, features a series of roof gardens originally installed in the 13th century. Throughout the Renaissance and Enlightenment, wealthy nobles commissioned the design and construction of elaborate roof gardens; notable examples included roof gardens at the Kremlin in Moscow and the Hermitage in Saint Petersburg. The existence of roof gardens in the great Aztec city Tenochtitlán was documented in the journals of Hernán Cortés's men, before the conquistadors systematically destroyed the gardens in 1521. In the second half of the 19th century, American settlers on the Great Plains built roofs from sod; although far from luxurious, these living roofs provided insulation and protection from the elements, while compensating for the settlers' lack of building materials.

During the reconstruction of northern Europe following WWII, green roof development gained increasing popularity. Germany emerged as a leader in the field, enacting federal and state legislation mandating green roofs for specific situations, as well as offering installation incentives. Its legislators produced detailed guidelines for green roofs, and by 2001 approximately 14% of all German flat roofs—more than 145 million square feet—supported rooftop gardens. Other northern European countries quickly followed suit, and this European model has been embraced in Canada and the United States. Building standards and protocols that encourage sustainable practices often include green roofs, and higher environmental ratings are given under the Leadership in Energy and Environmental Design (LEED) initiative developed by the U.S. Green Building Council. Some North American cities, such as Portland and Chicago, have fashioned innovative policies to promote and encourage green roofs. Green roof construction in California is rapidly becoming part of the LEED process and a growing sustainability culture. Rooftop gardens at the Kaiser Center in Oakland (1960), the Gap Inc. headquarters in San Mateo (2002), the California Academy of Sciences building in San Francisco (2008), and an increasing number of both large- and small-scale green roofs across the state foster a growing confidence that green roofs—especially ones adapted to California's mediterranean climate—will play a significant role in future California landscapes.

DESIGN AND INSTALLATION
Green roofs offer exciting new options for homes, office buildings, and other structures, but they do present significant design challenges and must be viewed as more than simply an elevated garden. Load-bearing tolerances, planting and maintenance access, growing media, irrigation requirements, microclimates, and building shadow and reflection are some of the issues to consider in the design process. Many of the plants typically favored for California landscapes cannot be used effectively on green roofs, and even designs that are appropriate for our mediterranean- and desert-climate

One of the best-known publicly accessible green roofs is the installation at the California Academy of Sciences. SAXON HOLT

areas will usually need an irrigation system.

Green roof construction is divided into two broad categories: extensive roofs with a soil depth of six inches or less, and intensive roofs with a soil depth greater than six inches. Extensive roofs have the advantages of lighter weight and lower cost, and they have better potential for use in retrofitting an existing rooftop. Plant selection, accessibility, design options, and human use are more limited with this method. Intensive roofs are much heavier, with significantly higher load-bearing requirements, but they allow a greater range of design possibilities. Though more expensive to design and construct, intensive green roof gardens allow for greater access and human use. Also, due to their deeper soil profiles, the potential for plant diversity increases significantly.

Installers of both extensive and intensive gardens follow the same basic steps: they start by placing a waterproofing membrane above the structural roof material; next, they lay down a root barrier, drainage layer and/or filter fabric; and finally they add a growing medium and vegetation. In loose laid or built-up systems these layers are typically installed separately, although sometimes a material will serve multiple functions as when a waterproofing membrane is also used as the root barrier. Modular systems combine layers, are often preplanted, and are frequently used in extensive green roof applications because they are much easier to transport and install.

The water requirements of green roofs can be wildly variable. An intensive roof in Burbank with birch trees and a lawn would be extremely water consumptive. An extensive roof planted with sedums on the same site would provide many of the same benefits with only a fraction of the water. Specific water requirements will depend on soil depth, soil composition, location, plant selection, and irrigation design. The majority of

Top: Thymes and other drought-tolerant plants beautify a roof-top patio on this multilevel home. SAXON HOLT
Bottom: A mosaic of sedums forms a living mantle on the roof of a rustic studio. MELISSA BERARD

California's green roof installations include irrigation systems, and even the most drought-tolerant plantings on roofs will likely need supplemental irrigation during dry spells or periods of excessive heat.

Each of this book's six design alternatives can be utilized on rooftops and terraces. Many of the plant choices that are featured in this book's Plant Profiles will adapt well to a rooftop garden.

Greenswards and meadows can grow on roofs with relative ease if water and access are available. Buffalo grass, blue grama grass, and red fescue are all good choices for a rooftop greensward. Buffalo and blue grama grasses have lower water requirements and greater heat tolerance than fescue, making them better suited for warmer interior locations. Whether the greensward will resemble a lawn or a meadow depends on mowing frequency and the mix of plants. A planting of clustered field sedge and Patrick's Point red fescue on a roof in San Francisco, for example, might require a weekly irrigation and an annual trimming. However, the same

meadow installed on a rooftop in Pasadena would require considerably more irrigation—perhaps as much as four times a week in summer—to maintain an equally rich appearance. Mowing frequency would increase as well to retain a tidy appearance.

Rock gardens present an equally varied range of possibilities. On a spacious rooftop, the plant selections could emulate a mix found on one of California's foothill rock outcrops, including needlegrasses, dudleyas, and a splash of color from annuals, such as California poppies. Smaller-scale roofs with adequate access might feature a rock garden with a collection of alpine plants, perhaps featuring rock buckwheat and sulfur buckwheat. On a partially shaded roof with a bit more water, a combination of western coral bells would be suitable.

Rooftop designs using succulents, such as a mass of sedums or a vivid assortment of ice plants, would require little or no water if planted near the coast and only occasional water in interior valleys. Maintenance would also be modest, consisting of little more than deadheading and watching out for aphids, ants, and mealybugs.

Tapestries and carpets, as well as kitchen gardens, hold great potential for rooftop landscapes. A collection of low-growing thymes might be joined with sages, oreganos, and rosemaries, serving both as a tapestry and as a source of herbs. A carpet of strawberries could offer a perennial crop, while a steady rotation of lettuce, spinach, and other leafy greens could supply one's salad bowl year-round. Easy and safe access to these types of green roof installations would be essential.

MAINTENANCE AND SPECIAL ISSUES

The maintenance of a green roof is design dependent and can be quite variable from one location to another. Roofs with poor access and dangerous exposures will require designs with lower maintenance requirements. Roofs with free access and safe railings or parapets allow much greater freedom; in these situations design choices are limited only by the maintenance and water budgets. All roofs will require occasional weeding as wind and visiting birds can deposit an assortment of weed species. Other maintenance tasks common to traditional gardens would also apply to green roofs: irrigation repair, deadheading, plant replacement, monitoring nutrient needs, and even redesign are all part of a roof garden's life.

On the urban and suburban fringe of California, wildfire considerations will influence irrigation, maintenance, and design decisions. Allowing grasses used in a rooftop meadow to go summer dormant in a fire-active area would pose an irresponsible risk to the structure as well as the neighborhood. A well-maintained green roof of succulents, such as sedums, however, would provide a measure of fire prevention. Rooftop irrigation systems might also extend additional protection, assuming water pressure would be available as a fire approaches. All homes located in areas with high fire exposure will need to consider their plant selection carefully and be particularly mindful of plant dormancy.

SELECTED PLANT PALETTE FOR GREEN ROOFS

The following list is suggested for extensive green roofs since the potential plant palette for intensive roofs is unlimited. The plant selection reflects a bias toward species that will tolerate dry conditions. The optimal California climate zones for growing each plant appear in brackets after the plant name and are abbreviated as follows: c = coastal; i = inland; cv = Central Valley; ld = low desert; hd = high desert; m = mountain; all = all zones. (For more information on the zones, see page 57.) California native plants appear in green type.

Trees in containers adorned with succulents are set within a meadow planting on this Bay Area green roof. DAVID FROSS

Achillea clavennae, Greek yarrow [all]
A. filipendulina and cultivars, fernleaf yarrow [all]
A. hybrids, yarrow hybrids [all]
A. millefolium and cultivars (not all are native), common yarrow [all]
A. tomentosa, woolly yarrow [all]
Achnatherum hymenoides, Indian rice grass [c, i, cv, hd]
A. speciosum, desert needlegrass [c, i, cv, hd]
Agrostis pallens, dune bent grass [c, i, cv]
Aristida purpurea, purple three-awn [all]
Bouteloua curtipendula, side-oats grama [all]
B. gracilis, blue grama [all]
Buchloe dactyloides and cultivars, buffalo grass [all]
Carex divulsa, Berkeley sedge [c, i, cv, m]
C. flacca, blue sedge [c, i, cv, m]
C. pansa, dune sedge [c, i, cv]
C. praegracilis, clustered field sedge [all]
C. subfusca, mountain sedge [all]
Deschampsia cespitosa var. *holciformis,* Pacific hairgrass [c, i, cv, m]
Dudleya anthonyi, Anthony dudleya [c, i]
D. brittonii, Britton dudleya [c, i]
D. densiflora, Fish Canyon dudleya [c, i]
D. edulis, ladies' fingers dudleya [c, i]
D. pulverulenta, chalk dudleya [c, i]
D. virens ssp. *hassei,* Catalina Island dudleya [c, i]
Erigeron karvinskianus and cultivar, Santa Barbara daisy [c, i, cv, ld]
Eriogonum grande var. *rubescens,* red-flowered buckwheat [c, i, cv]
E. umbellatum, sulfur buckwheat [all except ld]
Festuca glauca and cultivars, blue fescue [all except ld]
F. idahoensis and cultivars, Idaho fescue [all except ld]
F. mairei, Maire's fescue [all except ld]
Leymus triticoides and cultivar, creeping wild rye [all except ld]
Muhlenbergia capillaris, pink muhly [all]
M. emersleyi, bull grass [all]
M. lindheimeri, Lindheimer's muhly [all except m]

M. pubescens, soft blue Mexican muhly [all except m]
M. rigens, deer grass [all]
Nassella cernua, nodding needlegrass [c, i, cv]
N. lepida, foothill needlegrass [c, i, cv]
N. pulchra, purple needlegrass [c, i, cv]
Nepeta × faassenii and cultivars, catmint [all]
Origanum dictamnus, dittany of Crete [c, i, cv, ld]
O. laevigatum and cultivars, oregano [all]
O. rotundifolium, round-leaved oregano [all]
Portulacaria afra 'Prostrate', Prostrate elephant's food [c, i, cv]
Sedum acre, common stonecrop [all except ld]
S. adolphii, coppertone stonecrop [c, i, cv]
S. album and cultivars, white stonecrop [all except ld]
S. dasyphyllum, Corsican stonecrop [all except ld]
S. rupestre 'Angelina', Angelina stonecrop [all except ld]
S. × rubrotinctum, Christmas cheer [c, i, cv]
S. spurium and cultivars, two-row stonecrop [all except ld]
S. stefco, stonecrop [all except ld]
Sempervivum arachnoideum, cobweb houseleeks [all except ld]
S. montanum, montane houseleeks [all except ld]
S. tectorum, hen-and-chickens [all except ld]
Senecio mandraliscae, blue chalksticks [c, i, ld]
S. serpens, little blue chalksticks [c, i]
Sporobolus airoides, alkali sacaton [all]
S. heterolepis, prairie dropseed [all]
Yucca nana, dwarf yucca [all]
Zauschneria californica and cultivars, California fuchsia [all]
Z. septentrionalis, Humboldt County fuchsia [all]

A recycled conveyor belt serves as a pathway through this naturalistic greensward of creeping red fescue and deer grass (background). SAXON HOLT

CHAPTER TWO

HOW TO MANAGE, REDUCE, OR REMOVE YOUR LAWN

For practical, aesthetic, emotional, or other reasons, many gardeners desire an area of turfgrass in their yard. Some will want to include a lawn within a new landscape, while others have an existing lawn that they would like to renovate or reduce in size—even though the notion of maintaining a lawn may conflict with their desire to save water, time, and money. If you are one of these gardeners, the good news is that this dilemma has straightforward solutions. By implementing a few simple but effective practices, you can manage your turfgrass with fewer resources and reduce lawn-care costs as well.

If you are ready to get rid of your lawn, you may want to skip the following pages and go directly to the section titled "Removing Your Lawn" on page 52, which describes the different techniques for killing a lawn.

Conserving Water

Regardless of the size of your lawn, you can save water by using more efficient and site-specific irrigation techniques. Most landscape professionals contend that overwatering of lawns is all too common. Determining how often to water and how much water to apply depends on several factors, including the type of lawn and soil you have, your climate zone, current weather conditions, and mowing height. Follow these tips to use water wisely:

- Walk on the lawn. If your footprint does not bounce back within a few seconds, the lawn needs water. If in doubt, sample the soil with a soil probe to see whether it is dry or moist in the root zone. If you do not own a soil probe, a simple screwdriver serves as a handy alternative; if your soil is moist (and not heavily compacted clay), the screwdriver will penetrate it easily.
- Water in the early morning rather than during the heat of the day, when the potential for evaporation is high. Nighttime watering eliminates evaporation, but favors pathogens that thrive on moist foliage. Pathogens are especially problematic in wet coastal sites but less so in inland areas where the humidity is much lower. In addition, it is much more difficult to detect broken or misaligned sprinklers after dark.
- Adjust spray heads so that only the lawn receives irrigation. Eliminate overlap onto sidewalks, the driveway, or other adjacent areas.

- Keep the shape of your lawn simple by avoiding awkward angles or curves that are difficult to irrigate.
- Avoid watering when it is windy, but be sure to water in advance of forecasted Santa Ana conditions.
- Lawns growing in sandy soils respond best to shorter, more frequent irrigation cycles. For lawns on clay soils, water deeply and less often.
- Water long enough for moisture to penetrate at least 3 to 4 inches deep; 6 to 8 inches is preferable. This will ensure that the roots receive adequate hydration.
- If you are having problems with runoff, program the irrigation system for several short cycles instead of one long cycle.

Early morning irrigation using well-adjusted sprinkler heads saves water on this new installation of clustered field sedge.

Time clocks are a mixed blessing. If you are forgetful or away on vacation, they will automatically remember to water for you. However, they need periodic reprogramming to reflect seasonal weather patterns; otherwise they will waste water. Like other electronic devices, time clocks are not foolproof. They can malfunction in myriad ways, leading to either under- or overwatering. Remember to inspect them periodically to insure that they are working properly. Some automatic irrigation systems now come with "smart" controllers, which are technologically sophisticated water-saving tools. They respond to a constant stream of local weather data, supplied courtesy of satellites. They water according to the information you provide about your particular situation, such as soil type, amount of sunlight, and type of turf.

They cost more initially, but pay for themselves quickly with water savings.

Grass Varieties

In addition to smart irrigation practices, gardeners in climate zones with high summer temperatures can conserve water by converting their current lawn to a different type of grass. In the hot regions of California, warm-season grasses, such as buffalo or hybrid Bermuda grass, require 20% to 40% less water than a cool-season turf, such as tall fescue or Kentucky bluegrass. The best time to perform this conversion is late winter or early spring, when warm-season grasses emerge from dormancy and begin a new growth cycle. (If you plan to remove your lawn in the future, you may not want to convert it to Bermuda grass or its hybrids, because they are very difficult to kill.)

The process for replacing a cool-season grass is relatively simple: remove the sod or kill it (these techniques are described beginning on page 52) and install the new lawn by planting plugs or liners of warm-season grass. Stoloniferous species, like buffalo grass, will typically fill in during the first warm season if planted on 6-inch centers; wider spacing of 12 or 18 inches will yield results less quickly. Rhizomatous species, like blue grama grass, are slower to reach full coverage unless the plugs or liners are spaced on 2- or 4-inch centers. Careful attention to weeding and providing some additional water will be required while the new turf is getting established. A warm-season lawn will naturally go dormant (and look bleached-brown) in winter, and some gardeners are comfortable with this appearance. Those who want year-round green will need to overseed their turf each fall with an annual grass, such as annual bluegrass, also known as rye grass.

If your lawn is composed of a cool-season grass, especially one like tall fescue that can handle some drought, another strategy for water conservation is to stop irrigating in summer and let the lawn turn brown. This technique is primarily suited for climate zones with mild summers, such as those near the coast. In these areas, a lawn composed of cool-season grasses that has been deprived of summer water will typically bounce back with new green growth when the rains resume in fall. By embracing the natural seasonal shift of the cool-season grasses, you can enjoy tremendous water, energy, and labor savings.

Lawn Care and Maintenance

Next to overwatering, the second most common turf-care mistake is applying too much fertilizer. Excess fertilizer promotes lush new growth that requires correspondingly greater amounts of water, as well as more frequent mowing. It also encourages insect and disease infestations and contributes to the buildup of thatch. Although most lawn grasses are heavy nitrogen feeders, there are ways you can supply this important plant nutrient without negative impacts.

To start with, be sure that you are applying fertilizer at the recommended season and proper dose for your particular lawn. Then consider what kind of fertilizer you plan to use, because this decision will have an effect on your surrounding environment and will also influence your lawn's water needs. Inorganic fertilizers add potentially damaging salts to the soil and often break down so quickly that they leach into the groundwater before the grasses' roots can absorb them. As much as 60% of the synthetic nitrogen fertilizer applied to lawns ends up volatilizing into the atmosphere or polluting groundwater. In contrast, judicious use of organic fertilizer will keep your lawn healthy by feeding the beneficial microorganisms in the soil. This network of

Buffalo grass (seen here) and other warm-season grasses use less water than cool-season varieties, even in hotter regions.

Purple needlegrass, seen here in a front yard, is a cool-season grass that grows best without water during summer dormancy.

fungi, bacteria, and other microscopic creatures recycle organic matter below ground and make nutrients, such as nitrogen, available to plant roots. In addition, many organic fertilizers add structure to the soil and improve drainage as well as water retention.

Mowing the lawn may seem like a straightforward task, but the way you go about this chore will make a difference in how your lawn performs. Turfgrasses respond better to frequent rather than infrequent mowing, but excessive mowing promotes water loss by decreasing shade and increasing evaporation. It may also create openings where weeds can become established. If you let your grass grow, however, the longer blades will have more leaf surface available to conduct photosynthesis. This, in turn, promotes strong roots that enable the grass to withstand drought and fend off pests and diseases. To encourage optimum blade length, set the mowing height as high as possible for your particular turf—most grasses are best when kept at 2 to 3 inches high—and mow often enough so that you remove no more than 1/3 of the overall height. Several new cultivars of traditional lawn grasses are lower-growing selections that require significantly less mowing frequency. For example, Bella bluegrass and some Bermuda grass hybrids like 'FloraDwarf' and 'MiniVerde' are lower growing, and the need to mow them is reduced by as much as half.

Another way to limit resource consumption while maintaining a lawn is to replace your gas-powered mower with an electric model. It is quieter, consumes roughly 50% less energy than a gas mower, and reduces air pollution. Or, if you want to save fuel while simultaneously getting physical exercise, you could switch to a manual (also known as reel) lawn mower, and the only calories burned in the process of mowing the lawn will be yours. Regardless of mower style, make sure your machine's cutting blades are sharp, and only mow when the grass is dry. Leave the cut grass to decompose in place; it contains valuable nutrients. A mulching mower will chop the clippings into smaller pieces and speed up the recycling process.

Lawns eventually develop thatch between the soil and the grass blades. Once this layer of dead grass becomes more than ½-inch deep, it interferes with water and nutrient penetration into the soil. Remove it either by raking it away or by using a special de-thatching machine. Follow up by broadcasting lawn seed to fill in where needed; then cover the seed with a thin layer of compost and water the treated area. Be sure to avoid over-fertilizing, which contributes to thatch buildup. Use of organic fertilizers fosters a healthy soil food web—teeming with earthworms and beneficial microorganisms—that will help decompose the thatch and recycle its nutrients back into the soil.

If your lawn is growing in clay soil and gets a lot of traffic, it may become compacted over time. This,

A native plant tapestry (background) is an attractive alternative to a tired Bermuda grass lawn (foreground). STEPHEN INGRAM

too, will impede percolation of water and nutrients and result in an unhealthy lawn. Correct this problem by using a manual or power-driven aerator that extracts soil cores, and then fill the resulting holes with compost. It is best to tackle this rather laborious task during spring or fall when soil and air temperatures are milder.

A weed-free lawn is *de rigueur* for some gardeners. Other lawn owners are more relaxed about the occasional weed, and some actually encourage the growth of clover or other nitrogen-fixing plants in their turf. Bacteria living in nodules on the roots of these plants pull nitrogen out of the air and release it into the soil, thereby making nitrogen available to plant roots. (Clover is highly attractive to bees, and if you are allergic to their sting, you may not want this legume to flourish in your lawn.) If you cannot tolerate a few weeds here and there, do not automatically reach for chemical herbicides to eradicate them. Hand weeding is effective on a small scale, and applications of natural herbicide products, such as horticultural vinegar or corn gluten meal, have been used with success by some gardeners.

There is a long list of insect pests and diseases that can plague lawns. Even a thoughtfully maintained lawn may succumb to an occasional infestation. By following the principles of integrated pest management, you will likely solve the problem without having to use toxic chemicals. First, accurately diagnose the cause. Next, try changing your cultural practices to see if that fixes the problem. For example, lawns with insufficient nitrogen are susceptible to rust fungi. An additional, careful application of fertilizer should take care of this infection. A thick layer of thatch creates an ideal environment for chinch bugs; get rid of them by removing the thatch. Other insect pests, such as sod webworms and white grubs, can be controlled with parasitic nematodes.

If you rely upon a professional gardening service to maintain your lawn, be sure to insist that their equipment is free of weeds, insects, and diseases each time they perform any work on your property. All sorts of pest problems are spread from one garden to the next by such "unprotected" mowing.

REDUCING YOUR LAWN

If you are contemplating a reduction or modification of an existing lawn, the first step is to analyze its current size, function, and site. Then ask yourself the following questions: Do I really need to devote all that space to turf? What other uses might I make of the area currently occupied by the lawn? Are there problem spots where the lawn never looks good because there is too much shade, too steep a slope, or too much root competition from trees and shrubs?

After considering the answers to these questions, you may realize that you could cut back on the amount of grass you are maintaining by at least half or more. Perhaps you have always wanted a rock garden or a patch of succulents; you can shrink the lawn by ceding some of its space to these or other new uses. If water runs off because your turf sits on a slope, confine it to level ground and re-landscape the slope with a carpet or tapestry planting. When a specimen tree or a shrub provides too much shade, replace the grass beneath it with shade-tolerant herbaceous perennials. If roots from adjacent trees or shrubs suck up too much moisture and nutrients, eliminate lawn around them and cover the area with a layer of mulch, such as chipped bark. By reducing the lawn's square footage, you can quickly lower your water use, even without removing your entire lawn.

Lawn Alternatives Under Trees

One of the first places to consider removing lawn is where it has been installed beneath a tree. A stately tree within a manicured lawn is a staple of our landscapes, but closer inspection often reveals that turf under a tree is languishing. That's primarily because the turf must compete with the tree's roots for water and nutrients. In addition, some types of grass may not thrive in the shade of the tree's canopy.

When you replace turf or engage in other landscaping activities beneath a tree, extra care is called for. Most of a tree's roots are only 1 to 2 feet deep and the feeder roots, which take up water and nutrients, are usually within the top foot of soil. Therefore, avoid any of the lawn-removal techniques (see page 52) that entail the use of a rototiller or solarization. After the lawn is gone, do not change the original soil level beneath the tree canopy or bury any structural tree roots that are visible on the soil surface. Adding soil, especially around the base of the tree trunk, can cause crown rots, suffocates the roots, and creates conditions that are favorable to a host of soil-borne pathogens.

Respect the tree's root system during any construction activity, especially around mature specimens, as older trees are generally less tolerant of disturbance than younger ones. If you build a new deck, patio, or pathway, be flexible when designing these hardscape features by adjusting dimensions, layout, and footings. The same consideration applies when installing a new irrigation system. Severing even one major tree root can cause a 15% to 25% loss of the tree's overall root system. To minimize severing tree roots, do as much digging as possible by hand rather than using a power-driven trencher. Keep heavy equipment out of the critical root zone during construction. This zone is defined as the area from the trunk of the tree extending three feet beyond the outer edge of the canopy. When planting, try to use nursery stock that comes in 4-inch containers or 1-gallon pots; this way you can minimize the size and depth of the planting holes in the root zone.

Selecting plants for the new landscape under a tree involves finding specimens that will tolerate some shade, handle root competition from the tree, and be com-

Above: Drought-tolerant foxtail agave thrives in the dry shade beneath this mature coast live oak. Left: The flowers of Douglas iris contribute seasonal color to shady areas under trees.

Mulch and water-thrifty blue chalksticks are good choices for covering the ground beneath this valley oak.

patible with the tree's water needs. From an aesthetic standpoint, you may want a plant palette that works well with key features of the tree, such as its foliage, form, texture, flowers, fruits, or bark. For example, the mottled bark and vibrant summer flowers of a crape myrtle could be complemented with a carpet of rosette-forming succulents. The dark foliage and bold structure of a coast live oak might combine nicely with a selection of California's native grasses and evoke a woodland setting. In some situations, the best design solution is one without plants. The strong lines of a conifer with graceful boughs that arch to the ground could be offset by a layer of bark or gravel mulch to create a calm, understated effect.

Although many tree species can tolerate a surprisingly wide range of conditions, keep in mind that your tree was probably accustomed to regular irrigation when the lawn was present. The new plants around the tree may require less water than the lawn, but it's best for the tree if you gradually reduce the frequency of irrigation; this allows it to adjust to a drier environment over time. Continue to provide supplemental irrigation over one or two summers, watering less frequently but more deeply. Some trees, such as cottonwood, birch, and Chinese elm, will not survive our long, dry summers without adequate moisture in the soil. Removing the lawn under these trees may not significantly affect your water bill, but it will certainly reduce other attendant lawn-care chores such as mowing, fertilizing, and weed management. A number of plants featured in this book are "water-neutral" and can therefore adapt to either dry or moist shade beneath mature trees. These include agapanthus, barberry, bergenia, carex, hellebore, strawberry, and wire grass.

Our native oak trees deserve special mention. If you have a lawn that was installed beneath an oak that preexisted development in the area, it is a good idea to remove the turf. California's oaks evolved with our mediterranean climate's natural rhythm of winter-wet

and summer-dry seasons. Regular summer irrigation under an oak often induces oak root fungus or crown rot, which can weaken and kill the tree. The unneeded irrigation also promotes summer growth that is susceptible to powdery mildew, a disfiguring foliar disease. The list "Dry Shade" on page 135 provides good choices for landscapes under oaks.

The Hardscape Option

In some cases, the best way to reduce or replace a traditional turfgrass lawn may not rely entirely on plants. Instead of exclusively using "softscape"—a green industry term for living materials—you may prefer a design that blends plants with non-living, or "hardscape," materials, such as concrete, bricks, flagstone, or wooden decking. Compared to plants, hardscape has some distinct advantages: it never needs to be watered, mowed, pruned, or fertilized; potential insect or disease problems are minimal to none; and replacement may rarely, if ever, be necessary. Hardscapes are also ideal for creating level surfaces for activities that can be enjoyed outdoors, such

Top: Deer grass lines a gravel pathway through a garden of drought-tolerant California native plants. SAXON HOLT
Bottom: Local rocks can be used to fashion a seasonally dry streambed, such as the one shown here with autumn moor grass (foreground). JOAN BOLTON

Silver carpet fills the spaces and harmonizes with the colors of the stones in this patterned outdoor terrace.

as reading, dining, or socializing. Decks or terraces, for example, are especially valuable for replacing a sloping lawn that is challenging to mow and irrigate.

The disadvantage of using hardscape is that the cost of materials and construction can be quite high. Installing features such as patios, decks, steps, or retaining walls often requires exacting and extensive site preparation. Proper drainage, perfectly level grades, and careful placement of footings to avoid tree roots or underground utilities are some of the issues that a hardscape project may need to address. Regardless of what feature you are designing, it is a good idea to match the scale of the project with your actual needs. Too often, our tendency is to overbuild hardscape installations. You do not need to pave an area the size of a dance floor when the objective is to create a space for an outdoor dining nook.

If your goal is to have a more sustainable landscape, you may want to evaluate and compare various hardscape materials before you build. Every hardscape product that you import to your yard has an inherent impact on the environment, whether it comes from extraction, harvesting, processing, transportation, or installation. Concrete, for example, is a material that has a high environmental cost. That's because its core ingredient—cement—is manufactured by first mining a variety of minerals and then heating them in industrial kilns that emit significant amounts of carbon dioxide into the atmosphere. In addition, the aggregates that are mixed with cement to make it into concrete are usually removed from the beds of rivers and creeks.

The adage "right plant, right place," which serves gardeners so well in creating healthy and successful plant combinations, can also be applied to the selection of hardscape materials. Local materials can provide a tangible connection to the surrounding natural landscape and reinforce a sense of place. In Santa Barbara, for example, the region's indigenous sandstone fits seamlessly into area gardens when used for patios and walls. The coast redwood forests of central and northern California yield durable lumber for decking that feels right in coastal gardens but seems out of place in the desert. In arid locations such as Palm Springs, decomposed granite or other local aggregate is a more sensible choice for level surfaces. Since shipping often represents the highest energy cost for a product, the more local a material, the lower the transportation cost will be. You may even have native materials on your site that can be put to work, such as rocks that can be gathered and rearranged into a seasonally dry streambed. When properly compacted and canted for drainage, a path that consists of nothing more than your native soil may be the most satisfactory material of all.

Most new garden plans that entail lawn removal or reduction are likely to include some type of hardscape in the form of pathways. Navigating between the various spaces in our gardens is a key component of the overall design. A network of paths is both practical and essential; it connects the dots by visually linking house and garden. The choice of paving materials and patterns subtly affects our mood and speed. If designed to slow us down, as in a Japanese stroll or tea garden, pathways foster contemplation and invite a closer look at your surroundings. Alternatively, paths may hasten our step and beckon us onward to a tempting destination. In either case, the ideal path is easy to walk on and provides sure footing, even when wet.

There are a number of widely available materials to use for walkways and other hardscape features that are versatile and potentially reusable. Brick and tile—both derived from clay—can lend a formal element to paths and patios. Their warm colors and regular shapes allow for all sorts of creative patterns, whether they are laid flat or on end. Concrete pavers come in many preformed shapes, sizes, colors, and textures. Aggregates, such as crushed rock, gravel, decomposed granite, cobble, and pebbles, are attractive pervious materials that work well on level ground. For uneven surfaces, however, aggregates are often prone to erosion unless you add a binding or stabilizing agent, which makes them impermeable. The natural colors and textures of flagstone are hard to beat for aesthetic beauty. Unfortunately, harvesting this material by quarrying or extraction means destroying a natural outcrop elsewhere.

Recycled materials offer alternative options for hardscape projects. One of these products is called urbanite, which consists of broken-up chunks of concrete removed during the demolition of roads, driveways, sidewalks, patios, and other paved places. It can be used in myriad applications, such as walkways, planting beds, retaining walls, and entire patios and can even be stained. Urbanite is not available from vendors of hardscape products, so you will need to be resourceful to locate a supply for your project. Check with local contractors, in classified ads, or with neighbors to find out where and when a concrete-removal job is scheduled or underway. Trees are another renewable source for hardscape construction materials. Lumber that has been independently certified to signify that it has been sustainably grown and harvested is carried by a number of home and garden supply outlets in California. You may also want to inquire about local sawyers who are producing lumber from street trees that have been culled from the urban forest—trees that in the past would have gone to the local landfill or been turned into wood chips. Lumber made from wood waste and discarded plastic, such as soda containers, is a recycled material that is useful for decks, railings, and edging for garden beds.

Top: Recycled concrete pavers set in pervious gravel frame a greensward of blue grama. SAXON HOLT
Bottom: Low clusters of blue fescue grow between concrete strips in a driveway designed to reduce runoff. STEPHEN INGRAM

When it comes to capturing run-off from precipitation, even a lawn is better than a hardscape made of impervious material. Unless you need to have a uniformly smooth outdoor surface, try to construct your hardscape with permeable materials, such as aggregates or pavers that allow water to seep easily through and around them to reach the soil underneath. You can also fill the earthen spaces between flagstone, bricks, and urbanite with tough, ground-hugging plants, such as thyme, Greek yarrow, or silver carpet. Such plantings can provide a softening effect, visually unify the various landscape elements, and help keep a hardscape area cooler on hot days. When an uninterrupted solid surface is desirable for a patio or other outdoor feature, consider pouring a slab of pervious concrete. This is a type of concrete that is made with little or no sand, and it allows water to move through it at high rates. Pervious concrete is also strong enough to be used for weight-bearing elements, such as driveways.

REMOVING YOUR LAWN

If you have decided to get rid of your lawn, you have probably also wondered about how to do it. There are several effective ways to remove a lawn, but all of them should begin with a close analysis of your particular turfgrass. Chances are, your current lawn is composed of one or more common commercial grasses. Mixed in with these—especially if it is an older lawn—you will often find various species of weeds. A number of perennial grasses and weeds are especially difficult to eliminate, including Bermuda grass, Kikuyu grass, St. Augustine grass, nutsedges, bindweed, and Bermuda buttercup. The presence (or absence) of these hard-to-kill grasses and weeds will likely determine the best method for eradicating your particular mélange of a lawn. No matter how you remove your turf, you will need to be vigilant to keep unwanted plants from getting re-established or introduced into your new landscape. To learn more about the types of grasses or weeds in your lawn, dig out a sample with a trowel and take it a local nurseryman or landscape contractor for assistance with identification.

Mechanical Removal

If your lawn is free from the worst perennial grasses and weeds, you may choose to eliminate it by using machinery. One proven method is to use a sod cutter. This piece of equipment is designed to penetrate your turf and cut the roots, so you can remove strips of sod without displacing too much soil. Cut strips may be either composted or flipped over and used as mulch. You may need to adjust the level of the newly cleared surface before you plant again.

Another mechanical way to remove the lawn entails the use of a rototiller or a tractor with a tiller attachment. Known as the "multiple-till and irrigation method," this process requires rototilling the lawn area at least four times over a four- to six-week period. The initial tilling should be sufficiently deep and thorough

to incorporate any amendments and break up the existing turfgrass. After tilling, water the area and allow weed seeds and bits of lawn to resprout. In one to two weeks, till again, but only to a shallow depth. Repeat these steps at least two more times to eliminate most weed seeds; more tilling and irrigation may be needed to get rid of all re-emerging grass roots. Be sure your soil is moist, but not too wet, when you work it with a tiller; cultivating soggy soils—especially heavy clay soils—will damage the soil's structure.

Solarization

Solarization harnesses the energy of the sun to remove the lawn. By trapping sunlight beneath a layer of clear plastic sheeting, you essentially steam-sterilize the upper few inches of your garden's soil and kill nearly every living thing in this zone. Solarization is an excellent alternative in hot areas, but it rarely does much good in cooler climate zones of California. For success with this method, you will need six to eight weeks of daytime peak temperatures reliably over 80°F and full sun expo-

Top, After: The young clustered field sedge greensward required regular weeding during its initial establishment.
Bottom, After: Two years later, the recently mowed clustered field sedge greensward resembles a mature lawn.

Before: A lawn of tall fescue was removed by repeated tilling to make way for a clustered field sedge greensward.

sure for at least six to eight hours each day.

Even in warm climates, solarization has some limitations. Seeds of plants in the legume family (Fabaceae) are often unaffected by solarization, and in some cases this technique can lead to a marked increase in these plants. This is fine if your lawn area contained seed from plants, such as lupines, that you want to retain as part of a new garden design, but it can be disastrous if you have burr clover, vetch, sweet clover, or other weedy, unwanted legumes. Also, some deeply rooted pest plants such as nutsedges, Bermuda grass, bindweed, and others will initially be set back by solarization, but they will often reappear from deeper roots or shoots that survived below the solarized level.

To begin the process of solarization, clear the lawn site of any materials that could puncture the plastic sheeting, including twigs or thorny vegetation. Level the area carefully to ensure there is as much direct contact between the plastic and the surface as possible. Dig a 6- to 8-inch-deep trench around the edge of the area to be solarized. Water the site deeply and thoroughly; then, wait a few days until you can safely walk on the area without fear of compacting the soil or getting muddy. The soil should be moist, not waterlogged. If it is too dry, water it again and proceed only when the soil conditions are appropriate.

Roll out enough 3- to 6-millimeter-thick clear plastic sheeting to cover the entire area. Be sure that your plastic sheeting is a type that is resistant to ultraviolet light, because it may otherwise fall apart before the soil has been successfully solarized. If the sheeting is not wide enough to cover the lawn completely, apply as many additional plastic sheets as necessary, making certain they overlap by a couple of inches. Pull the sheets tight to maximize contact with the lawn's surface, and then cover any seams with sand in order to retain moisture in the soil; duct tape could also be used for this purpose. The outer edge of the plastic sheeting should extend beyond the outer edge of the perimeter trench. Fill the trench with sand to weigh down the plastic.

During the following weeks, avoid unnecessary foot traffic on the plastic-covered surface, as the sheeting is thin and punctures easily. Any new holes or tears in the plastic should be quickly repaired with duct tape. If needed, apply additional sand to keep the margins and seams sealed. Note that these seam and edge areas will not receive the full benefit of solarization, and weeds will likely still be present along these lines when solarization is complete.

After a minimum of four to eight weeks, you can remove the plastic and proceed with your landscaping project. Remember that only the top 4 to 6 inches of the soil will have been solarized. Trenching, extensive grading, or digging holes for plants in gallon-sized or larger containers are activities that can penetrate below

the solarized soil and can bring deeply buried weed seeds close to the surface, where they are likely to germinate. Hand weeding can usually keep these new sprouts from getting established.

Sheet Mulching

Sheet mulching uses layers of organic materials to kill your lawn by smothering it. This process can be initiated at any time of the year, although it works best when the lawn is actively growing. In its most basic form, sheet mulching requires little more than layers of paper or cardboard, topped with a thick layer of organic matter. You can also enrich your soil during sheet mulching by including manure or compost in the mulch "sandwich" along with other nitrogen-rich materials, such as grass clippings. This technique is also referred to as sheet composting. If you plan to replace a large area of grass, you will need to acquire or stockpile a significant amount of biodegradable material to complete the job.

To start, water the existing lawn, making the soil moist but not saturated or muddy. Next, put down a layer of moistened newspaper at least five pages thick.

Top, Before: An uninterrupted front lawn presented a bland entrance to this suburban home. JOAN BOLTON
Bottom, After: Colorful borders containing Santa Barbara daisy, lavender, and other plants helped reduce the size of the lawn. JOAN BOLTON

Wetting the newspaper will help it break down faster and keep it from blowing away as you are building your layers. You can also use one or two layers of thick corrugated (but not waxed) cardboard instead of newspaper. Be sure these materials overlap at the edges so that coverage of the lawn area you want to kill is complete. Follow this with a thick layer of manure. (Some authorities recommended putting the manure layer first and adding the newspaper or cardboard on top of that.) Then pile on layers of whatever organic materials you happen to have on hand or can locally acquire: shredded leaves, lawn clippings (but not from stoloniferous species that can sprout, such as Bermuda or St. Augustine grass), pine needles, straw, alfalfa hay, compost, and even soil. As you build the mulch, try to alternate dry, coarse substances, such as straw, with moister layers that have more nitrogen content, such as fresh greens or manure. Rough, dry materials that are high in lignins and cellulose, such as chipped tree and shrub prunings, will take much longer to break down and function as a soil amendment; ideally they should be a minimal component in the mulch.

Initially, the finished height of the sheet mulch should be at least 12 to 24 inches. Keep your sheet mulch slightly moist for optimum rates of decomposition. As they break down, the various layers will lose height. You will need to wait at least four to six weeks until the sheet mulch has killed the turf beneath it and decomposed sufficiently before you plant. Once the new area is ready, simply pull back or part the mulch in places where you install plants and plugs or sow seeds.

Lasagna Bed Method

The "lasagna" method is a variation on sheet mulching and is the subject of several books by garden author Patricia Lanza. This technique has its origins in the "no-dig" philosophy, which was first popularized in the United States during the 1950s by New England gardener and mulching advocate Ruth Stout. The lasagna method is especially useful when your objective is to reduce the lawn by creating beds along its edges or islands within the turf. The process is essentially the same as sheet mulching, but instead of covering your entire lawn, you create distinct beds by laying down the same sequence of organic layers. If you construct lasagna beds on top of a lawn that was composed of aggressive perennial grasses or weeds, you will have to treat the remnant strips between the beds to keep the grass and weeds from spreading into your beds. The most resilient perennial weeds will eventually reappear—even within the beds—and sometimes will do so rather quickly, depending upon your actual site and conditions. It is always a good idea to control such pest plants before building a lasagna garden.

The lasagna method confers various advantages: the beds' high content of organic matter retains moisture and they therefore need less frequent watering; they require no initial digging or tilling to prepare; and once established, they have few weed problems. To avoid compacting your lasagna beds, design them so you can reach into their centers without stepping on them. For maximum drainage, lasagna beds can be initially built up even higher than the recommended 24-inch depth for sheet mulch. You can maintain a lasagna bed by periodically adding layers of organic material, as needed.

Herbicides

Applications of herbicides offer a proven way to kill a lawn, although many gardeners may want to try other methods before resorting to this approach. In some situations, spraying herbicides may be the only practical or feasible way to eradicate a lawn. This is especially true if the lawn is composed of Kikuyu grass or Bermuda grass (or its hybrids). This also pertains to lawns that contain noxious weeds, such as nutsedge and bindweed. Most commercially available herbicides are derived from petrochemicals, and traces of these chemicals turn up in our rivers and groundwater. Many toxicologists and ecologists believe these chemical weed killers have detrimental long-term effects on human health and the environment. Some gardeners refuse to use them, and they will be more comfortable trying one of the lawn-removal methods previously described in this chapter

There are a number of herbicides to choose from, including some non-toxic, plant-based products that have more recently come on the market. Be sure to match your target grass(es) and weed(s) with an appropriate herbicide. When using any herbicide, follow all label directions and safety protocols.

The following procedure is recommended for the elimination of a long-established lawn, especially one composed of Bermuda grass or with a serious infestation of nutsedges or other hard-to-kill weeds. This method is based on the use of a glyphosate-based herbicide (such as Roundup®), which is a systemic herbicide that is absorbed by green foliage and then translocated throughout the plant.

Step one: Mow your lawn closely, then apply a nitrogen fertilizer and water the lawn deeply and regularly for at least two weeks. You want to have the turf and weeds growing lushly.

Step two: After a few weeks, the lawn should be responding to the fertilizer and regular deep watering with vigorous new growth. Water the lawn thoroughly in the evening and then spray it with herbicide the next day—ideally when the grass surface has dried, the air temperature is 75F° to 85F°, and there is no wind. (Even a light breeze can cause your spray to drift onto vegetation beyond the targeted area, so be extra careful when applying herbicides near plants that you do not intend to kill.) Within a few days, the lawn will look

Top, Before: Frequent irrigation and applications of fertilizer were needed to maintain this expanse of lawn. WYNNE WILSON
Bottom, After: A vibrant tapestry of native and mediterranean-climate plants creates a low-water use landscape. WYNNE WILSON

fairly dead. But this can be deceptive, especially if your lawn had perennial weeds.

Step three: About two weeks after spraying (if the weather has been clear and warm), mow your dead and dying turf.

Step four: Start watering your treated lawn regularly and deeply. Within a week you will discover which weeds and parts of your lawn are still alive.

Step five: Encourage vigorous growth of these resprouts by giving them regular water.

Step six: After the resprouts are growing well, spray them again (under the conditions listed above), being sure to apply the herbicide to every spot with new green growth.

Repeat steps three to six until there are no further resprouts.

With the lawn now dead, you are ready to begin work on your new garden. Closely watch your subsequent new plantings for at least two years, especially if the area had been infested with any aggressive perennial weeds; it is likely that some new seedlings of these plants will appear. If these are seedlings (as opposed to resprouts), they should be promptly pulled out, and this

should be easily accomplished as there will not be a deep or complex root system to contend with. If they do happen to be deeply embedded resprouts and are resistant to removal by hand, you may need to carefully apply a spot application of herbicide.

The Case Against Artificial Turf

Artificial, or synthetic, turf has been around for many years. Developed for athletic playing fields as a low-maintenance alternative to natural turf, it is occasionally touted for residential sites for similar reasons. Although a lawn of synthetic turf requires no mowing or fertilizer, and only infrequent applications of water for cleansing, this material is hardly supportable from an environmental standpoint. Consider these facts:

- Artificial turf is made from polyethylene, the most widely used form of plastic. This is an oil-based product; its use contributes to depletion of the shrinking supply of fossil fuels.
- Artificial turf is not biodegradable; although it can be recycled, energy is necessary to convert it to something else.
- Installation costs are high, ranging from $8 to $15 per square foot. Estimates of its lifespan range from 8 to 20 years.
- Synthetic turf does not sequester atmospheric carbon, but a low-maintenance greensward will perform this pollution-reducing service.
- Artificial turf provides absolutely no wildlife habitat value.
- Leaves and other organic debris that accumulate on the surface will not be able to infiltrate the ground below as they break down, preventing an opportunity for natural nutrient recycling. Instead, property owners will likely keep their artificial turf clean by hosing it off or using a blower.
- Artificial lawns can harbor harmful bacteria (due to fecal matter from pets, etc.) and they also collect pollutant particles, soil, dust, and other inorganic debris.
- The impermeability of synthetic turf excludes any groundwater recharge and can even contribute to erosion on the property if runoff from major rain events is not taken into account during installation.
- Under high temperatures, the petroleum products used in manufacturing artificial turf can begin to off-gas as toxic substances, adding to air pollution and creating respiratory problems for people and pets.
- Artificial turf gets incredibly hot in the sun and compounds the urban heat island effect. Real lawns are up to 50% cooler by comparison. On an 80°F day, synthetic turf can easily get up to or exceed 130°F.
- Older formulations of artificial turf often contain lead, and as these products break down, they may release unhealthful levels of lead dust.

Every region of California contains gardens open to the public that showcase water-conserving designs. This demonstration landscape at Seaside Gardens in Carpinteria features Sunset rockrose and other Mediterranean Basin plants.

CHAPTER THREE

PLANT PROFILES

The following Plant Profiles contain horticultural information about a wide array of plants suitable for the design options presented in this book. This selection is not encyclopedic, but instead represents the best choices currently available for lawn alternatives in California. The primary criteria used in determining which plants to include are size, reliability, availability, aesthetic value, drought tolerance, and resistance to insect and pest problems. Preference is given to genera and species that are low-growing, durable, and versatile. The majority of the plants meet all of these criteria, and many would be effective in more than one of the design alternatives we feature: greenswards, meadow gardens, rock gardens, succulent gardens, carpet and tapestry gardens, kitchen gardens, and green roofs. For each design alternative presented in Chapter One, we provide a list of plants from the profiles that are especially recommended.

Although desirable and appropriate for many kinds of lawn alternatives, annuals and seasonally dormant bulbs were not included due to their ephemeral nature. The profiles also exclude vegetables and fruit trees, but other plants that are useful in kitchen gardens are noted.

We have not knowingly included any plants that can be considered invasive. We define these as nonnative plants that readily escape from gardens and naturalize in California wildlands. Some of the featured plants can be quite aggressive in a garden setting—and are so noted in the text—but they are not currently regarded as invasive species in our natural habitats. For more information on this topic, refer to the California Invasive Plant Council (Cal-IPC) at www.cal-ipc.org.

The Plant Profiles are arranged in alphabetical order by scientific (Latin) name. The "Index to Common and Scientific Plant Names" beginning on page 148 will help you locate a plant if you know its common name but not its scientific name. If you are seeking a plant for a particular landscape need or one that possesses a certain characteristic—such as plants that are aromatic or tolerate poor drainage—consult the lists in "Recommended Plant Selections," beginning on page 132.

At the start of each profile, readers will find a valuable summary of the plant's horticultural requirements and a brief description of its distribution. Our definitions and explanations of the terminology used in the summary information for the featured plants are given below.

Plant Type

The following standard terms are used to describe the featured plant: Shrub, Subshrub, Perennial, Grass, or Succulent.

Climate Zones

California gardeners should be able to successfully grow a plant in one or more of the six following broad climate zones if it is given proper siting and care.

Coastal: Cool ocean air is a major influence on both summer and winter temperatures. Examples: San Diego, Los Angeles, Santa Barbara, San Luis Obispo, Berkeley, San Francisco, Crescent City, and Eureka. (Comparable *Sunset* zones are 15 to 17 and 22 to 24.)

Many native grasses, such as purple three-awn, can grow in all of California's climate zones. STEPHEN INGRAM

Inland: Foothills and valleys with moderate to minimal ocean influence. Coast and Peninsular ranges typically block any consistent maritime influence. Examples: Hemet, Riverside, Ontario, San Gabriel, San Fernando, Simi Valley, Santa Ynez, King City, Paso Robles, Hollister, Santa Rosa, Covelo, and Grass Valley. (Comparable *Sunset* zones are 7, 14, and 18 to 21.)

Central Valley: The Sacramento and San Joaquin valleys. Examples: Bakersfield, Fresno, Sacramento, Redding,

Among the aloes, sages, and lavenders, a rich variety of selections is available for waterwise gardens.

Davis, Chico, Modesto, and Merced. (Comparable *Sunset* zones are 8, 9, and 14.)

Low Desert: This embraces the Sonoran Desert area within California, also regionally known as the Colorado Desert. Examples: Borrego Springs, Blythe, Brawley, Palm Springs, El Centro, and Indio. (Comparable *Sunset* zone is 13.)

High Desert: This comprises the Mojave Desert and Great Basin areas of the state. Examples: Twentynine Palms, Bishop, Barstow, Ridgecrest, Susanville, and Alturas. (Comparable *Sunset* zones are 1A, 10, and 11.)

Mountains: Yellow pine forest belt and higher. (Elevation for this zone varies with latitude and local conditions and typically begins between 3000 and 6000 feet.) Examples: Lake Arrowhead, Big Bear, Mammoth Lakes, South Lake Tahoe, and Truckee. (Comparable *Sunset* zones are 1A, 2A, 2B, 3A, and 4.)

When all the profiled species in a genus share the same recommended climate zones, this information is included in the summary at the start of the genus profile. When climate zone recommendations vary between different species or cultivars within a profile, the zones appear in brackets that follow the plant's description in the text. Where given in brackets, the climate zones are abbreviated as follows: c = coastal; i = inland; cv = Central Valley; ld = low desert; hd = high desert; m = mountain.

This information is offered as a guideline, and you are encouraged to experiment by trying a plant outside its recommended zone(s). For the many readers who are also familiar with the climate zones in the *Sunset Western Garden Book*, we have provided the corresponding

Top: This terraced yard utilizes an array of durable choices, including, from left: society garlic, blue fescue, Santa Barbara daisy, rosemary, and lily-of-the-Nile.
Bottom: Spanish lavender is a versatile ornamental.

Sunset zones for every featured plant in "*Sunset* Zones for Profiled Plants," beginning on page 142.

Light
Sun: Full sun.
Partial shade: Filtered light or shade for part of the day.
Shade: No direct sun.

Top: The overlapping bloom time for fernleaf yarrow (foreground) and autumn sage produces a colorful combination.
Bottom: Gaura can flower freely for months.

Soil

Adaptable: A plant that will tolerate a range of soil types. Well-drained: A plant that prefers or requires soil that drains well after water application. Some soils, such as rocky or sandy types, drain well based on their respective physical characteristics. Others, such as clay and silt-clay types, are normally poorly drained on level ground but are considered well-drained on slopes.

Water

The suggested water requirements in the summary text refer to established plants. Water needs vary considerably in California's diverse climates, and our categories are offered as a broad guideline to irrigation schedules during the warm season (generally April through October in most of the state). Once established, most of the species listed in the Plant Profiles require minimal to no supplemental irrigation during the rainy season, except during

exceptionally dry years. Plants grown within their native range usually require less supplemental irrigation.

Regular water: Every 3 to 7 days.
Moderate water: Every 10 to 14 days.
Occasional water: Every 3 to 4 weeks.
Infrequent water: Every 4 to 6 weeks.
Drought tolerant: Plants survive on rainfall once established except during periods of prolonged winter drought. (Please note that the common definition of "drought tolerant" is often misapplied to plants that depend upon supplemental irrigation to survive California's long dry summers.)

Origin

This summarizes the natural geographic distribution that the plant occupies in the wild. Many of the Plant Profiles include several species from a single genus, and in these entries, the range of the entire genus is given.

Garden Uses

This book features seven design alternatives to the lawn, and these correlate to the "Garden Uses" that are listed as appropriate landscaping options for each entry in the Plant Profiles. The Garden Uses are listed in a consistent order from one profile to the next and do not reflect any hierarchical preference.

Greensward: Grasses and sedges that fulfill the same functions as traditional lawns but are more environmentally appropriate for the regions covered in this book.

Meadow: A naturalistic, informal mixture of grasses, sedges, and herbaceous perennials.

Rock: A garden that features rocks as the primary visual backdrop or framework for a mixed planting.

Succulent: A garden dominated by succulent plants.

Carpet and tapestry: Carpets are large-scale plantings of one or a few taxa that form a homogeneous groundcover. Tapestries are typically low-stature plantings that use many taxa to create gardens with or without formal patterns.

Kitchen: A garden composed primarily of edible plants.

Green Roof: Not a garden style per se, but rather a technique with very specific installation and maintenance requirements. Plants listed here are appropriate for "extensive" green roofs (see page 41 for more information).

California Native Plants

California native plant names appear in **green type**.

Achillea
YARROW
Sunflower Family (Asteraceae)

Plant Type: Evergreen perennials.
Climate Zones: All.
Light: Sun to partial shade.
Soil: Well-drained.
Water: Drought tolerant to occasional.
Origin: Widespread in the Northern Hemisphere.
Garden Uses: Meadow, rock, carpet and tapestry, kitchen, green roof.

Island Pink yarrow. CAROL BORNSTEIN

The genus *Achillea* comprises a robust and versatile group of perennials that offer an array of species and cultivars for California gardeners. A small sampling of cultivar names provides a hint of the many flower colors available: 'Island Pink', 'Moonshine', 'Cerise Queen', and 'Terracotta'. Yarrows vary in height from a few inches to a few feet and have feathery green to gray-green foliage. Spring and early summer flowers are borne on erect stems with flattened clusters measuring ½ to 6 inches wide. Species with long stems make excellent choices for both fresh and dried flower arrangements. Modestly to aggressively rhizomatous, yarrows require minimal maintenance once established. They benefit from an annual pruning to remove spent flowers and an occasional division of older plants. Yarrows will serve well in a habitat garden; their spring flowers attract butterflies and bees, and their foliage provides winter forage for birds and lining material for cavity nesters. Gophers and rabbits are also attracted to yarrow, and plantings may require protection.

Moonshine yarrow (foreground) and Gold Plate fernleaf yarrow.

Greek yarrow *(A. clavennae)* forms low spreading mats 2 to 4 inches high and up to 18 inches wide. The dissected silver-gray leaves are a striking complement to bright white flowers that are borne on 4-inch-long stems from late spring to summer. Greek yarrow originates from southern Europe and is useful in smaller gardens where some of the more aggressive species might prove overwhelming.

Fernleaf yarrow *(A. filipendulina)* is a clumping perennial to 3 feet wide with finely dissected downy green leaves. Throughout summer, bright yellow 4- to 6-inch-wide flower heads are held on erect stems that can reach 4 feet tall. It is drought tolerant along the coast but will require summer water in warmer, interior sites. 'Gold Plate' is a vigorous selection with luminous yellow flowers, and 'Coronation Gold' features broad 6-inch-wide heads of bright yellow flowers on stems to 4 feet tall or more.

Common yarrow *(A. millefolium)* graces myriad habitats across Europe, North America, and western Asia. It often forms dense mats from spreading rhizomes and can easily be mowed into a pleasing lawn that will tolerate modest foot traffic. Flowers rise above the soft, feathery green to gray foliage on 2- to 3-foot-long stems and manifest a range of colors. Many cultivars are available: California native selections include 'Island Pink', 'King Range', and 'Sonoma Coast'; vigorous older European cultivars, such as 'Cerise Queen', 'Paprika', and 'The Beacon' also make good choices.

Woolly yarrow *(A. tomentosa)* exhibits a creeping habit. It has velvety gray-green leaves and displays golden yellow flower clusters on 6- to 10-inch-long stems. Durable and drought tolerant, woolly yarrow is a good choice for dry gravel and rock gardens and green roofs.

Yarrow hybrids *(A. hybrids)* are common in the genus and originate from a number of species; many have common yarrow *(A. millefolium)* as one of the parents. Robust and colorful, four of the best and most frequently encountered hybrid selections are: 'Moonshine', with bright yellow flowers; 'Salmon Beauty', which has pale salmon flowers; 'Terracotta', offering salmon blooms that mature to orange; and 'Taygetea', featuring pale yellow flowers.

Achnatherum
NEEDLEGRASS, SPIKE GRASS
Grass Family (Poaceae)

Plant Type: Deciduous, cool-season perennial grasses.
Climate Zones: Varies with species.
Light: Sun.
Soil: Well-drained.
Water: Occasional.
Origin: Central and southern Europe, eastern Asia, and western North America.
Garden Uses: Meadow, rock, succulent, green roof.

The genus *Achnatherum* embraces a broad-ranging group of bunchgrasses, but the two species featured here will be particularly valuable to desert gardeners. Both are excellent choices for hot, sunny, dry sites and are notable for their attractive spring inflorescences. Ripening seeds make the stalks even more ornamental and, as an added benefit, provide food for wildlife. Both species turn golden tan as the soil dries out in summer.

Indian rice grass (*A. hymenoides*) was once an important staple for native tribes in the desert Southwest, and today the rounded brown seeds are still ground into flour. This dryland bunchgrass brings an airy texture to the garden. Plants are typically 1 foot tall and wide, and the delicate inflorescences add another foot in height. [c, i, cv, hd]

Desert needlegrass (*A. speciosum*) forms clumps up to 18 inches wide by 2 feet tall. The flowers of this fine-textured grass are luminous when backlit and the beautiful inflorescences appear so silky soft they invite stroking. A single specimen next to a boulder or a large drift weaving through cacti is equally appealing. [c, i, cv, hd]

Indian rice grass.

Aeonium
AEONIUM
Stonecrop Family (Crassulaceae)

Plant Type: Evergreen succulent perennials.
Climate Zones: Coastal and inland.
Light: Sun to partial shade.
Soil: Well-drained.
Water: Drought tolerant to occasional.
Origin: Yemen, Africa, and Atlantic Islands.
Garden Uses: Rock, succulent, carpet and tapestry, green roof.

Aeoniums are admired for their geometrical form and reliability in gardens. They can also be somewhat whimsical in appearance, since many of the larger species display grand tilted daisylike rosettes of foliage atop bare stems. Plants in coastal locations prefer full sun, but further inland aeoniums grow best in partial shade. Flowers appear from late spring to summer. The species listed here branch freely and lend themselves to mass or pattern plantings.

Dinner-plate aeonium. STEPHEN INGRAM

Zwartkop aeonium (*A. arboreum* 'Zwartkop') has an upright growth habit that brilliantly shows off its 6-inch-wide rosettes of shiny near black leaves. It can reach 3 feet in height and is an outstanding choice for creating contrast with gray- to white-foliaged plants. This is an especially eye-catching species when long conical clusters of yellow flowers grace its branch tips.

Dinner-plate aeonium (*A. canariensis*) has stemless to nearly stemless flat rosettes up to 20 inches across. Foliage varies in color from bright green to reddish. Showy pyramidal inflorescences up to 3 feet tall carry hundreds of pale yellow flowers. After a rosette blooms, it dies. Plants may or may not form offsets.

Pinwheel aeonium (*A. haworthii*) forms dense clumps of 2- to 3-inch-diameter rosettes of gray-green succulent leaves that often have red margins. A mature plant may reach from 1 to nearly 2 feet tall with a slightly wider spread. The whitish to yellowish flowers are not particularly attractive.

Dwarf aeonium (*A. sedifolium*) grows into dense mounds less than 1 foot across; they are composed of packed half-inch rosettes of slightly sticky green leaves that are highlighted with red lines. Flowers are bright yellow. It is outstanding as an edging plant in rock gardens or in containers.

Pinwheel aeonium.

Kiwi aeonium.

A. simsii has toothed bright green leaves that are often marked with red and have long white hairs along their edges. Plants produce abundant offsets and quickly form low spreading clumps. The attractive flowers are bright yellow.

Kiwi aeonium (*A.* 'Tricolor') is a vigorous and reliable clone. The plant is freely branched and produces attractive rosettes of variegated cream to green leaves with prominent pinkish margins. When stressed, however, it turns plain green. This aeonium may reach from 1 to 2 feet tall and can spread wider.

Stalked aeonium *(A. undulatum)* is a bold choice for use in nearly frost-free gardens. As its common name suggests, each rosette is perched atop a thick, smooth 2- to 3-foot-tall stem. The loose 1½-foot-wide rosettes are composed of wavy-margined succulent green leaves. The effect is not unlike a large-flowered, somewhat wilted green chrysanthemum. Terminal 1½-foot-long clusters of yellow flowers appear in summer.

Agapanthus
LILY-OF-THE-NILE
Lily Family (Amaryllidaceae)

Plant Type: Evergreen or deciduous perennial herbs.
Climate Zones: Coastal, inland, and Central Valley.
Light: Sun to partial shade.
Soil: Adaptable.
Water: Infrequent to moderate.
Origin: South Africa.
Garden Uses: Meadow, rock, carpet and tapestry.

Lilies-of-the-Nile are ubiquitous in the cultivated California landscape, and their late-spring to early-summer flowers lend color to the streets and boulevards of our communities. Deciduous or evergreen, these durable and trouble-free perennials form clumps of glossy green strap-shaped leaves. In late spring and early summer, cylindrical clusters of funnel-shaped blue or white flowers arise on their elongated stems, well above the foliage. They are best in full sun along the coast and need some shade in hotter interior climates. Although they will endure long periods of drought, appearance and flowering is improved with regular irrigation. Snails and slugs can disfigure the plants and heavy infestations of these garden pests should be prevented.

African lily (*Agapanthus praecox* ssp. *orientalis,* syn. *A. orientalis*) puts forth a profusion of stiff flowering stems that rise 3 to 5 feet above the foliage and provide a dramatic display of pale blue blossoms. It is the most commonly grown species of the genus and some have suggested that all *Agapanthus* belong to this one species. African lily will form large clumps to 3 feet tall and 4 feet wide and has evergreen linear leaves 1 to 2 inches wide.

Lily-of-the-Nile hybrids (*A.* hybrids) offer a wide range of color and size choices. Some excellent evergreen

Agapanthus.

selections include: 'Peter Pan', a compact plant with blue flowers on 18-inch-long stems; 'Storm Cloud', a cultivar with dark violet-blue flowers on 4-foot-long stems; and 'Gold Strike', which has variegated leaves and blue and white striped flowers that open from dark blue buds.

Agave
AGAVE
Agave Family (Agavaceae)

Plant Type: Evergreen succulent perennials.
Climate Zones: Varies with species.
Light: Sun to partial shade.
Soil: Well-drained.
Water: Drought tolerant to occasional.
Origin: Southwestern United States to tropical South America.
Garden Uses: Rock, succulent, carpet and tapestry, green roof.

With their dramatic rosettes of thick, leathery succulent leaves, agaves are often viewed as living sculptures in a garden. Many are armed with vicious spines, so their placement in the garden requires careful consideration. All but the largest agaves also make excellent choices for big containers. After a period of time—often many years—an agave rosette will flower spectacularly and then die. The plant may continue to live on from pups or seeds. Pups sap the growth of the main rosette; remove them and the main rosette will continue to grow larger and will maintain its form. Nearly all agaves require some summer watering to look their best. In the winter months, many are sensitive to root and crown rots if

Medio Picta Alba agave.

they are too wet and cold. There are hundreds of agaves to choose from, and the following ones are especially recommended.

Medio Picta Alba agave (*A. americana* 'Medio Picta Alba') is, at 3 to 5 feet tall and wide, much more suitable to most gardens than its gigantic parent species (*A. americana*). Its sharply spined blue-gray leaves are wide, thick, and leathery and display a broad white stripe down their center. [c, i, cv, ld, hd]

Foxtail agave (*A. attenuata*) is a popular garden plant due to its soft pale yellow-green to gray-green leaves that are completely without spines. Mature rosettes may reach from 3 to 6 feet wide. When it blossoms, whitish flowers densely cover its tall stalk, which flops over near the top. Although the species is widely used, you may want to consider two of the more recent selections. 'Nova' (syn. 'Boutin Blue') has thicker, broader, bluer leaves and a wholly upright inflorescence. 'Variegata' offers blue-gray leaves liberally splashed and lined with yellow and cream-green; it is best grown in partial shade to avoid sunburn. [c, i]

Candelabrum agave (*A. bracteosa*) has foliage that is similar to octopus agave (below), but it is considerably smaller and much easier to accommodate in most gardens. It forms rosettes up to nearly 3 feet across. The pale green, gently arching 2-inch-wide leaves taper to a point but have no terminal spine. Flower spikes are 4 to 8 feet tall and carry numerous white to pale yellow 1-inch-wide flowers. [c, i, cv, ld]

Desert agave (*A. deserti*) is likely the most drought tolerant of the species listed here. Its natural range extends from California's Colorado Desert eastward into western Arizona and south into the Mexican states of Sonora and Baja California. Plants may be solitary or

Nova foxtail agave.

Candelabrum agave.

Joe Hoak agave.

Queen Victoria agave.

Artichoke agave. STEPHEN INGRAM

clumping, with green to blue, gray, or whitish foliage. A single rosette measures up to 2 feet tall and 3 feet wide. Its stout flower stalk is 8 to 12 feet tall and carries dozens of reddish to golden-yellow flowers in showy flat-topped clusters. [c, i, ld]

Smooth agave *(A. desmettiana)* has a distinctive gobletlike growth form that is especially effective in both pattern plantings and in containers. Rosettes may reach 2 to 3 feet tall and are 3 to 4 feet wide. The leaves are essentially unarmed, and their terminal spines are sharp but not vicious. Flower stalks reach from 8 to 10 feet tall and carry large clusters of light yellow blossoms. [c, i]

Twin-flowered agave *(A. geminiflora)* forms rosettes up to 4 feet across and carries innumerable linear succulent leaves that are up to 2 feet long. It resembles a green-foliaged form of chaparral yucca—without the severe terminal spines. The flower spikes display hundreds of paired yellowish to reddish flowers and may reach nearly 20 feet in height. [c, i, ld]

Joe Hoak agave *(A. 'Joe Hoak')* has thick creamy green variegated leaves with sharp black terminal spines. This plant's unique color makes it quite attractive. Mature rosettes may reach about 2 feet tall and 3

feet wide. [c, i]

Artichoke agave *(A. parryi)* demonstrates remarkable adaptability. It is surprisingly cold hardy (to about 0°F) and can be grown throughout much of California, even in gardens with regular snowfall. The attractive broad thick gray-green leaves are amply spiny and form rosettes up to 3 feet tall and wide. Place this plant away from garden paths. [all]

Queen Victoria agave *(A. victoriae-reginae)* is a choice specimen for the garden. Plants have chunky fingerlike leaves that often have showy irregular white edges. The leaves are densely packed into ball-like rosettes that may reach from 1 to 2 feet tall and wide. The terminal spines, while sharp, are short and weak when compared to others in this genus and frequently break off. The narrow inflorescence of this species, while distinctive, is not as showy as most agaves. [c, i, ld, hd]

Octopus agave *(A. vilmoriniana)* has twisted pale green leaves that lack sharp terminal spines. Rosettes of this completely unarmed plant will grow 3 feet tall and 5 feet wide. The flower stalk may reach from 15 to 25 feet tall and is densely packed with yellow flowers along most of its length. [c, i, cv, ld]

Agrostis pallens (syn. *A. diegoensis*)
DUNE BENT GRASS
Grass Family (Poaceae)

Plant Type: Cool-season perennial grass.
Climate Zones: Coastal, inland, and Central Valley.
Light: Sun to shade.
Soil: Adaptable.
Water: Drought tolerant to regular.
Origin: Western North America.
Garden Uses: Greensward, meadow, rock, green roof.

Dune bent grass. STEPHEN INGRAM

Dune bent grass has a fine-textured, delicate appearance that belies its range of garden tolerances. Spreading by rhizomes and growing to 4 inches high with short, light green leaves, it is found in a variety of habitats and often rambles through a woodland understory. The late spring to summer flowers are held in golden spikelike clusters on thin culms that can reach 2 feet high. In dry gardens, dune bent grass is fully summer dormant, but with water it can easily be maintained as an evergreen. It will tolerate moderate foot traffic, drought, sun, or shade.

Aloe
ALOE
Asphodel Family (Asphodelaceae)

Plant Type: Evergreen succulent perennials, shrubs.
Climate Zones: Varies with species.
Light: Sun to partial shade.
Soil: Well-drained.
Water: Drought tolerant to moderate.
Origin: Africa to Madagascar, Arabian Peninsula, and Atlantic Islands.
Garden Uses: Rock, succulent, carpet and tapestry, green roof.

Aloes range in size from rock garden gems measuring a few inches across to trees reaching 30 to 50 feet tall. Showy clusters of orange, red, or yellow tubular flowers adorn their succulent rosettes of attractive foliage, which may be spotted or have teeth. The blossoms are highly attractive to hummingbirds. An infestation of aloe mites *(Aceria aloinis)* manifests itself in the cauliflower-like growths that appear in the center of the plant and/or in the flowering stems. There is no effective cure other than to remove and destroy the affected growth or the entire plant.

Torch plant *(A. aristata)* is an especially decorative small succulent that is less than a foot tall and wide. The dark green leaves are attractively marked with white spots and bands. Showy red-orange flowers appear from late spring to early summer. [c, i, cv, ld]

Climbing aloe *(A. ciliaris)* has a sprawling habit. It reaches to 8 feet or more across and, with time, can mound up to 6 feet tall (though it is easily pruned and maintained at a height of 2 feet). With support, however, it can climb, lean, or clamber up to 20 feet high! The leaves are relatively thin for an aloe and have short stiff hairs along their margins. Attractive orange flowers are produced on 6-inch-long stems in spring, but occasional blooms may happen at any time of the year. [c, i, cv, ld]

Soap aloe *(A. maculata,* syn. *A. saponaria)* features thick succulent leaves with attractive pale-green to white

Soap aloe hybrid.

Gold tooth aloe.

Above: Fan aloe.
Left: Coral aloe.

inflorescences appear nearly year-round. They carry several headlike clusters of numerous orange tubular flowers that grade toward yellow at their tips. Established clumps may reach 3 feet across. [c, i]

Reblooming aloe *(A. sinkatana)* is most notable for its ability to rebloom several times during the year. Plants form rosettes up to 2 feet across. The green leaves are edged with small white teeth and variously marked with white spots and lines. Branched inflorescences reach up to 2 feet tall and carry as many as 6 or more 3-inch-wide conical clusters of tubular yellow, red, or orange blossoms. [c, i]

Coral aloe *(A. striata)* has showy branched clusters of coral-pink flowers that arise in late winter and last a long time. A mature plant measures 2 to 4 feet wide and about 2 feet tall and has a single rosette of broad, flat, triangular gray-green leaves. [c, i, cv, ld]

Aloe vera *(A. vera)* achieves widespread recognition as a highly touted plant of cosmetic and medicinal use. The typical foot-wide rosettes are composed of near vertical gray-green to dusky-colored leaves. This species quickly forms dense spreading colonies. Plants that are limited to a single rosette may reach 3 or more feet across, but will quickly shrink in size if the pups are allowed to proliferate. Branched inflorescences of dull-yellow flowers materialize from late spring to early summer and resemble those of red-hot poker. [c, i, cv, ld]

Arctostaphylos
MANZANITA
Heath Family (Ericaceae)

Plant Type: Evergreen shrubs.
Climate Zones: Varies with species.
Light: Sun to partial shade.
Soil: Well-drained.
Water: Drought tolerant to occasional.
Origin: Circumboreal south to Guatemala.
Garden Uses: Rock, carpet and tapestry.

The lower-growing, spreading manzanitas—which are the focus for this book—are studies in the color green. They range from the bright shiny green of *A. hookeri* to the dulled gray-green of *A.* 'Pacific Mist' to the rich ruddy tones of *A. edmundsii*. These groundcover manzanitas are a diverse lot, but all have nodding clusters of urn-shaped white to pink flowers that appear in winter to early spring. Most low-growing manzanitas perform better in coastal or high-mountain gardens. There are, however, some that succeed in a wider range of garden situations, and we have included several in the descriptions that follow.

Edmunds manzanita *(A. edmundsii)* grows naturally along California's Big Sur coast, but it is surprisingly

markings. It sends up branched flower clusters from late winter through early summer and produces blooms that can be quite variable in color, ranging from yellow, orange, or pink, to near red. These vigorous plants form dense colonies with time. Each rosette may reach from 1 to 2 feet across and 1 to 2 feet tall; the flower stalks generally ascend an additional 2 feet. [c, i, cv, ld]

Gold tooth aloe *(A. × nobilis)* has short, thick green leaves that create nearly globular rosettes up to a foot tall and wide. Plants freely form offsets and make an attractive, if lumpy, groundcover. Gold tooth aloe puts forth orange-red flowers in early summer. [c, i, cv, ld]

Fan aloe *(A. plicatilis)* is unique in the genus due to its two-dimensional fanlike arrangement of gray leaves. This slow-growing, thick-stemmed shrubby plant is usually equally broad as tall. With great age, it may reach a height of 15 feet, though most California specimens seem to top out at half that height. Attractive orange flowers bloom in spring. [c, i]

Red Riding Hood aloe *(A.* 'Rooikappie') is a hybrid involving the reblooming aloe (see below). Plants prefer full sun, but will tolerate partial shade. The 2-foot-tall

adaptable to the widest range of California gardens. This variable species reaches between 1 and 4 feet tall and spreads from 3 to 8 feet wide. 'Bert Johnson' (*A. emundsii* var. *parvifolia* 'Bert Johnson') is a small-leaved, mounding plant that freely produces small clusters of pink flowers; it is probably the most beautiful selection of this species. 'Carmel Sur' has rich green leaves, a lower and more vigorous growth habit, and fewer clusters of white flowers. [c, i, cv]

Emerald Carpet manzanita (*A.* 'Emerald Carpet') must be grown in acidic soils, and to perform well in central and southern California, it also needs significantly more water than other manzanitas. It is low growing, has dark glossy green leaves, and sparingly sets forth small clusters of white flowers. [c, i, cv]

Hooker manzanita (*A. hookeri*) has white flowers but is otherwise quite variable. It ranges in height from 6 inches to 6 feet and has widely ovate to narrow-lanceolate leaves in hues from gray to olive to green. This plant is adaptable to many garden conditions and is the

Above: Carmel Sur manzanita.
STEPHEN INGRAM
Left: Emerald Carpet manzanita.
STEPHEN INGRAM

Pacific Mist manzanita.

parent species of numerous selections. 'Wayside' produces bright green leaves and develops an upright mounding growth habit. Perhaps the most adaptable selection is 'Monterey Carpet', which has olive-green leaves and a more sprawling growth habit. [c, i, cv]

John Dourley manzanita (*A.* 'John Dourley') appears low growing at first, but as it ages, it mounds up and may eventually reach 4 to 5 feet tall and spread up to 10 feet across. Fortunately, this vigorous and garden-tolerant plant may be pruned judiciously on an annual basis to keep it in bounds. The outstanding foliage is slate blue in summer, and the new winter growth is beautifully bronzed. Rich pink flowers are freely produced and are followed by glowing red-orange fruits that disappear in a month or two. [c, i, cv]

Media manzanita (*A.* × *media*) is well suited for northern California gardens, particularly those from Sonoma County north. These vigorous, low-growing hybrids can easily spread from 3 to 8 feet across and normally top out at 2 to 3 feet. Flowers vary from white to pink. [c, i, cv, m]

Pacific Mist manzanita (*A.* 'Pacific Mist') makes an excellent choice for a larger area where its sprawling stems can spread unbound. A mature specimen may reach 2 feet in height and up to 15 feet across. Plants can be successfully grown in smaller areas, but will require judicious annual pruning to contain them. The narrow leaves are a pleasing gray-green color. Pacific Mist grows well in most gardens and produces few, if any, small clusters of pure white flowers. Young plants will look lanky for a year or two, but will then fill in without any pinching or pruning. [c, i, cv]

Dune manzanita (*A. pumila*) has small grayish leaves and usually grows no higher than 2 to 3 feet but spreads at least 3 feet wide. Although it is naturally found in semi-stabilized sand dunes in Monterey, it is widely adapted to different soils and garden environments. In sandy soils, the branches tend to layer or root easily. Small clusters of tiny white flowers are abundant. [c, i, cv]

Kinnikinnick. STEPHEN INGRAM

Kinnikinnick *(A. uva-ursi)* proves to be unreliable in many of California's hotter, drier climate zones, but this species and its many selections may perform well in gardens near the coast or high in the mountains. Small clusters of white to pink flowers are followed by attractive red berries. Kinnikinnick prefers acid, peaty soils. [c, i, cv, m]

Arctotis
AFRICAN DAISY
Sunflower Family (Asteraceae)

Plant Type: Evergreen perennials.
Climate Zones: Coastal, inland, and Central Valley.
Light: Sun.
Soil: Adaptable.
Water: Occasional to moderate.
Origin: Southern Africa.
Garden Uses: Rock, carpet and tapestry, green roof.

African daisies (*Arctotis* species) are noteworthy for their fast growth rate and springtime profusion of large, colorful 2- to 4-inches-wide daisies. The showy flowers can be just about any color other than blue. Although

African daisy and rockrose (upper right).

often short-lived, they make an excellent choice for use as temporary filler between long-term plantings. Many African daisies will not survive freezing temperatures, but they can be enjoyed as annuals everywhere. The lowest, most vigorous types, such as *Arctotis stoechadifolia* and *A. adpressa,* can tolerate limited foot traffic. Plants adapted to hotter, drier climates, such as *A. gumbeltonii,* typically develop lush foliage with the advent of the autumn rains and bloom prolifically in spring. During the hottest months they go into summer dormancy and require deadheading and cutting back. Just be sure to leave the small gray-green foliage rosettes intact, or the plants will not re-grow. Many of the hybrids are best adapted to coastal gardens, where they may grow and flower nearly year-round.

Aristida purpurea
PURPLE THREE-AWN
Grass Family (Poaceae)

Plant Type: Semi-evergreen to deciduous, warm-season perennial grass.
Climate Zones: All.
Light: Sun.
Soil: Adaptable.
Water: Drought tolerant to moderate.
Origin: Southern California to the Great Plains and northern Mexico.
Garden Uses: Meadow, rock, succulent, carpet and tapestry, green roof.

Purple three-awn is a fine-textured, free-flowering, easy-care bunchgrass that fits into a wide array of garden styles and possesses an elegant bearing. The young, wine-red flower stalks are quite showy and eventually age to an appealing blond color. The long awns atop each sharp-tipped seed can become embedded in pet fur or socks; avoid this nuisance by cutting plants back before the seeds ripen. Although purple three-awn

Purple three-awn. DAVID FROSS

thrives on minimal rainfall, it will tolerate supplemental irrigation, which can extend flowering to practically year-round in some regions. Overwatering and nutrient-rich soils, however, are not advisable.

Artemisia
SAGEBRUSH, WORMWOOD, MUGWORT
Sunflower Family (Asteraceae)

Plant Type: Evergreen and deciduous perennials or shrubs.
Climate Zones: Varies with species.
Light: Sun.
Soil: Adaptable, except poorly drained.
Water: Drought tolerant to occasional.
Origin: Europe, Asia, northern Africa and North America.
Garden Uses: Meadow, rock, succulent, carpet and tapestry, kitchen, green roof.

The artemisias favor arid and semiarid conditions, and one species in particular—Great Basin sagebrush—is so dominant in the Intermountain West that it is has been described as forming a "sagebrush ocean." Grown primarily for their striking silver and gray foliage and drought tolerance, these aromatic plants also have a long tradition of use for herbal, psychic, and religious purposes. A variety of plant sizes are available, ranging from creeping groundcovers to stately shrubs. Small, inconspicuous pale-yellow flowers are borne on erect stems, and the appearance of some species is improved with their removal.

Large wormwood *(A. arborescens)* spreads to 8 feet or more in width and reaches a height of 5 feet. This evergreen shrub from the Mediterranean Basin displays finely divided silver-white leaves and a billowing habit. Large wormwood makes a good choice for the back of a sunny border, as an accent, or woven into a dry tapestry. It tolerates a wide range of garden conditions and

Large wormwood.

Canyon Gray California sagebrush. STEPHEN INGRAM

requires little care beyond an annual pruning in fall or winter. [c, i, cv]

California sagebrush *(A. californica)* possesses soft, wonderfully fragrant fine-textured foliage. This coastal California shrub has a mounding to upright habit and grows to 3 feet tall. 'Canyon Gray' is a prostrate form, reaching 1 foot high and 10 feet wide, while 'Montara' is mounding to 2 feet tall and 4 feet wide. Pruning after flowering in late fall or early winter will improve its appearance, as will deep monthly watering in summer. [c, i, cv]

French tarragon *(A. dracunculus)* finds its way into many different culinary dishes. A flavorful herb from central Asia, it has shiny dark green leaves and spreads slowly by rhizomes. Plants form small colonies to 2 feet high with a 3- to 4-foot spread and can become woody with time. Cut it back on occasion for renewed vigor. French tarragon is winter dormant in most gardens. [all except ld]

Western mugwort *(A. ludoviciana)* grows across much of North America, and a number of subspecies are recognized. Subspecies *albula,* more commonly cultivated in California, is a rhizomatous perennial that reaches 3 to 5 feet tall and spreads vigorously—perhaps even with reckless abandon—in many gardens. Foliage varies among selections. 'Valerie Finnis', for example, exhibits broader silver-white leaves that have serrated edges near the tips, while 'Silver Queen' and 'Silver King' offer thinner leaves with silver-gray foliage. All are drought tolerant but look better with some water. Cut them to the ground in winter to renew spring growth. [all]

Powis Castle wormwood *(A. 'Powis Castle')* combines the best qualities of its probable parents, *A. arborescens* and *A. absinthium.* It boasts lacy silver foliage and has a mounding habit to 3 feet tall and 6 feet wide. This plant's garden tolerance and handsome foliage have made it one of the most popular wormwoods available in California. [all]

Sandhill sagebrush *(A. pycnocephala)* is a woody perennial or subshrub from the immediate coast of central and northern California. It has a sprawling habit and grows to 2 feet tall. The upright stems are clothed in soft silver-gray leaves and radiate away from the crown, creating a fountainlike appearance. Small yellow flowers form on elongated stalks and are best removed to create a tidier habit. 'David's Choice' is a compact, mounding selection to 6 inches tall with a 2-foot spread. [c, i]

Above: Great Basin sagebrush.
Left: Sandhill sagebrush.

Great Basin sagebrush *(A. tridentata)* covers millions of acres in its namesake region where it is a crucial source of food and habitat for many species of animals. This plant has silver-gray wedge-shaped leaves with three small lobes at the tips; they grow up to 1 inch long and cluster thickly along the stems. Autumn flowers are yellowish and are best removed at the end of the season. Great Basin sagebrush makes an interesting focal point in a gravel or rock garden. Older specimens can eventually reach 5 to 8 feet tall, with gnarled twisting trunks and peeling bark. The subspecies *vaseyana,* which typically grows 2 to 5 feet tall, is a good choice for residential gardens. [all except ld]

Sea Foam artemisia *(A. versicolor* 'Sea Foam') features a frothy habit to 12 inches tall and 3 feet wide and has threadlike silver-blue leaves. Drought and heat tolerant, it is a good choice in a gravel and rock garden or mixed with succulents. The tiny yellow flowers are insignificant and borne at the ends of the stems. Prune the older wood when new buds begin to swell. [all except ld]

Aster chilensis 'Point Saint George'
POINT SAINT GEORGE COAST ASTER
Sunflower Family (Asteraceae)

Plant Type: Evergreen herbaceous perennial.
Climate Zones: Coastal, inland, and Central Valley.
Light: Sun to partial shade.
Soil: Adaptable.
Water: Occasional to moderate.
Origin: Point Saint George, California.
Garden Uses: Meadow, rock, carpet and tapestry, green roof.

Point Saint George coast aster is a vigorous and assertive selection from California's far northwestern corner. It forms a dense 2- to 6-inch-high mat that can quickly colonize large areas. Pale violet flowers are held just above the foliage from summer to late fall and are followed by bristly seeds. Occasional mowing will maintain a lawnlike appearance and is recommended after flowering. This aster is tolerant of modest foot traffic and is particularly useful in coastal meadows, as part of a tapestry, or en masse as a carpet. The species *(A. chilensis)* is equally robust but grows taller to 3 feet high and has flowers ranging from white to blue. 'Purple Haze' is a dark-flowered selection.

Point Saint George coast aster. DAVID FROSS

Twin Peaks coyote brush. STEPHEN INGRAM

Baccharis
COYOTE BRUSH
Sunflower Family (Asteraceae)

Plant Type: Evergreen or deciduous shrubs.
Climate Zones: Varies with species.
Light: Sun.
Soil: Adaptable.
Water: Drought tolerant to occasional.
Origin: Western Hemisphere.
Garden Uses: Meadow, rock, carpet and tapestry.

Shrubs included in the large *Baccharis* genus are often found in dry, challenging habitats characterized by poor or saline soils and salt-laden winds. Their male and female flowers are borne on separate plants in white or gray heads, and the female plants produce copious seeds that can be a nuisance in the garden. Although most species are not used in cultivation, the species and selections listed here are tough, durable, and garden tolerant with a utilitarian character.

Centennial coyote brush (*B.* 'Centennial') is a good candidate for a desert garden. It grows to 3 feet tall and 5 feet wide and has narrow, linear leaves. This female hybrid can produce an ample supply of seedlings. [all except m]

Starn coyote brush (*B.* 'Starn') is similar in all respects to 'Centennial' except it is a male hybrid form and does not produce seed. [ld, hd]

Coyote brush (*B. pilularis*) grows naturally along the coast from Baja California to Oregon. This well-known California native has a variable habit; it can be low and mounding or stiff and upright, reaching a height of 8 feet. The green to olive green leaves are thick and resinous. 'Twin Peaks #2' is a spreading selection that can grow 3 feet tall and 8 feet wide, and 'Pigeon Point' is smaller with brighter green leaves. Supplemental water will improve the appearance of this species and its cultivars, and an occasional shearing helps maintain a dense and vigorous habit. Rejuvenate older, woody plants by coppicing. [c, i, cv, hd]

Bellis perennis
ENGLISH DAISY
Sunflower Family (Asteraceae)

Plant Type: Perennial, often treated as an annual.
Climate Zones: All except low desert.
Light: Sun.
Soil: Adaptable.
Water: Moderate to regular.
Origin: Europe and western Asia.
Garden Uses: Meadow, rock, green roof.

English daisy is a frequent volunteer in lawns, where it is often encouraged by gardeners who appreciate the color it adds to a repetitious run of green. The 1- to 2-inch-long dark green leaves arise from a basal rosette that may reach 8 inches wide. White to rose–colored flowers with a spot of yellow emerge 3 to 6 inches above the foliage in spring and early summer. Deadheading will prolong the flowering season. Plants grown in cool coastal climates

English daisy. SAXON HOLT

have a perennial habit while those in warmer areas are often annuals. A number of selections are available, some with double flowers and others with vivid red and pink blossoms.

Berberis (syn. *Mahonia*)
BARBERRY, MAHONIA
Barberry Family (Berberidaceae)

Plant Type: Evergreen shrubs.
Climate Zones: Varies with species.
Light: Varies with species.
Soil: Adaptable.
Water: Occasional to moderate.
Origin: Temperate zone worldwide (except for Australia).
Garden Uses: Rock, carpet and tapestry, kitchen.

Their handsome evergreen foliage is the main reason most gardeners choose to grow these California native barberries. As a bonus, all produce brilliant yellow, sweetly fragrant flowers in early spring that are followed by blue-black fruits, which are relished by birds, other wildlife, and humans. Compared to their larger relatives, the plants listed here will look and perform better when given more water.

Compacta Oregon grape *(B. aquifolium* 'Compacta') has shiny green leaves with somewhat spiny margins

Above: Compacta Oregon grape.
Left: Barberry fruit.

and a stiff, upright growth habit. This is the most vigorous of the barberries listed here. It tolerates full sun, but prefers partial shade in interior gardens. This plant typically reaches from 2 to 3 feet in height and spreads slowly to form clumps that are at least 2 to 3 feet wide. With age, Compacta Oregon grape often loses much of its lower foliage and can appear "stemmy." You can rejuvenate such plants with a hard pruning in late fall. They grow back nicely with the winter rains, producing copper-colored new growth that is especially attractive against the dark-green older foliage. [c, i, cv, m]

Longleaf barberry *(B. nervosa)* makes an excellent choice for use in shade or dappled shade. Of the plants highlighted here, this species has the showiest blossoms. The golden yellow flowers are produced in terminal racemes from 3 to 6 inches in length. Its dark green leaves have many stiff, leathery leaflets with spiny margins. Plants vary in height, but most reach from 2 to 3 feet tall and slowly spread to form loose, open colonies. To cover an area with longleaf barberry, your initial spacing of plants from 1-gallon containers should be about 4 to 5 feet apart. [c, i, cv, m]

Creeping barberry *(B. repens)* is an attractive but slow-growing species that performs best in dappled shade and can eventually establish large dense colonies. It grows from 1 to 2 feet tall and may reach 6 to 8 feet across. To counteract its slow pace of spreading, place 1-gallon plants about 3 feet apart. Flower production is sparse in most gardens. The compound leaves are composed of 3 to 5 oval to rounded leaflets that have weak marginal spines of no consequence. Foliage color varies from reddish brown new growth in spring to dusty green in the summer and purplish tones in the winter. [all except ld]

Bergenia
BERGENIA
Saxifrage Family (Saxifragaceae)

Plant Type: Evergreen perennials.
Climate Zones: All except low desert.
Light: Partial shade to shade.
Soil: Adaptable.
Water: Occasional.
Origin: Eastern Asia.
Garden Uses: Rock, carpet and tapestry, green roof.

There are few low-growing durable groundcovers that offer the grand bold texture of the bergenias. The fact that they will perform best in shade or dappled sunlight makes them all the more desirable. Giant, round, shiny leathery leaves are produced along thickened rhizomatous stems that slowly spread along the surface of the soil. Their bright pink or, rarely, white, flowers emerge from thickened upright stalks in early spring. There are many named selections to choose from. Snails, slugs, and thrips can damage and disfigure the foliage.

Bergenia.

Bothriochloa barbinodis
SILVER BEARDGRASS
Grass Family (Poaceae)

Plant Type: Semi-evergreen to deciduous, warm-season perennial grass.
Climate Zones: Coastal, inland, and Central Valley.
Light: Sun.
Soil: Adaptable.
Water: Drought tolerant to moderate.
Origin: Southern California to Oklahoma, Texas, and Mexico.
Garden Uses: Meadow, rock, succulent, carpet and tapestry.

Silver beardgrass is a showy, carefree, and reliable bunchgrass that merits much wider use in California gardens. Individual clumps reach 1 to 2 feet tall and wide and produce fluffy seed heads on rigid, 1- to 2-foot-tall canelike stalks. Flowering continues almost year-round if the plant receives supplemental irrigation. The silky inflorescences are soft to the touch and stunning when backlit. This grass is most dramatic when planted in large swaths. Cut the clumps back in fall and enjoy the burgundy-tinged resprouting new leaves as they emerge.

Silver beardgrass.

Bougainvillea
BOUGAINVILLEA
Four O'Clock Family (Nyctaginaceae)

Plant Type: Evergreen shrubby vines.
Climate Zones: Coastal, inland, low desert.
Light: Sun.
Soil: Adaptable.
Water: Occasional to moderate.
Origin: South America.
Garden Uses: Carpet and tapestry.

Flamboyant, bold, and shocking are adjectives often used to describe the colorful papery bracts that flank

Bougainvillea.

these popular plants' small tubular flowers. Only a few of the 14 species of this tropical and subtropical genus are grown commercially, and many of the plants cultivated are hybrids. Cultivars with names such as 'Scarlett O'Hara', 'Temple Fire', 'Raspberry Ice', 'Orange King', 'Jamaica White', 'Cherry Blossom', and 'Lavender Queen' signal the vivid range of colors available.

Bougainvillea's sprawling branches will quickly cover the ground and often send long thorny stems climbing over fences or walls. All are frost tender, but established and well-sited plants that freeze to the ground commonly reappear from the roots with the advent of warm weather. Pruning is recommended to control rampant growth and to encourage flowering that is borne on new wood. Planting is best done in the warmer months, and always use care to avoid damaging the sensitive roots. Fertilization encourages vigorous growth and should be used sparingly.

Bouteloua
GRAMA GRASS
Grass Family (Poaceae)

Plant Type: Warm-season perennial and annual grasses.
Climate Zones: All.
Light: Sun.
Soil: Adaptable.
Water: Drought tolerant to occasional.
Origin: Western Hemisphere.
Garden Uses: Greensward, meadow, rock, succulent, green roof.

Grama grasses belong to a wide-ranging genus that consists of about 40 species of annual and perennial grasses. They grow primarily in the warmer, drier portions of the Americas, and the two perennial species listed here are important components of the North American shortgrass prairie. Both offer significant garden value in the hot inland portions of California.

Side-oats grama *(B. curtipendula)* is a tufted perennial with an erect habit to ½ to 3 feet high. The narrow blue-green leaves flush with rose in colder temperatures and have a bleached appearance in dormancy. Late-spring culms bear one-sided purplish spikes of small flowers with bright orange anthers. A durable and extremely drought-tolerant grass, it is particularly valuable when used as an accent among rocks or as a component in dry borders and meadows.

Blue grama *(B. gracilis)* resembles side-oats grama, but spreads slowly from short rhizomes. The thin, sage

Blue grama. STEPHEN INGRAM

green to blue leaf blades grow 4 to 16 inches tall and have a delicate appearance. In late spring and early summer, its flower stalks are topped by delightful inflorescences that resemble eyebrows and curl gracefully as they age. Held horizontally, they are as colorful as they are charming and exhibit many hues: first shiny purple-red, then umber, next brown, and finally blond. Blue grama tolerates foot traffic and mowing and makes an exceptionally fine choice for lawns. It also accepts extremely dry conditions and serves well in meadows and dry borders.

Buchloe dactyloides
BUFFALO GRASS
Grass Family (Poaceae)

Plant Type: Warm-season perennial grass.
Climate Zones: All.
Light: Sun.
Soil: Adaptable.
Water: Drought tolerant to regular.
Origin: North American prairies, Montana to northern Mexico.
Garden Uses: Greensward, meadow, rock, green roof.

Short grass prairie weaves through the heart of North America, carrying a dense sod composed of two codominant species, buffalo grass and blue grama. Framed by the 100th meridian to the east and the Rocky Mountains to the west, this grassland once covered the

UC Verde buffalo grass.

vast, windswept high plains from Canada to Mexico and nourished the celebrated bison herds of American lore.

Buffalo grass has received considerable attention as a lawn grass suitable for dry conditions, and plant breeders have developed a number of selections and seed strains for this purpose. They all grow rapidly and spread via branching stolons. In the summer months, they reach 8 inches high; in the winter they become dormant, and the blades take on a taupe color for extended periods. They tolerate heavy soils and are best planted in full sun. Newer selections have improved the performance of buffalo grass in California. 'UC Verde' offers a finer texture, greener color, and greater tolerance of heat. 'Prestige' is a hardier selection recommended for the portions of the state that experience colder winters. Once established, they require minimal care in meadow applications but need regular mowing if a lawn is desired. They have not always performed well in the cooler climates along the immediate coast of California. Vegetatively propagated female plants are most commonly used for lawns, as they produce a more uniform and lower-growing habit.

Carex
SEDGE
Sedge Family (Cyperaceae)

Plant Type: Deciduous to evergreen perennials.
Climate Zones: Varies with species.
Light: Sun to shade.
Soil: Adaptable.
Water: Infrequent to regular.
Origin: Global.
Garden Uses: Greensward, meadow, rock, carpet and tapestry, green roof.

Sedges occupy an astonishing variety of habitats worldwide, from wind-swept dunes along the California coast to alpine deserts at 16,000 feet in Tibet. This vast genus offers myriad growth forms from diminutive creepers to large clumpers. The diverse palette of foliage colors includes green, gold, orange, amber, and chocolate. Although most sedges prefer some moisture, there is a species suitable for any California garden condition.

Berkeley sedge *(C. divulsa)* was sold mistakenly for many years as a California native *(C. tumulicola),* but it

Berkeley sedge.

has recently been identified correctly as a wide-ranging European species. Its arching dark green blades form dense mounds to 18 inches tall and at least 2 feet wide. Shear it hard after the spring flowering to remove fruits and prevent reseeding. This handsome, durable, garden-tolerant sedge is an excellent choice for woodland gardens, as plants sited in shade have a more graceful habit and reduced flower production. [c, i, cv, m]

Blue sedge or carnation grass *(C. flacca,* syn. *C. glauca)* grows naturally in dunes, estuaries, and dry grasslands in northern Africa and Europe. It is a vigorous rhizomatous species, but spreads slowly to form dense mats from 6 to 18 inches tall. Leaf color varies from blue to blue-green, although most cultivated forms have gray-blue foliage. Tolerant of moderate foot traffic, drought, poor soils, and competition from mature trees, this low-maintenance sedge is easily trimmed into a lawn and highly recommended for difficult sites. [c, i, cv, m]

Dune sedge *(C. pansa)* is a creeping species found along the immediate coast from northern California to British Columbia. It is remarkably similar to the closely related clustered field sedge, but it generally has a lower profile, reaching 8 to 12 inches tall. [c, i, cv]

Clustered field sedge *(C. praegracilis)* is often confused with dune sedge, a similar species with a more restricted distribution in North America. Freely spreading from rhizomes, clustered field sedge is suitable for lawns, erosion control, meadows, green roofs, and even driveways. It tolerates drought, inundation, poor soils, salt spray, heat, cold, and foot traffic. Once established, it is seldom troubled with weed infestations. The fine-textured dark green leaves reach 12 inches tall and

Clustered field sedge.

present a thick tousled appearance when left un-trimmed. A bit coarser than traditional turf, it can be mowed or string-line trimmed into a lawn as low and green as the outfield of Dodger Stadium. Away from the coast, plants will turn brown if grown with minimal summer irrigation. [all]

Mountain sedge *(C. subfusca)* spreads rapidly from thick rhizomes and forms a dense turflike cover of dark green leaves 8 to 12 inches tall. Native to moist habitats in western North America, it can be used effectively in both sun and shade. Mountain sedge is best grown with some moisture because dry plantings tend to turn brown during the summer months, especially in interior portions of the state. [all]

Orange New Zealand sedge *(C. testacea)* features colorful orange, golden brown, or amber-green foliage

Orange New Zealand sedge.

that responds to degrees of sunlight; or-ange tones are most promi-nent in full sun and green more common in the shade. The graceful 2-foot-tall tufts are tough and tolerate considerable drought. Fruiting stems elongate and should be removed for a tidy appearance. Plants re-seed in moist conditions and are often short-lived away from the coast. [c, i, cv]

Catlin sedge *(C. texensis)* forms low 6-inch-tall clumps that slowly broaden into small undulating drifts. It has fine-textured dark green leaves and is quite durable. Catlin sedge is effective as a small-scale lawn or meadow and has a cleaner appearance with the seed heads removed. [c, i, cv]

Ceanothus
CEANOTHUS, CALIFORNIA LILAC
Buckthorn Family (Rhamnaceae)

Plant Type: Evergreen shrubs.
Climate Zones: Coastal, inland, and Central Valley.
Light: Sun to partial shade.
Soil: Adaptable to well-drained.
Water: Drought tolerant to occasional.
Origin: North America.
Garden Uses: Meadow, rock, carpet and tapestry, green roof.

A storied genus of the California flora, *Ceanothus* of-fers a solid range of useful shrubs for an array of garden

Top: Anchor Bay ceanothus.
Bottom: Frosty Dawn ceanothus. TOM ELTZROTH

functions, and several low-growing species are excellent choices for lawn replacement. They are celebrated for their spring clusters of blue flowers and tolerance of drought. For success, they require only well-drained soils, occasional summer water, and adequate space to grow. Some of the wider spreading selections can be pruned or trained to conform to smaller gardens.

Centennial ceanothus *(C.* 'Centennial') is a natu-rally occurring hybrid from the Sonoma Coast with spreading stems 8 to 12 inches tall and 6 feet wide. The small glossy green leaves sparkle attractively in full sun. It produces cobalt blue flowers in rounded clusters from mid to late spring and often again in autumn. Surpris-ingly tolerant of shade, 'Centennial' is a good choice in woodland and cool coastal gardens.

Point Reyes ceanothus *(C. gloriosus)* features leath-ery dark green leaves with toothed margins. Plants range in height from a few inches to 5 feet and spread widely to 10 feet or more. Dense clusters of lavender-blue to blue flowers are produced in early spring. 'Anchor Bay' is an adaptable selection to 3 feet tall and 6 feet wide. 'Heart's Desire' has pale blue flowers and forms a dense groundcover 6 to 12 inches high with a 4-foot spread.

Hearst ceanothus. STEPHEN INGRAM

Hearst ceanothus *(C. hearstiorum)* is a prostrate species from the coastal bluffs above Arroyo de la Cruz in northern San Luis Obispo County. Young plants develop a starlike pattern before forming loose mounds or prostrate carpets up to 8 feet wide. The small green leaves have a warty texture with a sparkling, reflective surface and are complimented each spring with rounded clusters of pastel- to medium-blue flowers.

Joyce Coulter ceanothus *(C. 'Joyce Coulter')* grows rapidly to 3 feet high with trailing branches that often spread widely to 15 feet or more. This selection is well adapted to garden conditions and has handsome textured green leaves and sky blue flowers.

Maritime ceanothus *(C. maritimus)* has a low mounding habit to 2 feet tall and 8 feet wide. The leathery, olive green ½-inch-long leaves are held on rigid stems. Blue to lavender flowers open from appealing ball-like buds in late January to March. 'Frosty Dawn' with dark lavender-blue flowers and 'Point Sierra' with cotoneaster-like foliage are two durable and garden-tolerant selections well suited for use in coastal California.

Carmel creeper ceanothus *(C. thyrsiflorus var. griseus,* syn. *C. griseus var. horizontalis)* is one of the most commonly planted groundcovers in California. A coastal species in nature, it has been used successfully across much of the state, although plantings in interior sites are shorter lived. It forms mounds 3 to 5 feet high and spreads up to 10 or more feet wide. Carmel creeper has glossy dark green leaves and pale- to medium-blue flowers. 'Yankee Point' is the most popular selection and features smaller leaves, light blue flowers and a slightly lower growth habit. The intriguing 'Diamond Heights' possesses variegated lime gold foliage. It is a slow-growing, creeping form that reaches 12 inches high. 'Diamond Heights' requires shade in interior plantings and will tolerate heavy leaf litter in a woodland garden.

Cistanthe grandiflora (syn. *Calandrinia grandiflora*)
ROCK PURSLANE
Purslane Family (Portulacaceae)

Plant Type: Evergreen succulent.
Climate Zones: All except high desert and mountains.
Light: Sun to partial shade.
Soil: Well-drained.
Water: Drought tolerant to occasional.
Origin: Chile.
Garden Uses: Rock, succulent, carpet and tapestry.

Rock purslane's shocking magenta-pink flowers are stunning to behold. Opening one at a time atop 1- to 3-foot-long stalks, the satiny, cup-shaped 1- to 2-inch-wide blossoms provide vivid color from spring into summer in hot inland areas and on into fall along the coast. A single plant, composed of several blue-green basal rosettes, may grow up to 8 feet across and produce dozens of airy flower stalks. Group several together for even greater visual impact. After flowering, cut the inflorescences off.

Rock purslane.

Cistus
ROCKROSE
Rockrose Family (Cistaceae)

Plant Type: Evergreen shrubs.
Climate Zones: Coastal, inland, and Central Valley.
Light: Sun.
Soil: Well-drained
Water: Drought tolerant to occasional.
Origin: Mediterranean Basin.
Garden Uses: Rock, carpet and tapestry.

This drought-resistant group of fast-growing shrubs from the Mediterranean Basin and Canary Islands features attractive paperlike flowers with crinkled petals that range from white to pink to red. A central cluster of yellow stamens confers a roselike appearance to the blooms. Although each blossom is ephemeral, a new flush of flowers opens every day for a month or more from spring to late summer. Many of the rockroses listed will flower sporadically throughout the year. The green to gray leaves are variable and measure 2 to 5 inches in length; some have a coating of fragrant resin and others are covered in downy hair. Rockroses require minimal maintenance and are broadly tolerant of heat, drought, poor soils, salt-laden winds, and sun. Some gardeners choose to replace them after 5 to 10 years, when they become woody. Many promising new cultivars have been introduced into the trade during the last few years, adding an array of choices to the following classic selections.

White rockrose *(C. × hybridus)* has a long history of use in California. It forms mounds to 4 feet tall and spreads to 8 feet wide. The downy gray-green leaves have a distinctive resinlike fragrance on warm days, and from mid-spring to summer the plant is covered by 1½-inch-wide clear white flowers. This adaptable old standard remains a good choice for dry locations.

Sageleaf rockrose *(C. salviifolius)* features 1-inch-long sage green leaves with a white underside that have

Above: Sunset rockrose and sageleaf rockrose, (bottom right). Left: Sunset rockrose.

a crinkled texture. It is a spreading shrub to 2 feet tall and 6 feet wide. Profuse flowers measuring up to 1¼ inches wide cover the foliage with a spring shower of white petals. Sageleaf rockrose is a good choice for poor rocky soils and difficult sites.

Skanberg rockrose *(C. × skanbergii)* is a naturally occurring hybrid found in Sicily and Greece. It has a billowing habit and grows to 3 feet tall and 6 feet wide. In spring, the soft-pink 1-inch-wide flowers provide a pleasing contrast to the sage green leaves.

Sunset rockrose *(C. 'Sunset')* performs well across a broad range of California garden conditions. This popular selection creates mounds to 4 feet high and 6 feet wide. It features 2½-inch-wide magenta flowers and gray-green leaves.

Convolvulus
MORNING GLORY
Morning Glory Family (Convolvulaceae)

Plant Type: Evergreen shrubs and subshrubs.
Climate Zones: Varies with species.
Light: Sun to partial shade.
Soil: Well-drained.
Water: Moderate.
Origin: Europe, Asia, Africa, and North America.
Garden Uses: Rock, carpet and tapestry, green roof.

The two species of *Convolvulus* described here are well-behaved ornamentals, even though they are related to the rambling morning glory vine *(Ipomoea)* and the highly invasive field bindweed *(Convolvulus arvensis)*.

Sageleaf rockrose.

Above: Snow Angel bush morning glory. Left: Ground morning glory.

Much admired for their saucer-shaped flowers, these floriferous plants bloom from spring through fall and blend easily with a wide array of partners. A hard annual pruning helps to retain a dense shape and promote new growth.

Bush morning glory *(C. cneorum)* forms silvery mounds that measure 2 to 4 feet tall and equally wide. Plants have a sparkly appearance due to the silky hairs on the 1- to 2½-inch-long leaves. Milky white 2-inch-wide flowers open from pink-tinged buds and reveal a bright yellow eye. Native to rocky coastal sites in southern Europe, bush morning glory is well suited to seaside gardens and looks terrific next to boulders. Plants grown in heavy soils or with generous watering will be short-lived. 'Snow Angel' is a compact cultivar that grows 2 feet tall and wide. [c, i, cv, ld]

Ground morning glory *(C. sabatius,* syn. *C. mauritanicus)* is a sprawling groundcover, reaching less than 1 foot tall and up to 3 feet wide. Rounded, softly hairy green to gray-green leaves line the slender trailing stems, and lavender to light blue 1½-inch-wide flowers emerge at the stem tips. Plants can become woody and leggy over time, but they respond well to pruning. The long stems are effective when allowed to spill over boulders, walls or roofs. [all except hd]

Cotoneaster
COTONEASTER
Rose Family (Rosaceae)

Plant Type: Evergreen, semi-evergreen, and deciduous shrubs.
Climate Zones: Varies with species.
Light: Sun.
Soil: Adaptable.
Water: Drought tolerant to occasional.
Origin: China to northern India.
Garden Uses: Rock, carpet and tapestry, green roof.

Gardeners have long appreciated cotoneasters as utilitarian shrubs and groundcovers. Their growth forms vary from low and prostrate to tall and fountainlike. The small white or pink flowers that bloom in spring to early summer are not individually showy but do produce a pleasing display in mass. Red to orange berries ripen in fall and attract a variety of birds. The vigorous, low-growing species listed here are all drought tolerant, easy-care shrubs suitable for poor soils. Some cotoneasters are invasive, although the ones below have not proven problematic in California. Fire blight can affect cotoneasters.

Bearberry cotoneaster *(C. dammeri)* makes an excellent choice for erosion control because its fast-growing stems root as they spread. It is an evergreen species with bright green leaves and a prostrate habit, growing to 12 inches tall and 10 feet wide. 'Coral Beauty' is a lower profile selection with orange berries. 'Lowfast' is a popular groundcover selection that reaches 12 inches in height. 'Streib's Findling' features a creeping habit with a distinctive herringbone branching pattern. [c, i, cv, hd]

Rock cotoneaster *(C. horizontalis)* has a dense

Above and left: Coral Beauty cotoneaster.

growth form, reaching 3 feet tall and spreading up to 12 feet wide. The rounded glossy green leaves are deciduous and often provide a splash of orange and red fall color before they drop. The soft-pink spring flowers develop into luminous red berries by autumn. Mature plants attain a handsome layered appearance. 'Variegatus' has leaves with cream-colored margins. [c, i, cv, hd]

Rockspray cotoneaster (*C. microphyllus*) is an evergreen species with small glossy green leaves and a dense, twiggy habit to 3 feet tall and 6 feet wide. Some branches are erect while others creep along the ground, making it a good choice for rock and gravel plantings. The variety *cochleatus* is nearly prostrate and produces a heavy crop of rosy red fruit, while the variety *thymifolius* reaches 2 feet in height and has tiny wedge-shaped leaves and a stiff, upright habit. [c, i, cv]

Willowleaf cotoneaster (*C. salicifolius* 'Repens') is a fast-growing, drought-tolerant, and adaptable cultivar that offers a lush green appearance, white summer flowers, and long-lasting bright red berries. Narrow evergreen leaves cover the spreading branches and form a carpet 8 to 12 feet wide. With maturity, willowleaf cotoneaster develops a mounding form with crowns that reach up to 2 feet in height. A light pruning is recommended to control its rapid growth. [all]

Cotyledon orbiculata
PIG'S EAR
Stonecrop Family (Crassulaceae)

Plant Type: Succulent shrubs.
Climate Zones: Coastal, inland, and low desert.
Light: Sun to partial shade.
Soil: Adaptable, well-drained preferred.
Water: Drought tolerant to occasional.
Origin: South Africa.
Garden Uses: Rock, succulent, carpet and tapestry, green roof.

Pig's ear is an impressive shrub that adds bold texture to a garden year-round. It reaches 1 to 3 feet tall

and can spread to several feet wide. This succulent is often mistaken for silver jade plant because both plants have silvery gray to chalky white fleshy leaves that are typically rimmed with red. The confusion disappears in spring or summer when pig's ear's blooms. Its pendulous clusters of orange to salmon pink bell-shaped flowers are borne on 1-foot-long white stalks and are far different from silver jade plant's small star-shaped blooms. Plants of *C. orbiculata* var. *oblonga* (syn. *C. teretifolia*) have cylindrical, fingerlike leaves; *C. orbiculata* var. *oblonga* 'Macrantha' (syn. *C. macrantha*) has large rounded green leaves and coral-red flowers.

Crassula
CRASSULA
Stonecrop Family (Crassulaceae)

Plant Type: Succulent annuals, perennials, or shrubs.
Climate Zones: Varies with species.
Light: Sun to partial shade.
Soil: Well-drained.
Water: Drought tolerant to moderate.
Origin: Global, but the majority are restricted to South Africa.
Garden Uses: Rock, succulent, green roof.

Curious and peculiar plants are common among the 300 species of the diverse *Crassula* genus. Collectively, crassulas display a bewildering assortment of growth forms, from diminutive mat-forming species to erect 12-foot-tall shrubs. Leaf color is equally variable, ranging from silver-blue to glossy green. The oppositely arranged succulent leaves and creeping stems combine to create fascinating geometric patterns. Terminal clusters of flowers are seldom showy, although a number of the species listed here are exceptions. Crassulas require minimal care, but well-drained soils are recommended and many species are frost tender.

Silver jade plant (*C. arborescens*) can potentially reach 10 feet tall, but a height of 2 to 3 feet is more common in cultivation. The oval chalk blue leaves are

Pig's ear. CAROL BORNSTEIN

Silver jade plant. STEPHEN INGRAM

Above: Fairy crassula.
Left: Jade plant.

1½ inches wide and cluster closely along the branching stems. Mature specimens have a handsome mounding form. [c, i, cv, ld]

Campfire crassula (*C. capitella* 'Campfire') displays bright orange-red leaves in distinct tiers along its stem. The foliage color is much stronger in winter and when the plant is drought stressed. Campfire crassula has a flopping habit to 12 inches tall; it is best grown in full sun along the coast and partial shade inland. [c, i, cv]

Fairy crassula (*C. multicava*) roots easily from small cuttings and leaves and can spread quickly in a garden. It makes a durable groundcover and grows to 18 inches high with a 3-foot spread. The dark green leaves are topped with loose clusters of star-shaped, pink-tinged white flowers in late winter and early spring. It is tolerant of sun or shade and most soil conditions. [c, i, cv, ld]

Jade plant (*C. ovata*) has been grown for decades in southern California and is as common as it is durable. Large specimens up to 6 feet tall are not unusual. Jade plant's thick gray-brown stems have a muscled appearance and are topped with shiny, wedge-shaped green leaves that often have a reddish margin. 'Hobbit' is a smaller selection with cupped leaves and red margins, and 'Tricolor' has variegated foliage. [c, i, cv]

Airplane plant (*C. perfoliata* var. *falcata*, syn. *C. perfoliata* var. *minor*) has knifelike gray-green leaves up to 4 inches long. Thick and fleshy, they are arranged in overlapping pairs and give the plant a compelling flattened form. Dense clusters of bright red flowers are held above the foliage in summer. [c, i, cv]

Crassula schmidtii forms a mat of 6-inch-tall clustered rosettes with narrow linear red-striped leaves. Compact heads of dark pink flowers are held just above the foliage in summer. [c, i, cv]

Dalea greggii
TRAILING INDIGO BUSH
Pea Family (Fabaceae)

Plant Type: Evergreen subshrub.
Climate Zones: Coastal, inland, low desert, and high desert.
Light: Sun.
Soil: Well-drained.
Water: Drought tolerant to occasional.
Origin: Texas, New Mexico, Arizona, and Mexico.
Garden Uses: Rock, succulent, carpet and tapestry, green roof.

Trailing indigo bush makes an excellent groundcover for hot, dry sites. It grows up to 1 foot tall and 5 or more feet wide and has slender branches clothed with light gray leaves that are fine-textured and silky soft. Terminal clusters of small reddish purple flowers bloom from spring to summer and attract bees and butterflies. Trailing indigo bush cascades beautifully over retaining walls or boulders and combines well with succulents and mediterranean-climate plants. In its natural range, it receives summer rain, so provide modest irrigation during this season. Tip prune as needed to retain dense leafy growth.

Trailing indigo bush (on right). SAXON HOLT

Delosperma
ICE PLANT
Ice Plant Family (Aizoaceae)

Plant Type: Succulent perennials.
Climate Zones: Varies with species.
Light: Sun to partial shade.
Soil: Well-drained.
Water: Occasional to regular.
Origin: Africa, primarily south of the Equator.
Garden Uses: Rock, succulent, green roof.

Ice plants typically exhibit bright eye-catching blossoms; white, cream, yellow, orange, pink, and crimson are all flower colors found in this genus. Borne singly or in clusters, the flowers range in size from ¼ to 1 inch in diameter and bloom primarily from March to August in California. These succulent perennials offer an array of forms from diminutive clumping species to spreading groundcovers and even small shrubs. Once established, ice plants require little maintenance but they do need more water than most other succulents for a fresh garden appearance. As might be expected with a genus of this size, a diverse range of species and cultivars is available for use in California gardens. (There are many more excellent low-growing lawn substitutes in the ice plant family, Aizoaceae. Species and cultivars from genera such as *Drosanthemum, Lampranthus, Malephora, Chasmatophyllum, Ruschia,* and *Cephalophyllum* all offer intriguing possibilities in rock gardens, as a carpet, mixed in a tapestry, or on green roofs. Another genus in this family, *Carpobrotus,* is also referred to as ice plant, but two species *(C. edulis* and *C. chilensis)* should be avoided due to their highly invasive nature.

Blut ice plant (*Delosperma ashtonii* 'Blut') features lance-shaped leaves with pronounced edges unlike the rounded leaf forms common in the genus. Forming mats to 4 inches high, it will spread robustly to 2 feet or more. The attention grabbing color of the magenta-red flowers stands out like the brilliance of a neon sign and can dominate the summer garden. [c, i, cv, hd]

A variety of ice plant species in a tapestry planting.

Gold Nugget ice plant (*D. congestum* 'Gold Nugget') forms a tight carpetlike mat of rounded dark green leaves. It reaches a height of ½ inch and spreads to 8 to 12 inches wide. A summer-blooming alpine selection, it produces glossy yellow flowers with a distinct white center. Gold Nugget ice plant combines well with other low-growing *Delosperma* species to create a vibrant multicolor display. In warm interior portions of the state, afternoon shade and frequent irrigation is recommended. [c, i, cv, hd]

Mesa Verde ice plant (*D.* 'Mesa Verde') bears luminous salmon pink flowers throughout summer. The flowers remain closed in foggy, overcast weather, which makes this plant best suited to gardens away from the immediate coast. It is a vigorous hybrid that spreads rapidly and forms a thick mat 2 to 6 inches high. Mesa Verde ice plant can easily outcompete weaker selections, and care should be taken when combining it with other species. [all]

Oberg ice plant (*D.* 'Oberg') provides a refreshing change from the typically bright exuberant flower colors of the genus. Soft, ivory pink 1½-inch-wide flowers emanate from pale pink buds from spring to fall. The slow-growing mats of gray-green foliage create a pleasing maintenance-free groundcover to 2 inches high and 2 feet wide. [c, i, cv, hd]

Tufted ice plant *(D. sphalmanthoides)* is the smallest species in the genus and forms a dense, prostrate carpet 6 to 8 inches wide. Tiny, stemless gray-green leaves provide contrast to the ½-inch-diameter pink flowers that bloom from late spring to fall. It combines well with other small-scale groundcovers and is an excellent choice for gardens with limited space. [all except ld]

Blut ice plant. SAXON HOLT

Deschampsia cespitosa
TUFTED HAIR GRASS
Grass Family (Poaceae)

Plant Type: Evergreen cool-season perennial grass.
Climate Zones: All except low desert and high desert.
Light: Sun to shade.
Soil: Adaptable.
Water: Occasional to regular.
Origin: North America, Europe, and eastern Asia.
Garden Uses: Greensward, meadow, rock and gravel, green roof.

Tufted hair grass has a lush, verdant appearance and establishes neat mounds 1 to 2 feet tall. Fine-textured inflorescences crown the foliage in late spring and early summer with cloudlike masses of spikelets that gradually turn gold. Long-lived and undemanding, this clump-forming bunchgrass is useful in meadows and greenswards or for bordering a lawn. It naturally occurs in moist habitats and is therefore best suited for irrigated gardens.

A number of selections are available in a range of sizes; some even feature variegated foliage. Pacific hair grass (*D. cespitosa* var. *holciformis*) is a coastal native found from central California to British Columbia. It has a smaller tufted habit to 1-foot high and amber-brown inflorescences. Cut this variety back in fall, or mow it periodically to maintain it as a lawn.

Pacific hair grass.

Dierama pendulum
FAIRY WAND
Iris Family (Iridaceae)

Plant Type: Evergreen perennial.
Geographic Zones: All except low desert and high desert.
Light: Sun to partial shade.
Soil: Adaptable.
Water: Occasional to regular.
Origin: South Africa.
Garden Uses: Meadow, rock.

Fairy wand takes its common name from its 3- to 6-foot-long, wandlike flower stalks. This attractive, carefree perennial sprouts from corms and adds elegance

Fairy wand. SAXON HOLT

to the garden. The flower stalks arch above 2- to 3-foot-long, strap-shaped leaves and in spring and summer, they bear pendulous bell-shaped blossoms of white, rose, pink, or purple. Gossamer stems hold each flower cluster and dance with the slightest breeze, likely giving rise to the plant's other common name: angel's fishing rod. Use fairy wand singly or in drifts. Maintain it by removing spent flower stalks and grooming away dead leaves as they accumulate. *D. pulcherrimum* is another popular species with slightly more funnel-shaped flowers.

Dudleya
DUDLEYA, LIVEFOREVER
Stonecrop family (Crassulaceae)

Plant Type: Evergreen succulent perennials.
Climate Zones: Coastal and inland.
Light: Sun to partial shade.
Soil: Adaptable.
Water: Drought tolerant to occasional.
Origin: Southwestern Oregon to Northwestern Mexico, including parts of California, Nevada, and Arizona.
Garden Uses: Rock, succulent, carpet and tapestry.

Dudleyas originate primarily from California's mediterranean-climate area and make excellent subjects for a dry garden. These low-growing, summer-drought-adapted succulents have fingerlike to broadly strap-shaped leaves. Delicate to bold, the white to gray to green leaves form 1-inch- to 4-foot-tall rosettes that are a study in radial symmetry. Flower stalks are usually branched and may reach from 1 inch to 4 feet tall and carry numerous white, yellow, orange, or vibrant red flowers. The leaves of summer-stressed plants often take on colorful tints of yellow, orange, or red. The species listed here may be grown in full sun near the coast, but require partial shade in hot inland gardens. Nearly all dudleyas are available commercially, but many species are only found in selective nurseries, and some are not available every year. Botanic garden and cactus and succulent society plant sales are good places to look for them.

Top: Catalina Island dudleya. DAVID FROSS
Bottom: Chalk dudleya.

Fish Canyon dudleya *(D. densiflora)* features finger-like, succulent green to grayish leaves that form slowly spreading clumps up to 2 or more feet across. This rare species reliably produces showy clusters of white to pink flowers in early summer.

Ladies' fingers dudleya *(D. edulis)* resembles fish canyon dudleya in leaf shape and color, as well as overall size. Its flowers, however, are yellowish.

Coast dudleya *(D. farinosa)* has two primary color forms: one features green foliage, the other displays gray-white foliage, and both are excellent for garden use. This plant grows into a large branching mound up to 4 feet across and nearly 2 feet tall. Each mound is composed of dozens of 4- to 8-inch-wide rosettes of thick succulent leaves. Branched flowering stems are about 1 foot long and carry numerous pale yellow flowers. This species is best grown near the coast, as it is prone to crown rot in hot interior climates.

Chalk dudleya *(D. pulverulenta)* is a spectacular plant that is best used as a specimen or focal point since it typically forms a single rosette. It is a white-foliaged species with broad leaves, and it shares these traits with two other handsome relatives: **Anthony dudleya**

(D. anthonyi) and **Britton dudleya** *(D. brittonii)*. Compared to the other dudleyas listed here, these three species are less hardy and more prone to winter rot from cold and wet. In most cases, they are best planted on slopes or with their crowns tilted in order to drain water away from their centers and crowns.

Catalina Island dudleya *(D. virens* ssp. *hassei)* is the most dependable Dudleya species to use as a large-scale groundcover. This plant freely branches and forms nearly continuous carpets of silver to gray (rarely green) 6-inch-wide rosettes of plump, fingerlike leaves. In coastal or partially shaded inland gardens, established stands of Catalina Island dudleya thrive without supplemental water. Plantings in full hot sun may look desiccated and tired by the end of the dry season, but to avoid the possibility of rot, resist the temptation to water them. Some plantings of this species seem to bloom rarely, while others will reliably sport 6- to 12-inch-tall branched clusters of yellow flowers in late spring or early summer.

Dymondia margaretae
SILVER CARPET, DYMONDIA
Sunflower Family (Asteraceae)

Plant Type: Evergreen perennial.
Climate Zones: Coastal, inland, and Central Valley.
Light: Sun to partial shade.
Soil: Well-drained.
Water: Occasional to regular.
Origin: Western Cape of South Africa.
Garden Uses: Rock, carpet and tapestry, green roof.

Silver carpet is a dense, matting groundcover commonly used among pavers and stepping-stones. Thick creeping stems hold slender, 2-inch-long, waxy green leaves that have downy silver-white undersides. Small, daisylike yellow flowers are held closely amongst the foliage during the warm season. The appearance of silver carpet is water dependent: during periods of drought, the leaves curl at the margins revealing the silver-white

Silver carpet.

undersides; with regular water, plants have a more verdant appearance. Tolerant of moderate drought and foot traffic, silver carpet is maintenance free, aside from the need for occasional weeding.

Echeveria
ECHEVERIA
Stonecrop family (Crassulaceae)

Plant Type: Evergreen succulent perennials.
Climate Zones: Varies with species.
Light: Sun to partial shade.
Soil: Adaptable, well-drained preferred.
Water: Drought tolerant to occasional.
Origin: Texas, Mexico, and south to Argentina.
Garden Uses: Rock, succulent, carpet and tapestry, green roof.

The perfectly symmetrical rosettes of echeverias vary in size from tiny, 2-inch-high gems to visually commanding specimens that may reach 1 to 2 feet wide and 2 to 4 feet tall. There are literally hundreds to choose from. Depending on the species or cultivar, these plants may grow predominantly as either solitary rosettes or as dense mats of rosettes. Nearly all have handsome, interesting yellow, orange, pink, or red flowers that attract hummingbirds. Most prefer to be kept rather dry during the winter months when excessive moisture may cause them to rot. Many of the larger selections with fancy leaves are less cold hardy and do not perform well long-term, if left untended. Fortunately, tired-looking echeverias are easy to replace by propagation; simply behead them and reroot the rosette before replanting. The plants listed below are widely available and adapted to a variety of California garden conditions. Since there are so many echeverias to choose from, you may also want to consult local experts for additional selections that may be ideally suited to your specific needs and area.

Agave echeveria *(E. agavoides)* has chunky, erect to spreading leaves that vary considerably in color from bright green to red to near black. Although they appear to have pointed tips, the leaves are not at all sharp. Plants often form solitary rosettes from 4 to 8 inches wide or they may slowly produce pups to form clumps up to 2 feet or more across, depending on the clone. There are many named cultivars of, or involving, this species. [c, i, cv]

Painted lady echeveria *(E. derenbergii)* forms 3-inch-wide rosettes of light gray-green succulent leaves and short clusters of showy pale orange flowers. Plants quickly produce offsets and will spread up to 3 feet or more across. [c, i]

Elegant hen and chicks *(E. elegans)* is likely the most widely grown species in California gardens. Individual

Above: Elegant hen and chicks. Left: Agave echeveria.

gray, bluish, or whitish rosettes may reach from 4 to 6 inches across and spread vigorously to make a dense large-scale groundcover. Nodding pink flowers adorn unbranched 8- to 12-inch-tall stalks in spring. [c, i, cv]

Hen and chicks *(E. × imbricata)* makes an easy-to-grow, spreading groundcover with blue- to gray-green rosettes up to 8 inches across. Vigorous and reliable, this is one of the best hybrid echeverias for larger-scale groundcover plantings. [c, i, cv]

Echinocactus grusonii
GOLDEN BARREL CACTUS
Cactus Family (Cactaceae)

Plant Type: Evergreen succulent perennial.
Climate Zones: Coastal, inland, and low desert.
Light: Sun.
Soil: Well-drained.
Water: Drought tolerant to occasional.
Origin: Mexico.
Garden Uses: Rock, succulent, carpet and tapestry, green roof.

To create a garden that leaves an indelible impression, consider a pattern planting with golden barrel cactus. This plant's round, succulent stems grow to the size of a cushion or ottoman, and its ribs are lined with thick, stiff, golden yellow spines; these are crowned with buff to white hairs that make them look deceptively soft

Golden barrel cactus, Lotusland.

and inviting. Golden barrel cactus is easy to grow in drier parts of California where the temperatures do not fall below about 25°F. In colder and/or wetter gardens, plants may be lifted out of the ground and placed into a bright, cool, dry storage area; replant them outdoors after the frost season or when the soil dries. Some gardeners in colder climates protect their cacti in situ by installing a mini-greenhouse around them for the duration of the winter months.

Erigeron
FLEABANE
Sunflower Family (Asteraceae)

Plant Type: Evergreen perennials.
Climate Zones: Varies with species.
Light: Sun to partial shade.
Soil: Adaptable to well-drained.
Water: Occasional to moderate.
Origin: Global, especially North America.
Garden Uses: Meadow, rock, carpet and tapestry, green roof.

This showy genus, comprising about 200 species, takes its unusual common name from the belief that some fleabanes repel fleas. These plants are characterized by daisylike flowers, ranging in color from white to pink to blue with a yellow center. Primarily herbaceous perennials, they are valued for their long flowering season and ease of maintenance. Many of the smaller species are especially useful in rock gardens, but they often require well-drained soils. A number of *Erigeron* species freely reseed, and therefore some vigilance is required to keep them contained.

Seaside daisy *(E. glaucus)* naturally occurs along the West Coast, from California's Channel Islands north

Seaside daisy. STEPHEN INGRAM

to Oregon. Plants typically reach 1 foot tall and 2 feet wide and have flat green oval leaves. Flowering from spring to summer, the 1- to 2-inch-diameter blossoms are white to violet in color. Seaside daisy is a better choice for coastal gardens with heavier soils, since the foliage on drought-stressed plants will burn

Santa Barbara daisy.

in hotter climates. 'Cape Sebastian' is a low-spreading selection that reaches 6 inches tall and forms dense mats to 3 feet wide. 'W.R.' is a seaside daisy hybrid (second parent unknown) with larger leaves and lavender flowers; it performs better than the species in warmer sites. [c, i, cv]

Santa Barbara daisy (*E. karvinskianus*) develops a billowing habit to 18 inches tall and 3 feet wide and is seldom seen without its cheerful white to pink ½-inch-wide flowers. Graceful, drought tolerant, and durable, this native of Mexico requires only occasional coppicing to improve vigor and appearance. Plants reseed readily and it can become a pest in some gardens. 'Spindrift' is a compact, sterile selection, 8 to 12 inches tall, with flowers that open as white and fade to rose. [c, i, cv, ld]

Mat daisy (*E. scopulinus*) is a dense, mat-forming species to 1½ inches tall from the mountains of northern Arizona and New Mexico. From June to August, it produces small white flowers, which are held just above its diminutive spoon-shaped leaves. A choice plant for gravel and rock gardens, it does not tolerate long periods of drought and prefers some shade in hot interior valleys. [all]

Eriogonum
BUCKWHEAT
Buckwheat Family (Polygonaceae)

Plant Type: Shrubs, subshrubs.
Climate Zones: Varies with species.
Light: Sun.
Soil: Adaptable, well-drained preferred.
Water: Drought tolerant to occasional.
Origin: Southeastern and western United States and Mexico.
Garden Uses: Meadow, rock, succulent, carpet and tapestry, green roof.

Literally hundreds of buckwheat species occur in western North America. From tiny annuals to 8-foot-tall shrubs, they offer a wide array of shapes, sizes, and colors for California gardens. They are especially appealing for their abundant flowers and their ability to tolerate hot, dry sites. Buckwheats are distinguished by inflorescences composed of tiny yellow, pink, or creamy white flowers borne in dense ball-like heads, airy spires, or broad flattened domes. Although some species bloom in spring, many flower in summer and fall, adding welcome late-season color and supplying food for bees, butterflies, and other beneficial insects for months on end. The drying seed heads add warm earth tone colors and provide nutritious food for birds and mammals.

Buckwheats are undemanding plants. They thrive on neglect, needing only minimal pruning of spent inflorescences or wayward branches. Some species are incredibly long-lived, whereas others decline within three to four years and are best replaced with new plants. Powdery mildew can be troublesome during cool, damp spring weather. Avoid overhead watering to minimize this problem. Otherwise, buckwheats are relatively free of pests and diseases.

Although buckwheats are numerous in the wild, only a handful of species are routinely available in nurseries. Of these, the most desirable low-growing species are listed below.

Santa Cruz Island buckwheat (*E. arborescens*) occurs naturally on California's northern Channel Islands. This handsome shrub typically reaches 3 to 5 feet tall and wide. Its linear, 1-inch-long sage green leaves grow on charcoal gray stems. The pink-tinged or creamy white, flat-topped inflorescences are 3 to 6 inches across. [c, i, cv]

Ashyleaf buckwheat (*E. cinereum*) adds a cool element to gardens during the hottest months of the year with its pinkish white flowers and soft gray leaves. A mound-forming shrub from coastal southern California, it grows well on slopes and banks. Its arching branches reach 3 to 6 feet tall and spread 3 to 10 feet across. [c, i, cv]

Rock buckwheat (*E. compositum*) is a woody, semi-deciduous perennial with large basal gray-green leaves

Santa Cruz Island buckwheat. STEPHEN INGRAM

and stunning yellow or cream flowers on a long stalk. Plants vary from ½ to 2 feet tall. This comely western native warrants wider recognition. [all except ld]

Saffron buckwheat (*E. crocatum*) is a rare subshrub from the northwestern Santa Monica Mountains with densely hairy white leaves and chartreuse flowers. Mature plants form cushiony mounds that are 1 to 2 feet tall and 1½ to 2½ feet wide. [c, i, cv]

California buckwheat (*E. fasciculatum*) deserves its common name, since this utilitarian shrub naturally occurs throughout much of the state. It has narrow rosemary-like leaves and abundant flowers. 'Warriner Lytle', 'Theodore Payne', and 'Dana Point' are three low-growing selections with dark green foliage and masses of creamy white flowers in spring and summer. [c, i, cv, ld] The gray-leaved variety, interior California buckwheat (*E. fasciculatum* var. *polifolium*), is particularly suitable for desert gardens and colder areas. [i, ld, hd]

Red-flowered buckwheat (*E. grande* var. *rubescens*) has light to deep pink flowers in spring. This endemic from the California Channel Islands forms a loose mound 1 to 2 feet tall and spreads slightly wider. The ovate green leaves are coated with silvery hairs underneath. Plants reseed easily. [c, i, cv]

Above: Red-flowered buckwheat.
Left: Sulfur buckwheat.
STEPHEN INGRAM

Interior California buckwheat.

Coast buckwheat (*E. latifolium*) is the West Coast's mainland counterpart to red-flowered buckwheat. Although similar in overall appearance, it differs from its island cousin by having silvery gray to green foliage and creamy white or occasionally pink flowers that are held in tight 1-inch-wide pompoms. [c, i]

Sulfur buckwheat (*E. umbellatum*) forms low, dense mounds from ½ to 1½ feet tall and up to 3 feet wide. It is an exceedingly variable subshrub with sage to gray-green leaves and pale to bright yellow flowers. It occurs naturally in mid- to high-elevation sites and is one of the very few buckwheats that will grow satisfactorily in partial shade. [all except ld]

Wright's buckwheat (*E. wrightii*) is a variable subshrub with silvery gray leaves and small rounded tufts of white to pink flowers borne on slender stems. Plants range from prostrate cushiony mats to loosely upright mounds and can reach roughly 1 to 2½ feet tall and extend 2 to 3 feet wide. The attractive forms and dainty inflorescences of this widespread Western native make it a desirable addition to gravel or rock gardens. [all except ld]

Euphorbia
EUPHORBIA, SPURGE
Spurge Family (Euphorbiaceae)

Plant Type: Evergreen perennials or subshrubs.
Climate Zones: Varies with species.
Light: Sun to partial shade.
Soil: Adaptable.
Water: Drought tolerant to occasional.
Origin: Global.
Garden Uses: Meadow, rock, carpet and tapestry.

Euphorbias are defined by their unique and peculiar inflorescence: the small flowers lack petals, and they have a puzzling arrangement of stigma, stamens, fused bracts, and nectar-secreting glands. In many species both bracts and leaves are showy, as exemplified by one of the best-known euphorbias, poinsettia (*E. pulcherrima*).

Above: Wood spurge.
DAVID FROSS
Left: Tasmanian Tiger wood spurge.
DAVID FROSS

Euphorbias produce an irritating milky sap that, in some species, is poisonous to humans; avoid direct contact with the skin or eyes when working with them (severe permanent eye damage can occur) and carefully site plants in the garden in order to avoid casual contact with their foliage. The enormous *Euphorbia* genus contains nearly 2000 species and every plant type from annuals to succulents to trees. For the purposes of this book, we have presented several garden-worthy perennials and subshrubs.

Wood spurge *(E. characias)* develops an upright habit to 6 feet high and wide. Its erect stems bear tightly arranged whorls of blue-green leaves, and cylindrical heads of chartreuse flowers appear at the stem tips in early spring. Seedling production is common in most gardens, but they are easily removed. Cut back the older stalks to maintain garden appeal. The variegated 'Tasmanian Tiger' features cream-colored margins while 'Glacier Blue' has smoky blue foliage edged in cream. The subspecies *wulfenii,* with purple-tinted leaf tips in winter and lime green flowers, is the most commonly grown form of this species. 'Humpty Dumpty' develops a compact form, and the flowers have a red eye; 'Lambrook Gold' has larger flower heads. [c, i, cv]

Cypress spurge *(E. cyparissias)* has a feathery texture with thin, blue-green leaves. It grows to 1 foot tall and spreads by rhizomes. Chartreuse flowers are produced in late spring and early summer. This species is tolerant of drought, heat, and cold and has become invasive in some locales; be sure to contain it to the garden. In cooler regions, the plants become dormant in winter. [all except ld]

Martin spurge *(E. × martinii)* is a naturally occurring hybrid *(E. characias* and *E. amygdaloides)* from the south of France with reddish foliage and a compact habit 2 to 3 feet tall and wide. In late winter to early spring, it bears chartreuse flowers with an amber center. 'Red Martin' features a dense bushy habit with dark red foliage. 'Rudolf' has blue-green leaves with reddish winter bracts. [all except ld]

Myrtle spurge *(E. myrsinites)* makes a good choice for dry gravel and rock gardens because it is both heat and drought tolerant. This mounding perennial reaches 8 inches high and 18 inches wide. Its whorled blue-green to whitish leaves are held on decumbent stems that trail away from the central crown in a bowl-shaped fashion. Clusters of chartreuse flowers form at the branch terminals in late winter and spring. Remove the aging stems, as they turn brown. [all except ld]

Silver spurge *(E. rigida)* produces trailing stems that arch upward to create a pleasing undulating form. This perennial has semi-succulent stems with fleshy blue-gray leaves, and it reaches 2 feet tall and 3 to 5 feet wide. In spring, the lime-yellow flowers display a blush of pink as they age. This species reseeds in some gardens. [c, i, cv, hd]

E. seguieriana ssp. *niciciana* is a fine-textured evergreen perennial with thin, 1½-inch-long blue-green leaves. It forms mounds to 18 inches high and 2 feet wide and produces chartreuse inflorescences that cover the foliage in late winter or early spring. Native from the Balkans to Pakistan, it is drought and heat tolerant and grows best in full sun. [c, i, cv, hd]

Cypress spurge. DAVID FROSS

Festuca
FESCUE
Grass Family (Poaceae)

Plant Type: Evergreen cool-season perennial grass.
Climate Zones: Varies with species.
Light: Sun to partial shade.
Soil: Adaptable.
Water: Occasional to regular.
Origin: Global.
Garden Uses: Greensward, meadow, rock and gravel, carpet and tapestry, green roof.

Fescues have long been cultivated as turfgrasses and ornamental bunch grasses. The more than 300 members of this genus are primarily found in cold or temperate zones. Their habitats vary from moist alpine meadows to hot, dry plains, although most species are intolerant of hot, humid summers. Fescues can be clump forming or rhizomatous and grow from 6 inches to 3 feet in height. Their foliage color is also variable, ranging from luminous silver-blue to rich verdant green. The blue-foliaged forms are often shorter-lived in garden applications and require dividing or replanting after a few years to maintain a satis-

factory appearance. The species listed here are best in full sun along the coast and in partial shade in the interior.

California fescue *(F. californica)* displays a varied habit—some plants have short stout blades to 6 inches tall while others form loose mounds with thin leaves up to 40 inches long. The leaves can vary from dark green to blue, and some selections, such as 'Horse Mountain', even feature bicolored foliage. The wiry flower stalks rise 2 to 3 feet above the foliage in spring and are capped with airy panicles that age to blond. This durable California native grows best with some shade. You can improve its appearance with an annual raking to remove old leaf blades. [c, i, cv, m]

Blue fescue *(F. glauca)* deserves its common name. Densely tufted and clump forming, its narrow 6- to 10-inch-long leaves are usually blue to silver-blue. The upright to arching flower stems develop in late spring, starting out as blue-green in color and fading to straw. Many named cultivars are available; three of the best are 'Azurit', featuring steely blue leaves; 'Siskiyou Blue', with luminous blue leaves; and 'Elijah Blue', a durable choice. (Hybridization adds a perplexing twist to the taxonomic history of blue fescue, which is often listed as *F. ovina* var. *glauca* and *F. cinerea*.) [all except ld]

Elijah Blue fescue.

Idaho fescue *(F. idahoensis)* occurs across western North America in open forests, grasslands, and sagebrush-meadow communities. It is a tufted bunch-grass reaching 18 inches tall with blue to blue-green foliage. Idaho fescue is similar to blue fescue but is longer-lived and less likely to spread open in the center of the bunch. 'Stoney Creek' is a chalky blue selection from northern California with flower spikes to 3 feet tall, and 'Tomales Bay' is a durable choice with fine blue green leaves. [all except ld]

Maire's fescue *(F. mairei)* is a heat- and drought-tolerant species from the Atlas Mountains of Morocco. Its fine-textured, flat-green foliage forms graceful mounds to 2½ feet high. The arching culms are topped with slender panicles of golden flowers. Longer lived than

Top: Blue fescue. STEPHEN INGRAM *Bottom: California fescue and Siskiyou Blue fescue (lower left).* STEPHEN INGRAM

many fescues, it is an excellent mid-sized grass for dry meadows and rock and gravel gardens. [all except ld]

Creeping red fescue *(F. rubra)* offers gardeners a number of selections that can be utilized as lawn grasses.

These green turf selections are often combined with other species in blends, or they are used to overseed winter-dormant grasses, such as Bermuda grass. Most of the green-foliaged selections require regular water to maintain a fresh appearance. When left unmowed, they make an attractive addition to meadow plantings. Two handsome California native selections offer less water-consumptive options: 'Molate Blue' is drought tolerant and has gray-green foliage, and 'Patrick's Point' has blue foliage and a spreading habit. [all except ld]

Creeping red fescue.

Fragaria
STRAWBERRY
Rose Family (Rosaceae)

Plant Type: Evergreen herbaceous perennials.
Climate Zones: Varies with species.
Light: Sun to partial shade.
Soil: Adaptable, well-drained preferred.
Water: Infrequent to occasional.
Origin: Northern Hemisphere, Chile.
Garden Uses: Meadow, rock, carpet and tapestry, kitchen, green roof.

The large, plump strawberries that entice shoppers at grocery stores, farmers markets, and roadside stands are the result of decades of breeding, hybridization, and selection within this small genus. Although the flavorful fruit on our native strawberries is relatively small, gardeners value the plants because they are robust, fast-growing, and easy-care groundcovers. These perennials are generally freely stoloniferous, although a few selections lack stolons. In spring, they produce attractive white flowers,

Top and bottom: Beach strawberry.

up to 1¼ inches across that are held on leafless stalks. Declining vigor in older plantings is often an indication of strawberry virus, and the plants should be replaced.

Beach strawberry *(F. chiloensis)* has long been used as a substitute for lawns in California. It spreads quickly by reddish stolons, covering the ground with a mat of leathery, glossy green leaves. Established plantings can reach up to 10 inches high but are easily trimmed to maintain a tighter, carpetlike appearance. 'Aulon' is a vigorous non-fruiting selection with larger flowers and leaves. The fruit-producing 'Chaval' features a tighter, more compact habit that maintains its lower profile with very little mowing. [c, i, cv]

Woodland strawberry *(F. vesca)* is a variable species with a trailing habit that grows from 4 to 12 inches tall. It blossoms from early spring into summer, displaying clusters of white ½-inch-wide flowers that are followed by small, tasty red berries. An extensive range of cultivars is available. 'Albomarginata' possesses variegated foliage, and tuft-forming 'Semperflorens' (alpine strawberry) produces delicious fruit. Both are from the subspecies *vesca.* 'Montana de Oro', a vigorous California native from the subspecies *californica,* has a wide, spreading habit. [c, i, cv, m]

Gaura lindheimeri
GAURA, BUTTERFLY GAURA
Evening Primrose Family (Onagraceae)

Plant Type: Deciduous herbaceous perennial.
Climate Zones: All.
Light: Sun.
Soil: Well-drained.
Water: Drought tolerant to moderate.
Origin: Texas to Louisiana.
Garden Uses: Meadow, succulent, carpet and tapestry.

From spring through fall, gaura rewards gardeners with a generous, willowy display of 1-inch-wide white to pink flowers. The blossoms open a few at a time and are borne along leafy, wandlike 3- to 4-foot-tall stalks. This tough perennial needs little care; deadheading extends the long flowering period and prevents unwanted seedlings. Pruning back by half in late spring or early summer encourages sturdier, bushier plants that won't flop over while in bloom. Rust and powdery mildew infestations can affect the plant's appearance and vigor, especially near the coast. Gaura tends to self-sow, making it suitable for the naturalistic effect of a meadow garden. Several often indistinguishable cultivars offer variations in flower or foliage color: 'Siskiyou Pink' has deep maroon buds and mottled foliage, 'Whirling Butterflies' sports larger white flowers, and 'Pink Cloud' produces deep pink flowers.

Gazania
GAZANIA
Sunflower Family (Asteraceae)

Plant Type: Evergreen perennial.
Climate Zones: All except mountains.
Light: Sun.
Soil: Well-drained.
Water: Drought tolerant to occasional.
Origin: Sub-Saharan Africa to South Africa.
Garden Uses: Rock, carpet and tapestry, green roof.

Gazanias' vibrant flower colors and patterns bring Mexico to mind, but these fast-growing, free-flowering plants hale from the drylands of South Africa. Short-lived perennials, they are best used as a temporary filler when more permanent, slower-growing plants are still getting established. Depending on which gazania is selected, the narrow leaves can be gray or green and may be shallowly lobed. Some gazanias are clumping, while others have a trailing growth habit. All prefer full sun and well-drained soils.

Above: Siskiyou Pink gaura and gaura (right).
DAVID FROSS
Left: Gaura.

Gazanias.

Geranium
CRANESBILL
Geranium Family (Geraniaceae)

Plant Type: Annuals, perennials, or subshrubs.
Climate Zones: Varies with species.
Light: Sun to shade.
Soil: Adaptable.
Water: Moderate to regular.
Origin: Global.
Garden Uses: Meadow, rock, carpet and tapestry.

Cranesbill is a large genus that typically has foliage with lobed or toothed basal leaves rising from a thick crown. (The genus *Geranium* is occasionally confused with the genus *Pelargonium,* since plants in the latter are commonly known as geraniums.) Cranesbill flowers are borne on forked stalks and have five petals ranging in color from white to pink, to blue, magenta, and purple. Most of the species and cultivars from temperate climates prefer cool coastal conditions, although some of the South African species are suitable for warmer interior gardens. The majority will benefit from an annual shearing in fall.

Geranium × *cantabrigiense* spreads slowly to form small carpets and makes an excellent small-scale groundcover. This free-flowering hybrid has deeply lobed dark green leaves that measure 1½ to 2½ inches wide. The 6- to 12-inch-tall plants can be sheared at any time, and they quickly recover with an output of fresh foliage. 'Biokovo' is a particularly vigorous form with white flowers tinged with pink. [all except ld]

Frances Grate cranesbill (*G.* 'Frances Grate') has a billowing habit to 18 inches tall and 3 feet wide. The finely divided leaves are gray-green above and silver below; they provide a fine contrast to the pale mauve flowers, which appear from spring to fall. Seedlings can be a nuisance. [c, i, cv]

Carpet geranium *(Geranium incanum)* withstands dry, hot conditions better than most other cranesbills and is a good choice for warmer inland sites. This robust

Carpet geranium.

species from South Africa reaches 1 foot tall and 3 feet wide and has finely divided glossy green leaves. Its cup-shaped 1-inch-wide flowers are deep pink with darker colored veins. It reseeds with vigor and can be invasive in some gardens. [c, i, cv]

Graptopetalum paraguayense
GHOST PLANT
Stonecrop Family (Crassulaceae)

Plant Type: Evergreen succulent.
Climate Zones: Coastal, inland, and low desert.
Light: Sun to partial shade.
Soil: Well-drained.
Water: Drought tolerant to occasional.
Origin: Mexico.
Garden Uses: Rock, succulent, carpet and tapestry, green roof.

Ghost plant is a rosette-forming succulent whose closely overlapping, pointed leaves exhibit a wide range of colors depending upon light exposure. A glaucous

Biokovo cranesbill.

Ghost plant.

coating enhances the ghostly shades of silvery blue or conch-shell pink. When installed as a groundcover, ghost plant forms tight prostrate mounds that slowly spread to fill the allotted space. It is particularly effective spilling over rocks. The small, star-shaped pale yellow flowers are mottled with red.

Of the approximately 12 species in its genus, ghost plant is by far the most widely grown. Other desirable species include *G. amethystinum* with plump, rounded, silvery pink leaves and *G. pentandrum* ssp. *superbum* with flattened rosettes of mauve pink.

Helictotrichon sempervirens
BLUE OAT GRASS
Grass Family (Poaceae)

Plant Type: Cool-season perennial grass.
Climate Zones: All except low desert and high desert.
Light: Sun to partial shade.
Soil: Adaptable.
Water: Occasional to regular.
Origin: Western Mediterranean Basin.
Garden Uses: Meadow, rock, carpet and tapestry, green roof.

Blue oat grass is one of the best mid-sized grasses for the garden. Combining striking blue-gray leaves with a distinctive fountainlike appearance, this versatile 3-foot-tall species can be massed, sited as an accent, or used for

its rich blue foliage in a field of green. During late spring, it produces flowers on arching stems that extend 1 to 2 feet above the foliage; the stems are more plentiful in cooler, moister conditions. Blue oat grass will display some dormancy in colder locations but is evergreen in most California climate zones.

Blue oat grass.

Older straw-colored leaves are easily removed by combing the blades with a steel rake, but be cautious around the sharp leaf tips.

Helleborus
HELLEBORE
Buttercup Family (Ranunculaceae)

Plant Type: Evergreen to deciduous rhizomatous perennials.
Climate Zones: Varies with species.
Light: Partial shade to shade, unless noted otherwise.
Soil: Well-drained.
Water: Occasional to moderate.
Origin: Europe and China.
Garden Uses: Rock, carpet and tapestry, green roof.

Throughout the cooler months of the year, the luscious flowers of hellebores add a graceful presence to the garden. The open-faced to nodding 1- to 3-inch-wide blossoms range in color from pale green to cream, white, pink, mauve, or deep blackish purple and may persist well into spring or early summer. Although seemingly dainty, these perennials are actually tough, long-lived plants when properly sited and tended. They thrive in the dappled or deep shade under trees or on the north side of structures. Some forms offer handsome foliage year-round. Once established, many will persist with little to no summer irrigation. Volunteer seedlings are a welcome sight and may yield intriguing new color forms.

The popularity of hellebores continues to increase on the West Coast, thanks in part to better availability and the realization that they can indeed grow successfully here. They require minimal care, other than removal of spent flower stalks and browning leaves. Aphids and thrips occasionally infest the flowers or undersides of the leaves and may disfigure the flowers. Sadly, hellebores' reputation for being deer-proof is untrue. Note that all parts of the plant are poisonous, and some people get dermatitis on contact, so wear protective clothing when pruning or working around them.

Corsican hellebore (*H. argutifolius*) reaches 1 to 3 feet tall and spreads equally wide. It is considered the best species for southern California and has evergreen,

leathery bluish green leaves with prominently toothed margins. Large clusters of 2-inch-wide pale green flowers are held above the foliage and may be so heavy that plants will need staking. The cultivar 'Silver Lace' has silvery

Corsican hellebore. SAXON HOLT

blue-gray leaves and grows up to 18 inches tall and wide. [c, i, cv, m]

Bear's foot hellebore *(H. foetidus)* tolerates sun and has long, narrow, deeply divided leaves. Pale green 1-inch-wide flowers with red margins top the 2-foot-tall leafy stalks. As its Latin name suggests, the leaves are malodorous but only when bruised. [c, i, cv, m]

Lenten rose *(H. orientalis)* features shiny, medium to dark green coarsely toothed leaves. This semi-deciduous species displays 2- to 3-inch-wide flowers on separate stalks that may stand at or above the 1- to 2-foot-high mantle of leaves. Blossoms vary from cream to pale green with hints of pink, or they may be splotched with maroon. The myriad hybrids sold under this name expand the color range to shades of purple and burgundy. In general, this species and its hybrids prefer more summer water unless the soil is high in clay or organic matter. [all but ld]

Helleborus × *sternii (H. lividus* × *H. argutifolius)* is a hybrid that varies considerably in size and color. This plant reaches ½ to 3 feet tall and grows equally wide. Its leaves may be green, blue, silver, or mottled. Flower color ranges from peachy cream to pale green or mauve. [c, i, cv, m]

Hemerocallis
DAYLILY
Daylily Family (Hemerocallidaceae)

Plant Type: Evergreen to deciduous perennial.
Climate Zones: All.
Light: Sun to partial shade.
Soil: Adaptable.
Water: Occasional to moderate.
Origin: Central Europe east to Japan.
Garden Uses: Meadow, carpet and tapestry, green roof.

There are, it seems, tens of thousands of different daylilies to choose from, and dozens of new selections are named and marketed every year. The best of these garden workhorses provide showy, open-faced, lilylike flowers from spring through summer. Each flower lasts but a single day (rarely two), but there are many blooms on a single flower stalk. Plants produce fountainlike clumps of grassy, yellow-green to dark green foliage. Flowers and shoots are edible, though the tuberous roots are toxic unless properly prepared. Dwarf cultivars that rebloom frequently make excellent choices. Three of the best are: 'Bitsy' with yellow flowers, and the color-descriptive selections 'Terra Cotta Baby' and 'Cranberry Baby'. Remove spent flower stems as they occur, and cut back tattered foliage to the ground as needed in the winter. Plants that are drought stressed produce fewer flowers.

Hesperaloe parviflora
RED YUCCA
Agave Family (Agavaceae)

Plant Type: Evergreen semi-succulent perennial.
Climate Zones: All.
Light: Sun.
Soil: Adaptable.
Water: Drought tolerant.
Origin: Texas to Mexico.
Garden Uses: Rock, succulent, carpet and tapestry, green roof.

Red yucca works wonderfully in inland gardens but is saddled with a misleading common name: it is neither a yucca nor red. This species has leathery, semi-succulent dark green to grayish leaves held in loose basal clumps that are 1 to 3 feet tall and may reach more than 6 feet wide. From spring to summer, flower stems rise from 4 to 6 feet above the foliage and carry numerous, small, creamy yellow or coral pink to red bell-shaped flowers

that are prized by hummingbirds. It adores heat and performs poorly in cool coastal gardens. Plants growing in hot, dry, or interior locations perform better with occasional summer irrigation. Red yucca requires minimal maintenance; cut off the flower stems when you tire of them and you are done for the year.

Daylily.

Red yucca. SAXON HOLT

Hesperoyucca whipplei (syn. *Yucca whipplei*)
CHAPARRAL YUCCA
Agave Family (Agavaceae)

Plant Type: Evergreen semi-succulent perennial.
Climate Zones: All.
Light: Sun.
Soil: Well-drained.
Water: Drought tolerant.
Origin: California, northwestern Baja California.
Garden Uses: Rock, succulent, carpet and tapestry.

Chaparral yucca creates a focal point in the garden when used as a single specimen, but a mass planting makes a bold and daring statement. The visual impact of these stiff silver-blue balls of rigid needle-tipped leaves

Above and left: Chaparral yucca.

is unquestionably dramatic. And the care of chaparral yuccas provides its own form of drama: will the gardener survive weeding and cleanup around these plants without becoming impaled on its spines? Since this plant is physically dangerous in the garden, it should not be used where unsuspecting children and pets may encounter it.

Chaparral yuccas are remarkably variable in size, color, and longevity. The smallest have rosettes about 18 inches across, whereas the largest are easily over 10 feet wide. *Hesperoyucca,* when literally translated, means "western yucca." This species is indeed the westernmost of all the yuccas, even though it is no longer considered a member of the genus Yucca. Some populations are strictly monocarpic: they flower just once; then the entire plant dies and the next generation grows from seeds. Others produce pups and form colonies over time, but the actual rosette that blooms always dies after flowering.

Heuchera
CORAL BELLS, ALUM ROOT
Saxifrage Family (Saxifragaceae)

Plant Type: Evergreen perennials.
Climate Zones: Varies with species.
Light: Sun to shade.
Soil: Adaptable, well-drained preferred.
Water: Occasional to moderate.
Origin: North America.
Garden Uses: Meadow, rock, carpet and tapestry, green roof.

Coral bells are clump-forming perennials whose slender flower stalks rise above the basal foliage and carry small, loosely arranged red to white blossoms. They are especially effective when planted in mass, mixed into meadows, or added as a splash of color in a woodland garden. Many species will tolerate full sun along the immediate coast, but varying degrees of shade are recommended in interior gardens. Although adaptable to a wide range of garden conditions, coral bells perform best when sited in well-drained soils that are rich in organic matter.

Elegant coral bells *(H. elegans)* makes a perfect choice for partially shaded gravel and rock gardens. It forms dense rosettes of bright green basal foliage to 4 inches high, and the cespitose clumps can spread to 2 feet wide. In late spring to early summer, 6- to 12-inch-tall flower spikes bear small pink and white flowers. This plant is drought tolerant along the coast and in the mountains, but elsewhere it requires occasional supplemental irrigation. [c, i, cv, m]

Island alum root *(H. maxima)* is a native of California's Channel Islands, and on the mainland it performs particularly well under deciduous trees. At 2

Canyon Delight coral bells.

Above: Wendy coral bells. STEPHEN INGRAM
Left: Island alum root.

feet wide and high, it is somewhat larger than other Heucheras. The plant has heart-shaped pale green leaves that rise from a fleshy rootstock and 2- to 3-foot-tall flower stalks that hold airy, cream-colored blossoms. Cut it back every few years to improve vigor and flower production. [c, i]

Rancho Santa Ana hybrids (*Heuchera* hybrids) represent a series of crosses between Arizona scarlet coral bells (*H. sanguinea*) and alum root (*H. maxima*) that have produced a group of vigorous hybrids with strong garden performance. They form clumps of dark green foliage measuring up to 2 feet tall and wide and produce flowers with colors ranging from red to white. 'Wendy' has pale green leaves and a profusion of rosy pink flowers; 'Opal' produces white flowers that fade to pink. 'Santa Ana Cardinal' features lush green leaves and bright red flowers. [c, i, cv]

Canyon series coral bells (*Heuchera* hybrids) are a group of crosses between Arizona scarlet coral bells (*H. sanguinea*) and elegant coral bells (*H. elegans*). Their tight rosettes of dark green leaves form mats of foliage graced with bright white to red flowers that are held aloft on 6- to 18-inch-long stalks. 'Canyon Belle'

has distinctive red flowers. 'Canyon Pink' is a vigorous medium-pink flowered form. 'Canyon Delight' features deep pink flowers. [c, i, cv, m]

Hypericum
SAINT JOHN'S WORT
Saint John's Wort Family (Hypericaceae)

Plant Type: Evergreen and deciduous shrubs or perennials.
Climate Zones: Varies with species.
Light: Sun, partial shade in interior.
Soil: Adaptable.
Water: Moderate to regular.
Origin: Global.
Garden Uses: Rock, carpet and tapestry, green roof.

Saint John's wort is a popular genus containing 400 species of annuals, perennials, and shrubs, including many with a long history of cultivation. The broad geographical distribution of this genus and the multitude of habitats in which its species grow yield an array of forms, which range from small creeping perennials to shrubs 10 feet tall. Cheerful yellow to gold flowers with a central cluster of prominent stamens characterize all species and bloom during spring and summer. Saint John's wort prefers moist conditions in spring and at least moderate summer water. Rust can be a problem in cool, damp climates and overhead irrigation should be avoided when possible. Although most species are deciduous, the following low-growing ones are evergreen.

Creeping Saint John's wort (*H. calycinum*) grows to 1 foot tall and spreads assertively by creeping stolons. This vigorous species from Turkey has 4-inch-long leaves that are medium-green in sunny locations but have a yellow-green cast when grown in the shade. Vivid yellow 3-inch-wide flowers bloom through late spring and summer, although flowering is not as pronounced in shade. Creeping Saint John's wort competes well with

*Above and left:
Saint John's wort.*

tree roots and is a good choice for planting in the partial shade of deciduous trees. An annual mowing or trimming during the winter will improve its appearance. [all]

Yellow coris (*H. coris*) has bright green needlelike leaves that grow into a dome-shaped form measuring up to 12 inches tall and 2 feet wide. Small, star-shaped yellow flowers appear on the branch tips throughout summer. Yellow coris performs best in full sun with well-drained soils and moderate summer moisture. [c, i, cv, m]

Himalayan Saint John's wort (*H. reptans*) is a mat-forming perennial with ½-inch-long leaves and rooting stems. It grows up to 2 inches tall and extends 18 to 24 inches wide. Its ground-hugging habit makes Himalayan Saint John's wort a suitable rock garden plant. Bright gold flowers up to 2 inches wide with feathery stamens appear in summer. Protect this plant from frost in colder climates. [c]

Iris
IRIS
Iris Family (Iridaceae)

Plant Type: Evergreen perennials.
Climate Zones: Varies with subgroup.
Light: Sun to partial shade.
Soil: Adaptable.
Water: Drought tolerant to occasional.
Origin: Northern Hemisphere.
Garden Uses: Meadow, rock, carpet and tapestry, green roof

This widely known and colorful group of plants is aptly named after the Greek goddess of the rainbow. There are several major groups of irises that are especially good choices for drought-tolerant California gardens. Listed here from shortest to tallest, they are: Pacific Coast irises (our native west coast species and their hybrids); winter iris *(Iris unguicularis);* arilbred irises (hybrids of Middle Eastern species); bearded iris (*Iris germanica* hybrids); and butterfly iris (*Iris spuria* and hybrids). All of these irises have sword-shaped leaves that are produced in a fanlike arrangement at the tips of branched rhizomes. They require some cleanup to keep them looking better during summer and fall.

Pacific Coast irises are a remarkably diverse group in size, vigor, flower color, and adaptability. Most bloom from April to May. Among these, the best for most gardeners to start with are **Douglas iris** *(Iris douglasiana)* and its white-flowered cultivar 'Canyon Snow'. There are hundreds of others to investigate, and these selections are usually lumped together under the label of Pacific Coast Hybrid (PCH) iris. Plants are usually at their best where they get full sun in the winter and either

dappled shade or full afternoon shade in the summer. They vary in height from 6 inches to 2 feet. [c, i, cv, m]

Winter iris blooms very early in the year and its blue to violet flowers are similar in appearance to our native species. The fragrant flowers grow on short stems and may be obscured by the foliage;

Douglas iris.

*Above: Canyon Snow
Douglas iris.
Left: Bearded iris.*

range from miniature dwarf bearded irises that grow to a height of 8 inches to the familiar tall bearded iris (the irises of the artist Van Gogh) that may reach 2½ to 4 feet when they are in bloom. Most bearded irises flower from spring to early summer, though there are increasing numbers of reblooming irises that bloom off and on from spring through fall. The flowers have a distinctive pleasing fragrance—unlike any other floral scent. Tall bearded irises are among the most durable and dependable garden plants for California gardens, and there are hundreds of named selections to choose from. [all]

Butterfly irises are taller than the others listed here and may reach heights of 3 to 5 feet. The white to yellow to blue-violet flowers are distinctively three-parted and appear at the top of the tall stems. Their strong, stiff vertical growth habit makes them an excellent choice for creating contrast in the garden. Use them with the rounded forms of rockroses, rosemaries, santolinas, and California sages. [all]

Iva hayesiana
POVERTY WEED
Sunflower Family (Asteraceae)

Plant Type: Evergreen subshrub.
Climate Zones: Coastal, inland, and Central Valley.
Light: Sun to partial shade.
Soil: Adaptable.
Water: Drought tolerant to occasional.
Origin: San Diego County to northwestern Baja California.
Garden Uses: Succulent, carpet and tapestry, green roof.

Poverty weed, despite its common name, gives good value to gardeners looking for a reliable, carefree plant. This somewhat nondescript groundcover has light green

aromatic foliage and insignificant flowers. The loosely arching branches reach 1 to 3 feet tall and sprawl up to 12 feet across. The slightly fleshy leaves make it an effective partner for cacti and other succulents and afford some resistance to wildfires. Prune lightly to shape or more aggressively to rejuvenate older specimens.

Poverty weed.

some gardeners cut the foliage back by half during late fall so that the forth-coming flowers will be more readily visible. These plants are well suited to dappled shade and are about a foot or so tall. [c, i, cv]

Arilbred irises like full sun and summer heat and prefer to be dry in summer. Their thick rhizomes and flattened fans of leaves are similar to those of tall bearded garden irises, but these plants are usually much smaller. Arilbred irises produce globe-shaped flowers that are often stippled and lined with contrasting colors; these glorious blooms make them an outstanding addition to the garden. [all]

Bearded irises come in nearly every color imaginable except for true reds. Plants in this category are further grouped into seven classes that are governed by the size of the plant and the size of the flowers. These

Juncus patens
WIRE GRASS, CALIFORNIA GRAY RUSH
Rush Family (Juncaceae)

Plant Type: Evergreen perennial.
Climate Zones: All except low desert and high desert.
Light: Sun to shade.
Soil: Adaptable.
Water: Occasional to regular.
Origin: California to Southern Oregon.
Garden Uses: Meadow, rock garden, green roof.

Wire grass is a fitting common name for this adaptable species whose rigid, steely gray to green cylindric stems are often used as foundation material in Native American basketry. This plant initially forms dense clumps and then spreads slowly to establish small drifts. It thrives with moisture, and dry conditions will restrict the colony size and growth rate. The upright to slightly arching stems reach 1 to 2 feet tall, with small clusters of brown bracts and flowers forming near their tops. After a period of time (usually years) wire grass clumps can look increasingly disheveled. They are easily rejuvenated by using sharp shears or pruners to cut the plants back to a few inches tall in late fall; give them a very

Wire grass.

light dose of nitrogen fertilizer, and by spring they will regain their attractive appearance. You can also dig up the clumps, discard the older portions, and replant the vigorous sections in fall.

Wire grass has a vertical character that makes it a useful design element in a meadow or among rocks in a gravel garden. 'Carmen's Gray', 'Elk Blue', and 'Occidental Blue' are selections that offer more gray or blue tones in the foliage.

Juniperus
JUNIPER
Cypress Family (Cupressaceae)

Plant Type: Evergreen shrubs.
Climate Zones: All.
Light: Sun to partial shade.
Soil: Varies with species, well-drained preferred.
Water: Drought tolerant to moderate.
Origin: Northern hemisphere.
Garden Uses: Rock, succulent, carpet and tapestry, green roof.

Junipers belong to a highly variable group of conifers possessing needle- or scale-like evergreen leaves and somewhat fleshy berrylike fruits. A handful of species make excellent groundcovers for California gardens, despite their origins in colder regions. Useful as large swaths or singular accents, their compact or trailing forms add year-round texture. Foliage colors range from light to deep green, and depending on species, may also have tones of yellow, gray, or silvery blue. Pruning demands are minimal if the plants are sited properly. Aphids, twig borers, and spider mites can be problematic. Control juniper blight, a disease that kills twigs and branches, by keeping the foliage dry, avoiding over fertilization, and pruning only to remove dead or infected tissue. Junipers are susceptible to root rot when grown in heavy soils that stay waterlogged. Some people are sensitive to the oils in the foliage, which can cause dermatitis.

Chinese juniper (*J. chinensis*) typically has an upright habit, but a couple of cultivars—'San Jose' and 'Parsonii'—stay within 1½ to 2 feet in height and spread up to 6 and 8 feet, respectively. These cultivars tend to be slow growing.

Shore juniper (*J. conferta*) tolerates exposure to salt spray, so it is particularly useful for seaside gardens. Native to coastal bluffs in Japan, this prostrate species grows 6 to 8 feet wide. Despite recommendations to the contrary, it does not tolerate hot inland sites or heavy soils. 'Blue Pacific' is a popular selection.

Creeping juniper (*J. horizontalis*) grows naturally across the northern United States and Canada. Cultivars

Above: Shore juniper.
Left: Nana Japanese juniper.

from 4 inches to 1 foot tall are available in a broad array of colors, and many have leaves that turn plum or bronze during cold weather. 'Bar Harbor' (8 to 10 feet wide), 'Blue Chip' (6 to 8 feet wide), 'Prince of Wales' (8 to 10 feet wide), and 'Wiltonii' (6 to 8 feet wide) are just a few of the named selections.

Nana Japanese garden juniper *(J. procumbens 'Nana')* is a popular, 1-foot-tall by 4- to 6-foot-wide selection; its branches radiate from the center, eventually reaching 6 or more feet across.

Savin juniper *(J. sabina)* grows naturally in colder parts of Eurasia. Several cultivars with bright green to blue-green foliage are available. Twig blight is a fungal disease that can be problematic for this species in some areas. To minimize infection, avoid overhead irrigation and prune only when foliage is dry. Savin juniper ranges in height from ½ to 3 feet tall, and its selections include 'Arcadia' (6 to 8 feet wide), 'Broadmoor' (to 10 feet wide), and 'Buffalo' (to 8 feet wide).

Kalanchoe
KALANCHOE
Stonecrop Family (Crassulaceae)

Plant Type: Succulent perennials.
Climate Zones: Varies with species.
Light: Sun to partial shade.
Soil: Well-drained.
Water: Drought tolerant to occasional.
Origin: Africa, Madagascar, and Asia.
Garden Uses: Rock, succulent, carpet and tapestry, green roof.

Kalanchoes are an impressive lot, rivaling other succulent genera in beauty and diversity. The genus includes both low-growing forms perfect for groundcovers and tall, upright species desirable as dramatic focal points. The species vary widely in shape, size, texture, and color. Most have attractive flowers in addition to their colorful and handsome foliage.

Feltbush *(K. beharensis)* takes its common name from the densely hairy, grayish brown foliage. This striking shrubby species grows 4 to 12 feet tall. Its bold-textured, triangular, wavy-margined leaves—which measure up to 15 inches long—make up for the lackluster flowers. The cultivar 'Fang' is notable for white toothy projections borne on the underside of the leaves. [c, i, ld]

Rainbow scallops *(K. fedtschenkoi,* syn. *Bryophyllum fedtschenkoi)* is aptly named. This showy groundcover sends up numerous 1- to 2-foot long stems that bear closely overlapping, scalloped blue-green leaves that are occasionally marked with pink or white. Pendulous coral to orange flowers dangle above the leaves in late winter. Aerial roots add visual interest, and new plantlets often form on the leaf margins. [c, i]

K. grandiflora grows 2 to 4 feet tall. The rounded blue-green leaves of this somewhat shrubby species are held tightly along the stem and occasionally have a rosy glow. Its fragrant yellow flowers bloom rather erratically. [c, i]

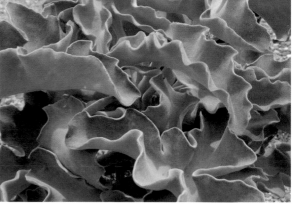

Feltbush.

Above: Paddle plant. Left: Flour dust plant (top) and elegant hen and chicks.

Paddle plant *(K. luciae)* grabs attention with its basal rosette of broad, flattened vertical leaves that are up to 6 inches tall and wide. Strong sunlight and cool temperatures intensify the two-tone contrast between the pale blue-green surface and the orange or rusty red marginal band. In spring, the white-coated flower stalk adds 2 to 3 feet in height and bears pale yellow flowers. Snails and slugs can disfigure the impressive foliage. *K. thyrsiflora* is a similar, more compact species with fragrant yellow flowers. [c, i]

Copper spoons *(K. orgyalis)* is named for its exceptionally attractive foliage. The upper surface of young leaves is felted with coppery cinnamon hairs; the up-rolled margins reveal the contrasting silvery underside. Plants grow slowly to 3 to 6 feet tall and wide. The small yellow flowers appear in winter or spring. [c, i]

Flour dust plant *(K. pumila)* has bright pink flowers that add sparkle to a garden in winter and early spring. This diminutive species reaches 1 foot tall and features chalky gray-green leaves that age in color to wine or plum. [c, i]

Panda plant *(K. tomentosa)* is a popular houseplant that grows well outdoors in warm-weather areas. The fuzzy silver-gray leaves are dotted with chocolate or cinnamon brown spots along the margins. Plants may eventually become small, multibranched shrubs up to 2 feet tall. [c, ld]

Lantana
LANTANA
Verbena Family (Verbenaceae)

Plant Type: Evergreen shrub.
Climate Zones: All except high desert and mountains.
Light: Sun.
Soil: Adaptable.
Water: Occasional.
Origin: Tropics of Central and South America, and Southern Africa.
Garden Uses: Rock, carpet and tapestry, green roof.

Lantana is often maligned by serious gardeners but is truly loved by the public at large—and for good reasons. It is an easily grown plant with myriad growth habits, it blossoms nearly every month of the year, and it offers an array of vibrant flower choices, including white, red, yellow, orange, and lavender. In general, the rough-textured green to gray-green leaves are unremarkable. The flowers are very popular with hummingbirds, butterflies, and bees. A number of birds relish the shiny black, succulent berrylike fruits and serve as effective seed dispersal agents. This is the reason lantana has

Above: Spreading lantana. Left: Lantana flowers.

become a pest plant in many tropical climates, although it is not a pest plant in California.

Many lantanas will need pruning to keep them in bounds. Light pruning can be done at any time of the year, although heavy pruning is best done in late winter or early spring after any chance of frost. Some people find the aroma of bruised lantana foliage objectionable, and touching the leaves may cause contact dermatitis for people with sensitive skin. In another cautionary note, lantanas are poisonous plants, and the immature fruits are especially toxic. The lantanas listed below are selected from the vast array of choices available in nurseries. (In addition to the plants featured here, there are several yellow-flowered selections, such as 'Landmark Yellow', 'Lucky Yellow', 'Gold Rush', or 'Spreading Sunshine').

Lantana cultivar, daylily, and octopus agave.

Miss Huff lantana (*L.* 'Miss Huff') has bright yellow-red-orange flowers that take on a pinkish hue as they age. This plant tolerates colder temperatures than most other lantana species and hybrids that have orange-red-flowers. Miss Huff lantana can grow 5 to 6 feet tall and spread equally wide. To keep it shorter, cut it back to about 1 foot in height in early spring.

Spreading lantana *(L. montevidensis)* is widely grown as a groundcover. The species has lavender flowers and gray foliage, although there are cultivars with white ('Alba' and 'White Lightnin' ' ®) or lavender and white flowers ('Lavender Swirl'). It typically reaches from 1 to 2 feet tall and may spread considerable distances as stems in contact with moist soil often take root. Plants of this species tend to be more cold hardy, and once established, often come back from the roots after a hard freeze.

Radiation lantana (*L.* 'Radiation') is an older reliable selection with vibrant red-orange flowers. It may even be pruned into a small patio tree. This plant may reach a height and width of 8 feet, but you can easily restrain its size with a hard annual early spring pruning.

Lavandula
LAVENDER
Mint Family (Lamiaceae)

Plant Type: Evergreen subshrubs to shrubs.
Climate Zones: Varies with species.
Light: Sun
Soil: Well-drained.
Water: Drought tolerant to occasional.
Origin: Atlantic Islands, Mediterranean Basin to Somalia and India.
Garden Uses: Meadow, rock, carpet and tapestry.

The lavenders comprise an immense wealth of species, hybrids, and cultivars, and California is the easiest place in the country to grow them. This beautiful and diverse group of plants is known for its long-lasting inflorescences, which are produced from spring to summer. Large scale plantings of lavenders are evocative of fields of wheat or barley: erect thin stems carry thick terminal masses of flowers that dance in the wind.

All of the lavenders listed here will do best if they are cut back by $^1/_2$ to $^2/_3$ after flowering, except for Spanish lavender, which should only be lightly pruned after it blossoms. Plants that are not sheared on an annual basis are frequently short-lived. Use rock, gravel, or other inorganic materials when mulching lavenders because organic mulches usually cause problems, such as crown rot or fungal diseases of the foliage. These plants readily hybridize and there is considerable taxonomic and horticultural confusion about them.

English lavender *(L. angustifolia)* possesses the quintessential sweet scent most people associate with the name "lavender." It is likely the most frequently grown species and can be quite variable, with foliage ranging from greenish to gray to white, depending on the plant and the season. Flowers vary from white to pink

Candicans French lavender. DAVID FROSS

Above:
Lavender mix.
DAVID FROSS
Left: Spanish
lavender.

flower stems with interrupted flower clusters. Blossom color ranges from blue to lavender-blue to violet blue. [c, i, cv, ld]

Spanish lavender *(L. stoechas)* has showy, long-lasting pinkish to purplish bracts atop its dense clusters of small dark flowers. These plants tend to be long-lived and more drought tolerant than the English lavenders. Though variable, expect plants of this species to reach from 2 to 3 feet tall and wide. 'Otto Quast' has green to gray-green foliage and showy violet bracts. [all except m]

Lessingia filaginifolia [syn. *Corethrogyne filaginifolia*]
CALIFORNIA ASTER
Sunflower Family (Asteraceae)

Plant Type: Evergreen herbaceous perennial.
Climate Zones: Coastal, inland, and Central Valley.
Light: Sun to partial shade.
Soil: Adaptable, well-drained preferred.
Water: Drought tolerant to occasional.
Origin: Oregon, California, Baja California.
Garden Uses: Meadow, rock, succulent, carpet and tapestry, green roof.

California aster is widespread in grasslands, oak woodlands, and coastal scrub. This silver-leaved herb comes in myriad shapes, sizes, and flower colors. 'Silver Carpet' is a particularly desirable mat-forming selection that grows 4 to 8 feet wide. It can be completely covered with 1-inch-wide lavender pink flowers in late summer and fall. Not quite as silvery and more upright is 'Smart Aster', a mounded selection roughly 2 to 3 feet tall and slightly wider. In addition, there are unnamed selections that may have greener foliage, pale purple or pink to almost white flowers, and either upright or trailing shapes. The species and its cultivars all attract butterflies. Prune California aster after it flowers to maintain a dense habit and promote abundant blooms the following year.

to lavender-blue. Mature specimens may be 1 to 2 feet tall and typically spread a bit wider than tall. Despite its common name, English lavender's native range is in mountainous areas of southern Europe. Some of the older selections are now seed-grown and are therefore no longer uniform clones; 'Hidcote' and 'Munstead' are the best examples of this unfortunate trend. [all]

French lavender *(L. dentata)* offers especially attractive foliage: its green to gray-green leaves are lance-shaped and have crenulated margins. This species has the longest bloom season, and the flowers vary in color from white to pink to lavender-blue. This the largest of the lavenders listed here, it grows from 3 to 4 feet tall and 5 to 6 feet wide. The cultivar 'Candicans' is widely grown for its beautiful gray-white foliage. [c, i, cv, ld]

Lavandin *(L. × intermedia)* varies considerably due to its hybrid origin. It is the second most commonly grown lavender in California and is a hybrid between English lavender and spike lavender *(L. latifolia).* Lavandin is larger than English lavender and has branched

Silver Carpet California aster.

Great Basin wild rye. STEPHEN INGRAM

Canyon Prince wild rye.

Creeping wild rye *(L. triticoides)* works well for large-scale plantings, including greenswards, because it can quickly fill an area. For smaller spaces, contain it with a root barrier. This aggressive species has narrow leaves and grows 2 to 4 feet tall. It looks better with supplemental irrigation in summer and annual pruning. 'Grey Dawn' is a selection with glaucous blue leaves. [all except ld]

Leymus
WILD RYE
Grass Family (Poaceae)

Plant Type: Semi-evergreen to evergreen grasses.
Climate Zones: Varies with species.
Light: Sun to partial shade.
Soil: Adaptable.
Water: Drought tolerant to moderate.
Origin: North America, Europe, and Asia.
Garden Uses: Meadow, carpet and tapestry, green roof.

Three of California's six native species of wild rye are durable ornamental grasses. Their spikelike flowers attract beneficial insects, and their seeds provide food for birds and mammals. These species benefit from periodic hard pruning in late summer or fall to promote new growth and to remove dried stalks and leaves that present a fire hazard.

Great Basin wild rye *(L. cinereus)* reaches 6 to 8 feet tall in bloom and makes a fine vertical accent or commanding naturalistic drift. This bold-textured upright species has broad blue-green to gray-green leaves and usually lacks rhizomes. It is especially suitable for inland gardens with cold winters. [all]

Giant wild rye *(L. condensatus)* is a coarse-textured medium-green species that soars to 9 feet tall when in bloom. It is useful in large-scale meadows or as a temporary screen. 'Canyon Prince', a striking blue-gray selection, is popular for its unusual foliage color and more compact habit. Plants reach 3 to 4 feet tall and spread slowly by rhizomes. [c, i, cv]

Muhlenbergia
MUHLY
Grass Family (Poaceae)

Plant Type: Evergreen perennial grasses.
Geographic Zones: Varies with species.
Light: Sun to partial shade.
Soil: Adaptable, unless otherwise noted.
Water: Drought tolerant to moderate.
Origin: North America and southern Asia.
Garden Uses: Meadow, rock, carpet and tapestry, green roof.

The genus *Muhlenbergia* includes over 150 species, and a few have acquired an honored place in California gardens. These cool- and warm-season grasses form medium to large, fine-textured mounds that are topped with decorative inflorescences in spring, summer, or fall. Unlike many other bunchgrasses, muhlys do not need annual pruning. Rejuvenate them in winter or early spring every few years or whenever the buildup of brown leaves compromises their appearance.

Pink muhly *(M. capillaris)* bears gauzy pink plumes and is easily the most colorful of the species listed here. Native to Mexico, the West Indies, and the eastern United States, it typically grows 2 feet tall and equally wide. Although it is drought tolerant, this late-summer-flowering beauty appreciates occasional to moderate irrigation in California. 'Regal Mist' is a particularly deep pink selection, while the cultivar 'White Cloud' has a name that says it all. [all]

Above: Pink muhly.
DAVID FROSS
Left: Lindheimer's muhly.

Deer grass.

Bamboo muhly *(M. dumosa)* differs from other muhlys because it has threadlike wispy leaves and cane-like stems. Growing 4 to 6 feet tall and wide, its delicate appearance and slightly weeping habit belie this plant's undemanding character. Use it as a solitary potted specimen, a foil for succulents, or a light, informal screen—if its brief absence can be tolerated following rejuvenative pruning. Plants may not reliably respond to a hard pruning. [all except m]

Bull grass *(M. emersleyi)* remains undervalued, even though it is a durable and striking bunchgrass. In summer, purple-tinged flower stalks rise 2 to 4 feet above the 2-foot-tall by 3-foot-wide mounds of gray-green foliage and eventually bend under the weight of the feathery plumes. Bull grass is very drought tolerant. [all]

Lindheimer's muhly *(M. lindheimeri)* is an elegant blue-gray grass that reaches 3 to 5 feet tall when in bloom. Slender, upright purplish inflorescences turn silver-gray upon ripening. Although drought and heat tolerant, this semi-evergreen muhly prefers moderate watering. [all except m]

Soft blue Mexican muhly *(M. pubescens)* is a handsome bunchgrass forming 1- to 2-foot-tall by 2- to

3-foot-wide mounds. Place it where you can stroke the velvety blue-gray to gray-green leaves and the downy blue flower stalks. Plants grow best in well-drained soils under sunny, dry conditions and rarely need to be cut back. [all except m]

Deer grass *(M. rigens)* has become increasingly popular as gardeners discover how easy it is to grow this reliable species. It has a widespread distribution and tolerates a broad range of moisture conditions and soil types. The olive-green leaf blades are upright or slightly arching and eventually create mounds 3 to 4 feet tall and wide. The 4- to 6-foot-long upright flower spikes emerge in late spring or summer and ripen to a silver or straw color; they are prized for use in basketry. Although a single plant makes an eye-catching vertical statement, deer grass is outstanding in mass or pattern plantings and is particularly useful bordering a greensward. [all]

Myoporum parvifolium
CREEPING MYOPORUM
Myoporum Family (Myoporaceae)

Plant Type: Evergreen shrub.
Climate Zones: Coastal, inland, Central Valley, and low desert.
Light: Sun to partial shade.
Soil: Adaptable.
Water: Infrequent to moderate.
Origin: Australia.
Garden Uses: Carpet and tapestry, green roof.

This vigorous, fast-growing 6-inch-tall shrub forms vegetative carpets from 10 to 20 feet across. The thick, nearly succulent, narrow shiny leaves are up to 1½ inches long and densely clothe the stems and branches.

Although fragrant, the small clusters of white to pink flowers are not the reason most people grow creeping myoporum. Gardeners value it most as a groundcover, especially on slopes and banks. Creeping myoporum needs space and the freedom to spread. Where it grows alongside paths and sidewalks, selectively thin or head back wayward branches, rather than shear the entire plant, to avoid an awkward look. Though its soft, carpetlike appearance is inviting, resist the impulse to walk on it, as these plants do not tolerate foot traffic. Due to its low stature, weeds can be a problem—especially as young plants are filling in. This species and its cultivars ('Burgundy Carpet', 'Davis', 'Putah Creek', 'Tucson', etc.) are considered to be resistant to myoporum thrips, a destructive insect pest that distorts the new growth on other myoporums.

Creeping myoporum.

Nandina domestica
HEAVENLY BAMBOO
Barberry Family (Berberidaceae)

Plant Type: Evergreen rhizomatous shrub.
Climate Zones: All.
Light: Sun to partial shade.
Soil: Adaptable.
Water: Drought tolerant to moderate.
Origin: China and Japan.
Garden Uses: Rock, succulent, carpet and tapestry, green roof.

A staple in California gardens, heavenly bamboo is a tough shrub that offers year-round appeal. A host of cultivars can fulfill essential functions in the landscape, from narrow screens to groundcovers to accents. The pinnately compound leaves emerge with a blush of bronze or pink before turning light to medium green or blue-green; they typically become infused with plum or bronze tones during the cooler months. In spring or early summer, 6- to 12-inch-long clusters of white to light pink flowers top the stems and are followed by glossy berries, which on rare occasions are white. Plants look best with moderate irrigation but withstand dry conditions, including competition from tree roots. On taller selections, the canelike stems eventually lose their lower leaves and can become top-heavy. Prune them to the ground in late winter to stimulate new basal shoots. Too much shade or poor air circulation favors powdery mildew, whereas full sun combined with high temperature can cause puckering and discoloration of the foliage.

The following heavenly bamboo cultivars illustrate the wide range of sizes, textures, and foliage colors gardeners can chose from, although many other selections are available.

Compacta heavenly bamboo (*N. d.* 'Compacta') doesn't quite match its name, growing up to 4 or 5 feet tall and to 3 feet wide. The profusion of canes and leaflets and the overall lacy texture of this plant make it particularly useful for screens or other mass plantings.

Filamentosa heavenly bamboo (*N. d.* 'Filamentosa') is a slow-growing, mid-size cultivar, topping out at 2 to 3 feet tall. Its unique feature is the intricate network of highly dissected leaflets. The entire plant turns dramatic shades of coppery red in fall.

Firepower heavenly bamboo (*N. d.* 'Firepower') packs a wallop on short 2-foot-tall stems; its summer-long display of rosy red foliage intensifies through winter.

Above: Gulf Stream heavenly bamboo.
SAXON HOLT
Left: Heavenly bamboo flowers and berries.

Gulf Stream heavenly bamboo (*N. d.* 'Gulf Stream') grows up to 3 feet tall and 2 feet wide. Its blue-green summer foliage takes on vivid red tones in both spring and fall.

Harbour Dwarf heavenly bamboo.

Harbour Dwarf heavenly bamboo (*N. d.* 'Harbour Dwarf') is a low-growing selection that reaches 1 to 2 feet tall. It is useful as a groundcover but spreads slowly.

Nassella
NEEDLEGRASS
Grass Family (Poaceae)

Plant Type: Deciduous to semi-evergreen, cool-season perennial grasses.
Climate Zones: Varies with species.
Light: Sun to partial shade.
Soil: Adaptable.
Water: Drought tolerant to occasional.
Origin: North and South America.
Garden Uses: Meadow, rock, succulent, carpet and tapestry, green roof.

Several species of needlegrasses, including three California natives, make excellent candidates for dry meadow gardens. These fine-textured, stately grasses are most effective when used in naturalistic drifts, although a strategically placed individual can lend just the right willowy softness to a boulder or serve as a counterpoint in a bold succulent garden. They share many characteristics: narrow, medium-green leaf blades; loosely upright, tufted forms that reach up to 3 feet tall when in bloom; and the eponymous seeds with long, needlelike glistening awns. In the wild, they turn flaxen as the soil dries out in summer, remaining dormant until the rains return in fall. Indeed, too much supplemental water during the dry season may kill them. Better to appreciate this quiet phase; enjoy watching the dried inflorescences sway with each breeze, and observe birds as they harvest the copious seeds. Rejuvenate plants at summer's end by cutting them back to the ground, which also removes any dry tinder.

Nodding needlegrass (*N. cernua*) is considered by some aficionados to be the prettiest native species. Its pendulous flower stalks are tinged with purple and

Above and left: Purple needlegrass.

the long, wavy awns account for its overall graceful character. [c, i, cv]

Foothill needlegrass (*N. lepida*) has a more refined bearing, with slightly thinner blades and shorter awns. [c, i, cv]

Purple needlegrass (*N. pulchra*) serves as the official state grass of California. Before European settlement, it was likely one of the most widespread and prominent bunchgrasses in the state. It is the most popular native species for meadow gardens. The purple-tinged young seeds and strongly twice-bent awns with straight segments distinguish it from the other species. [c, i, cv]

Nepeta
CATMINT
Mint Family (Lamiaceae)

Plant Type: Herbaceous, rhizomatous perennials.
Climate Zones: All.
Light: Sun to partial shade.
Soil: Well-drained.
Water: Occasional to moderate.
Origin: Europe, Asia, and North Africa.
Garden Uses: Meadow, rock, carpet and tapestry, kitchen, green roof.

Whether you approve of cats in gardens or not, there is probably no argument among gardeners about the aesthetic value of catmint. Members of this aromatic, floriferous genus provide months of pastel color and appealing fragrance, and their blooms supply nectar

Above: Catmint in bloom with rosemary.
Left: Six Hills Giant catmint.

for hummingbirds, bees, and other beneficial insects. Plants may need protection from foraging or frolicking cats, although some cats do not seem the least bit interested in this natural feline stimulant. As an added bonus, deer and rabbits leave the plants alone. The catmints' low stature and billowing habit make them ideal for edging or informal short hedges. Shear plants after flowers fade to promote a second bloom and to prevent seed germination (many forms can become invasive otherwise). If necessary, shear again in winter or early spring to remove last year's stems as new growth emerges.

Catnip *(N. cataria)* is typically relegated to herb gardens. Considered inferior to the more colorful species and cultivars, its small creamy white to pink flowers are nevertheless attractive. If not disfigured by cats, plants attain 2 to 3 feet in height and width. Some gardeners use the leaves to flavor tea, particularly the lemon-scented cultivar 'Citriodora'. The dried leaves can also be sprinkled on cat food or used to stuff cat toys.

Catmint *(N. × faassenii)* is a sterile hybrid that grows from 1 to 2 feet tall and 3 to 4 feet wide. The soft, heart-shaped gray-green leaves have scalloped margins, and the small lavender-blue flowers are held along lax spikes in spring and summer. Of the numerous cultivars, 'Six Hills Giant' remains one of the most

popular. This robust selection has greener leaves and plants can reach 3 feet tall. 'Blue Wonder' stays within a foot tall and has long-lasting violet blue flowers.

Walker's Low catmint *(N. racemosa* 'Walker's Low') displays vivid deep-lavender-blue flowers from spring through fall. It is named after its original locale—a garden in Ireland—and is actually a taller selection, growing 2 to 3 feet high and spreading equally wide.

Oenothera
EVENING PRIMROSE
Evening Primrose Family (Onagraceae)

Plant Type: Deciduous to evergreen herbaceous perennials.
Climate Zones: Varies with species.
Light: Sun.
Soil: Adaptable, unless otherwise noted.
Water: Drought tolerant to moderate.
Origin: Western hemisphere.
Garden Uses: Meadow, rock, succulent, carpet and tapestry, green roof.

Growing evening primroses is a rewarding endeavor. Their big, bold, beautiful flowers are enticing and require little investment. Flower colors range from white to pink, yellow, or orange, and many species are quite fragrant. Despite their common name, some species bloom during the day, whereas others open in the late afternoon or evening and close by morning. The night bloomers are pollinated by hawk moths—you can spot them at twilight as they hover above the plants.

Fragrant evening primrose *(O. caespitosa)* typically opens its prized, sweetly scented white flowers in the evening. Come morning, the flowers have collapsed and faded to pink. Rosettes of lance-shaped, irregularly lobed, hairy gray leaves grow 1 to 2 feet wide and even-

tually develop a woody caudex. This sun-loving, evergreen, drought-tolerant species needs well-drained soil and is well worth trying. The similar and equally beautiful **California evening primrose** *(O. californica)* is

California evening primrose.
STEPHEN INGRAM

Mexican evening primrose.

a deciduous species that spreads via rhizomes to form mats at least 2 to 3 feet wide. Both species bloom in late spring to early summer. [all except c]

Ozark suncups *(O. missouriensis)* is a deciduous species native to the central and southern United States. It bears bright yellow 4-inch-wide flowers that stay open all day. From late spring into fall, a continual parade of flowers unfolds on the tips of each stem. Plants grow up to 6 inches tall and 2 to 3 feet wide and prefer sunny sites. [all]

Mexican evening primrose *(O. speciosa,* syn. *O. berlandieri)* has fragrant pink to white flowers that bloom during the day. The 1-foot-tall plants spread quickly by rhizomes, forming colonies that can become invasive if not controlled. The colony blooms from late spring or early summer into fall and dies back in winter, although plants in warm-winter areas retain some green at the base year-round. This native of Mexico and the southwestern United States is very drought tolerant. It makes an excellent groundcover in challenging sites and is also useful in curbing erosion on slopes. The cultivar 'Siskiyou' has soft pink flowers; 'Woodside' (syn. 'Woodside White') has clear white petals and a chartreuse center. [all]

Opuntia
PRICKLY-PEAR
Cactus Family (Cactaceae)

Plant Type: Evergreen succulent perennials and subshrubs.
Climate Zones: All except coastal.
Light: Sun to partial shade.
Soil: Well-drained.
Water: Drought tolerant.
Origin: North America to South America.
Garden Uses: Rock, succulent, carpet and tapestry.

When well sited in the garden, these handsome cacti can provide bold structure, brilliant flowers, and added

security. Due to their barbed spines, prickly-pears are sometimes used in mass plantings at the base of a fence or beneath a window to deter unwanted access. These plants have stems that resemble flattened paddlelike pads and range in color from green to gray to nearly purple. The leaves appear briefly in spring, measuring ¼ to ½ inch long; they look like tiny green to reddish brown succulent cones. The beautiful, exotic flowers attractively display numerous satiny petals, which can be magenta, yellow, orange, red, or white, depending on the species.

Beavertail cactus *(O. basilaris)* has gray-green pads that can be colorfully blushed with purple. Plants are often low growing, ranging from 8 to 24 inches tall; over time, they form small clumps up to 3 feet across. The flowers are typically magenta, though white-flowered forms are known. This species rarely produces long spines, but does have lots of glochids; these very small tufts of hairlike spines will readily—and painfully—penetrate skin when the plants are handled or brushed.

Mojave prickly-pear *(O. polyacantha* var. *erinacea)* hides its pads beneath a thick coating of long white, brown, or blackish spines. Although it may appear intimidating, this is actually one of the easier cacti to garden around since its spines are rather thin and flexible and not as barbed as most. The pads are usually 3 to 4

Above: Beavertail cactus.
Left: Santa Rita cactus.
STEPHEN INGRAM

inches long, and develop a more oblong shape when the plant gets some shade. Mature garden specimens may reach 18 inches tall and up to 5 feet across. Although its yellow flowers are lovely, this variety is primarily grown for its showy cover of spines.

Santa Rita cactus *(O. santa-rita)* possesses round pads with long spines. The pads are usually purplish and are especially vibrant during the winter months. Flowers are yellow with orange-tinged highlights. Plants may reach up to 4 feet tall and will spread up to 6 feet wide. 'Tubac'™ has especially colorful pads.

Origanum
OREGANO
Mint Family (Lamiaceae)

Plant Type: Evergreen to semi-evergreen herbaceous perennials and subshrubs.
Climate Zones: Varies with species.
Light: Sun, unless otherwise noted.
Soil: Well-drained.
Water: Drought tolerant to moderate.
Origin: Europe and Asia.
Garden Uses: Meadow, rock, succulent, carpet and tapestry, kitchen, green roof.

Kitchen gardeners grow oregano for its culinary value, but even if you never pinch a leaf to season a meal, the charming floral displays and attractive foliage of this aromatic genus will appeal to your visual aesthetic. Most oregano species grow in hot, dry rocky sites in the wild and spread slowly via rhizomes. The leaves vary from glaucous blue-green to gray-green to golden yellow. The flowers attract bees and butterflies and range in color from creamy white to pink or purple. They emerge from showy bracts that are typically flushed with pink or maroon. Some liken the inflorescences to pine cones or hops, and both fresh and dried sprigs add zest to floral arrangements. Shearing off the flowers promotes leafy growth. Prune plants to the ground at the end of the

Dittany of Crete.

Top: Wild marjoram. Bottom: Kent Beauty oregano.

growing season to retain a tidier appearance and to promote abundant blossoms next spring and summer.

Dittany of Crete *(O. dictamnus)* makes an excellent candidate for rock gardens or serves as a soft counterpoint to the bold texture of upright succulents. Felted, baby-soft round leaves clothe the arching foot-long stems of 8-inch-tall by 1½- to 2-foot-wide plants. The pinkish purple flowers bloom from summer to fall. Plants need excellent drainage, full sun, and dry conditions. [c, i, cv, ld]

O. laevigatum forms mats of slightly blue-green leaves and sends up 1- to 2-foot-tall inflorescences in late spring. Masses of small purplish pink flowers protrude from the slightly larger bracts and bloom for several months. Two popular cultivars whose leaves turn purple in cool weather are 'Hopley's' and 'Herrenhausen'. [all]

Sweet marjoram *(O. majorana)* is primarily grown as flavoring for a variety of foods. The downy gray-green leaves are used either fresh or dried. Plants grow 1 to 2 feet tall and wide, and tiny round buds precede the rather inconspicuous white flowers. [all except m]

Round-leaved oregano *(O. rotundifolium)* has smooth, blue-green leaves and pink flowers. 'Kent Beauty' is an exceptional, compact cultivar, reaching only 4 inches tall and spreading a foot or more in width. Each arching stem bears several nodding inflorescences of lime green bracts—deeply blushed with rose pink—that almost overshadow the pinkish purple flowers. [all]

Wild marjoram, or oregano *(O. vulgare)*, is the most widespread species, growing as far north as the British

Isles. Many of the wild forms are scentless; look for aromatic selections if seasoning is your motivation. The

leaves of this highly variable species are typically dark green, but cultivars with yellow foliage or white variegation are common. The yellow forms are best in part shade to avoid burning the leaves. Flower color ranges from white to pink. [all]

Yellow-leaved selection of wild marjoram.

Pelargonium
GERANIUM
Geranium Family (Geraniaceae)

Plant Type: Evergreen perennials.
Climate Zones: Coastal, inland, and Central Valley.
Light: Sun to partial shade.
Soil: Adaptable.
Water: Occasional to moderate.
Origin: Mainly southern Africa, but also eastern Mediterranean Basin to South Asia, Madagascar, Australia, New Zealand, and St. Helena and Tristan da Cunha islands.
Garden Uses: Carpet and tapestry.

These plants are commonly known as geraniums, and though they are in the geranium family, they are actually pelargoniums—a much more useful group of plants for water-thrifty mediterranean-climate gardens. When compared to true *Geranium* species and hybrids, *Pelargonium* species and hybrids tolerate higher soil pH, warmer days, and cooler nights, which makes them ideal for most California gardens. The majority have showy flowers that are produced in dense headlike clusters. For best performance, cut the plants back by ½ to ¾ between mid-November and mid-January. To control geranium budworm caterpillars *(Helicoverpa virescens),* dust the inflorescences with *Bacillus thuringiensis* ssp. *kurstaki* (DiPel®).

Angel geraniums (*Pelargonium* cultivars) are noteworthy for their drought tolerance and long flowering season. They typically have pansylike flowers and fragrant foliage. Plants vary considerably in size, though an average would be about 1 to 2 feet tall with a slightly wider spread. The following are some of the best cul-

tivars for California: 'Antares' is one of the larger angel geraniums and has orange-red flowers; 'Aurelia' blooms for almost 10 months of the year, has a dwarf growth habit and light pink flowers; 'Gary's Nebula' blooms nearly year-round, has a dwarf growth habit, and sports red-pink flowers; 'Veronica Contreras' blooms for about half of the year and displays distinctively attractive pale pink and magenta flowers.

Ivy-leaved geranium *(P. peltatum)* has shiny green leaves that are nearly succulent. The plants naturally have a sprawling, low-growing habit. They may cascade over the edges of low walls and pots, but they can also be trained to grow upward like a vine. This geranium is most suitable in cooler coastal gardens; both its foliage and flowers burn in intense sunlight and the plants generally do not tolerate reflected heat. In hotter areas these plants suffer from edema, resulting in unattractive corky patches on the leaves. The red-flowered cultivar 'Sevilana' handles the heat better than most.

Peppermint geranium *(P. tomentosum)* does indeed smell like peppermint when lightly rubbed, but that is just a small part of why this plant is such a popular garden subject. All of its vegetative parts are covered with soft white hairs, which makes the plant appear as if sheathed in velvet. Luxuriously tactile, the leaves and stems are delightful to touch. Peppermint geranium is an outstanding plant for use in dry partial shade, although it does not tolerate hard freezes. It has a

Above and left: Ivy-leaved geranium.

Top: Peppermint
geranium.
Bottom: Choco-
late geranium.

Oriental fountain grass (foreground). DAVID FROSS

prostrate growth habit, is usually less than 18 inches tall, and can spread up to 4 to 6 feet wide. For best results, cut the plant back every year or two; avoid cutting old woody growth, however, since it may not respond. Peppermint geranium produces small white flowers.

Chocolate geranium (*P. t.* 'Chocolate') is named for the large chocolate-colored blotch on the center of the leaf. This plant prefers partial shade to full shade wherever it is grown in California. It does not seem to be quite as wide spreading as the species (above).

Pennisetum orientale
ORIENTAL FOUNTAIN GRASS
Grass Family (Poaceae)

Plant Type: Deciduous, warm-season grass.
Climate Zones: All except low desert.
Light: Sun.
Soil: Adaptable.
Water: Occasional to moderate.
Origin: Asia.
Garden Uses: Meadow, rock, succulent, carpet and tapestry, green roof.

The sheer number of plumose flower stalks produced by oriental fountain grass is impressive. Factor in their beauty and longevity and this bunchgrass becomes even more desirable. The stalks carry creamy white to pale pink fluffy flowers and adorn the 2-foot-tall by 2½-foot-wide mounds of green or gray-green foliage from summer through fall. The entire plant turns straw-colored in winter. Use this carefree grass liberally in drifts or as an accent, and cut plants back to the ground at the onset of new growth. Unlike some

members of its genus, oriental fountain grass has no record of being invasive in California.

Phyla nodiflora (syn. *Lippia repens*)
LIPPIA
Verbena Family (Verbenaceae)

Plant Type: Evergreen perennial.
Climate Zones: All except mountains.
Light: Sun to partial shade.
Soil: Adaptable.
Water: Occasional to regular.
Origin: California to the eastern U.S. south to South America.
Garden Uses: Meadow, rock, carpet and tapestry, green roof.

Lippia is native to California, although most of the forms seen in the state's gardens likely originate from South America. It is often found in older landscapes and gardens and makes an excellent low-growing evergreen groundcover that will even take foot traffic. From spring to fall, this plant produces an abundance of tiny mauve-pink flowers. These blossoms are held in cloverlike heads and are especially attractive to bees. Lippia tolerates regular mowing, although this will diminish flower

Lippia.

production. It loves warm weather and can look a bit sparse during the winter months but quickly fills in and greens up in the spring, especially if given a dash of fertilizer.

Portulacaria afra
ELEPHANT'S FOOD
Stonecrop Family (Crassulaceae)

Plant Type: Succulent shrub.
Climate Zones: Coastal, inland, and Central Valley.
Light: Sun to partial shade.
Soil: Well-drained.
Water: Drought tolerant to occasional.
Origin: South Africa.
Garden Uses: Rock, succulent.

If you plant it, will they come? Not likely, unless you live in Africa, where *Portulacaria* is indeed a staple food for African elephants. Easily mistaken for, and even sold as a smaller-leaved version of jade plant, this succulent has ½-inch-wide round leaves with a somewhat glossy surface. Combined with the reddish limber branches, the overall effect is less stiff than jade plant.

A variegated from of elephant's food. STEPHEN INGRAM

Elephant's food grows at a moderate rate, but it can eventually become 12 feet tall and wide. Use it as an informal screen or clipped hedge. In California's climate zones, this plant's tiny pink flowers are rarely seen. 'Variegata', also known as Rainbow bush, is a cultivar with yellow-green leaves and a mounded habit. It grows to roughly 3 feet tall and is effective as a groundcover or cascading over walls or boulders. 'Prostrate' is a lower-growing selection that doesn't exceed 1 foot tall. Its trailing stems are covered with bright green rounded leaves that are typical of the species.

Ribes viburnifolium
CATALINA PERFUME, EVERGREEN CURRANT
Gooseberry Family (Grossulariaceae)

Plant Type: Evergreen shrub.
Climate Zones: Coastal, inland, and Central Valley.
Light: Partial shade to shade.
Soil: Adaptable.
Water: Drought tolerant to moderate.
Origin: Santa Catalina Island and northwestern Baja California.
Garden Uses: Carpet and tapestry, kitchen, green roof.

Catalina perfume is an excellent groundcover for dry shade. This unassuming, sprawling shrub has arching branches that bend earthward and may root at their tips upon contact with moist soil. Plants typically grow 3 feet tall or up to 5 feet with support. The irregularly toothed, glossy deep green leaves are evergreen, an anomaly among currants and gooseberries. They are also deliciously aromatic, with a spicy scent when crushed. The equally fragrant maroon twigs hold their color year-round, and the tiny, star-shaped maroon flowers are quite showy when borne in profusion. Although rarely abundant, the translucent edible orange berries are attractive and provide food for wildlife. Virtually carefree, Catalina perfume benefits from periodic light pruning to retain a dense habit. Rejuvenate older straggly colonies by coppicing, although results are unpredictable.

Catalina perfume.

Rosmarinus officinalis
ROSEMARY
Mint Family (Lamiaceae)

Plant Type: Evergreen shrubs.
Climate Zones: All except mountains.
Light: Sun.
Soil: Adaptable, well-drained preferred.
Water: Drought tolerant to moderate.
Origin: Mediterranean Basin.
Garden Uses: Rock, carpet and tapestry, kitchen, green roof.

Above: Lockwood de Forest rosemary. Left: Renzels rosemary.
DAVID FROSS

The aromatic oils in rosemary leaves and flowers have a long history of medicinal and culinary uses. Its Latin name, *Rosmarinus,* means "dew of the sea" and evokes this plant's native habitat—bluffs and hills near the Mediterranean Sea. Rosemary is an adaptable, durable, and drought-tolerant species with resinous, dark green 1-inch-long leaves and blue to white flowers. Its form can be quite variable, ranging from a prostrate groundcover to a 6-foot-tall shrub. Pruning will help direct growth, but avoid cutting into aged wood as it may not resprout. The following cultivars prefer well-drained soils and can become rank and woody with excess water and fertilizer.

Boule rosemary (*R. o.* 'Boule') changes shape as it grows. A young plant has an undulating character, but it develops into a mounding "boule" (ball) shape at maturity. This delightful selection reaches 3 feet tall and has medium blue flowers.

Collingwood Ingram rosemary (*R. o.* 'Collingwood Ingram') has gracefully arching stems and grows up to 2½ feet high and 6 feet wide. Its bright blue flowers have violet veining. Other selections are a better choice for culinary use since 'Collingwood Ingram' has a distinct piney flavor.

Golden Rain rosemary (*R. o.* 'Golden Rain') offers variegated leaves edged in gold; leaf color is more pronounced in cool weather and in coastal climate zones. It features an upright habit to 4 feet tall and displays violet-blue flowers. There are a number of selections available with variegated foliage similar to 'Golden Rain'.

Ken Taylor rosemary (*R. o.* 'Ken Taylor') displays a profusion of lavender-blue flowers in early spring and is considered one of the showiest rosemary cultivars. It has trailing stems and develops a mounding form that reaches 1 to 2 feet tall and 5 feet wide. A bit tender, this selection is best used in areas where winter temperatures are milder.

Prostratus rosemary (*R. o.* 'Prostratus') is a garden classic. Its low, creeping form makes it ideal for use as a groundcover or for a planting where it will cascade over a wall. About 2 feet tall and 8 feet wide, prostrate rosemary's foliage is lighter green than many other selections and the flowers are pale blue. Lockwood de Forest rosemary (*R. o.* 'Lockwood de Forest', syn. 'Santa Barbara', 'Lockwoodii', 'Forestii') is similar to 'Prostratus' but with richer green leaves and darker blue flowers.

Renzels rosemary (*R. o.* 'Renzels', syn. 'Irene') forms a tight mound to 2 feet tall and 5 feet wide and is one of the best low-growing selections available. Vigorous and garden tolerant, it produces deep lavender-blue flowers.

Ruscus
BUTCHER'S BROOM
Butcher's Broom Family (Ruscaceae)

Plant Type: Evergreen shrubs.
Climate Zones: All.
Light: Partial shade to shade.
Soil: Adaptable.
Water: Infrequent to moderate.
Origin: England through the Mediterranean to Iran.
Garden Uses: Rock, carpet and tapestry, green roof.

Butcher's brooms are good looking, sturdy, dependable, durable, and long-lived. They are ideal candidates for use in the difficult garden conditions typically found under trees: dry shade with root competition. So, why don't we see these plants everywhere? More often than not, it is because they are slow growing and therefore command a higher price than more common and easily propagated groundcovers. These plants spread underground by rhizomes and have cladodes, which are flattened stems that resemble, and take the place of, leaves. Small greenish flowers appear at the center of the cladode and are followed by showy, long-lasting, bright red (rarely yellow) berries. Most plants are dioecious, so both a male and a female plant must be present in order for the female plants to produce berries; however, there are monoecious clones that will always produce fruits.

Butcher's brooms are capable of thriving in deep shade, but they will not survive in wet or boggy soils. The stems are long lasting in flower arrangements. Cut dead or unsightly old stems individually to the ground as necessary. Plants generally do not respond well to coppicing.

Common butcher's broom *(R. aculeatus)* can grow from 2 to 4 feet in height. It has erect, branched dark green stems and small spine-tipped cladodes, which make it an effective barrier plant.

Poet's laurel *(R. hypoglossus)* has unbranched green to yellow-green arching stems and cladodes that measure up to 4 inches long and 1½ inches wide. It typically spreads much faster than common butcher's broom and reaches heights of 1½ to 2 feet. This unarmed (spineless) species is one of several different plants that is cited as the "laurel" of Caesar and the Romans.

Poet's laurel.

Salvia
SAGE
Mint Family (Lamiaceae)

Plant Type: Semi-evergreen to evergreen perennials, subshrubs, shrubs.
Climate Zones: Varies with species.
Light: Sun to partial shade.
Soil: Adaptable.
Water: Drought tolerant to occasional.
Origin: Worldwide except for Australia and Antarctica.
Garden Uses: Meadow, rock, carpet and tapestry, kitchen (some species).

Salvia, which means "to save," is an appropriate name for a genus associated with medicinal uses. We also celebrate the sages for their horticultural attributes. Beautiful flowers, fragrant foliage, and a diverse array of pollinators—hummingbirds, bees, and butterflies—are among the hallmarks of this large genus. Today, with nearly 1,000 species and hundreds of named varieties, there are myriad ways to "save" your garden with sages. The following plants are among the better choices for drought-tolerant gardens. This selection includes black, purple, and hummingbird sages, which are also used for culinary purposes.

Bee's Bliss sage (S. 'Bee's Bliss') is simply one of the very best low-growing native California sages for our gardens. Bee's Bliss grows from about 6 inches to 2 feet tall, and spreads from 4 to 8 feet wide. The foliage appears gray-green while in active growth and turns grayer in the summer months. This groundcover sage has thick clusters of large lavender-blue flowers, but unlike other native sages with large flowers, the flower stems of Bee's Bliss wither and disappear into the foliage of the plant—they do not need to be pruned. Mildew can sometimes affect the foliage during the winter months (or when grown in nursery containers), but quickly disappears with the advent of warm, dry weather. [c, i, cv]

Germander sage (S. chamaedryoides) offers the visually arresting combination of silver-gray foliage and spikes of small cobalt blue flowers. This easy, fast-growing sage may reach from 1 to 2 feet in height and forms clumps at least 2 to 3 feet across. Clumps spread slowly from underground rhizomes, but the plant is rarely, if ever, considered aggressive. Rejuvenate germander sage, if it opens up and begins to lose vigor, by cutting the plant back hard (to 1 or 2 inches) before new growth begins in late winter or early spring. [c, i, cv]

Autumn sage (S. greggii) has a dense shrubby growth habit, grows quickly, and is especially floriferous. As its common name implies, this plant blooms during fall, although in many gardens it also blooms heavily in spring; a few blossoms even sporadically appear in hot summer months. The flowers are typically a vibrant red,

Above: Bee's Bliss sage (foreground). Left: Germander sage.

Above: Mexican sage. Left: Autumn sage.

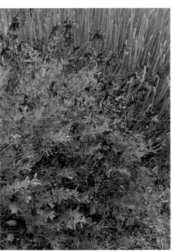

although numerous selections and some hybrids feature other colors, including white, pale yellow, peach, orange, mauve, pink, and rose. To keep your plants from becoming too woody, cut them back fairly hard on an annual basis when the new growth appears in late winter or early spring. Unpruned plants quickly decline in vigor and garden value and are best replaced. Selections of this plant are highly variable, but well-maintained plants can be expected to reach 2 to 4 feet in height and width. In desert gardens, this plant performs best in partial shade. 'Furman's Red' proves to be successful in many locales and has deep red flowers. [all except m]

Mexican sage *(S. leucantha)* is commonly seen in gardens and is justly popular. This colorful species is easy to grow and care for and offers blooms from late spring through fall, or even year-round in many coastal areas. The plant forms erect clumps that reach from 3 to 6 feet tall and spread equally wide. The distinctive fuzzy purple calyces of Mexican sage flowers give the inflorescence a soft appearance. Typical flowers are white, but 'Midnight' and some other cultivars have purple flowers. 'Eder' has variegated leaves, and 'Santa Barbara' is a more compact, less vigorous form. In winter, cut back all stems to the ground, and new growth will quickly emerge to replace them. Plants prefer moderate water for best performance. [c, i, cv, ld]

Point Sal Spreader sage *(S. leucophylla* 'Point Sal Spreader') is the best of the many selections of purple sage for use as a low-growing groundcover. The leaves of this cultivar are especially gray-white and amply cover the plant's stems, since they have short internodes. Rosy pink flowers are produced in dense whorl-like clusters in

spring. To produce a more compact plant, prune it lightly any time after flowering until November. A single specimen may attain heights of 2 to 3 feet (more if it is crowded) and will grow from 6 to 8 feet wide. It will spread even more if the plant's stems take root where they touch the soil; this occurs in many, but not all, gardens. [c, i, cv]

Terra Seca black sage *(S. mellifera* 'Terra Seca') was selected for its low growth habit. This durable and long-lived cultivar makes an excellent cover on dry slopes, where it will easily spread from 6 to 10 or more feet wide. The plants closely hug the ground, and over time they typically mound up in the middle to about 2 feet high. Shiny green foliage is produced during the winter months, although this may be year-round on specimens grown in partial shade or near the coast. [c, i, cv]

Red canyon sage *(S. microphylla)* occurs naturally across a wide area of the Chihuahua Desert. This plant can exhibit a broad range of growth forms, foliage, and flower colors. In general, its appearance is similar to autumn sage, and a number of hybrids exist between these two species. However, red canyon sage is usually

Hummingbird sage.

Above: Lavender cotton.
Left: Green santolina.

longer-lived and less prone to winter damage than autumn sage. Give this sage a hard pruning during late winter or early spring, before new growth appears, by cutting it back to less than 1 foot tall. 'Hot Lips' features variable red and white flowers; this selection grows up to 4 feet tall and spreads to 6 feet wide. [all except m]

Hummingbird sage *(S. spathacea)* truly deserves its common name: the whirring wings of hummingbirds are often seen, and heard, as these diminutive birds seek nectar from this sage's deep blossoms. A stunning and useful plant, it delights the senses with large showy red flowers, pungent fruity fragrance, and coarse-textured, lightly sticky green leaves. This is the only California native sage that spreads via underground stems to make large colonies. To rejuvenate an older planting, or to create a cleaner look, cut back your plants with a string-line trimmer in the fall before new growth begins. This species typically does best in partial shade, but it can tolerate full sun. [c, i, cv]

Santolina
SANTOLINA
Sunflower Family (Asteraceae)

Plant Type: Evergreen shrubs.
Climate Zones: Varies with species.
Light: Sun.
Soil: Well-drained.
Water: Drought tolerant to moderate.
Origin: Mediterranean Basin.
Garden Uses: Rock, succulent, carpet and tapestry, green roof.

Often partnered with lavender and rosemary, santolinas complement a wide array of water-thrifty plants. When grown with little to no supplemental water, they can be incredibly long-lived, developing picturesque gnarled trunks over time. These fine-textured mounding shrubs are effective as solitary specimens; they can also be used as edging along paths or as large-scale ground-covers. The aromatic, simple or pinnately compound leaves vary from rich green to whitish gray, and the buttonlike spring flower heads are cream to pale or deep yellow. Plants tolerate heavy shearing, a fact that has made them popular subjects for formal herb gardens. Prune them back to the ground when they become leggy or sparse. Otherwise, these versatile shrubs are carefree.

The nomenclature of santolinas is difficult at best. The most widely grown species and cultivars are described below.

Lavender cotton *(S. chamaecyparissus)* has deeply divided woolly white leaves with tiny leaflets and bright yellow flowers. Plants form 2-foot-tall undulating mounds that can sprawl several feet across. [all]

Lemon Queen santolina *(S. 'Lemon Queen')* and Little Nicky santolina *(S. 'Little Nicky')* are two cultivars whose parentage is unclear. 'Lemon Queen' has creamy yellow flowers atop gray-green foliage. 'Little Nicky' is a dwarf selection with bright green foliage that grows 6 to 8 inches tall by 8 to 12 inches wide. [all]

Green santolina *(S. rosmarinifolia)* still sells occasionally under its old name *S. virens,* and both species names aptly describe the plant's rosemarylike, bright green foliage. Green santolina forms a billowy 2-foot-tall by 3-foot-wide mound. It is particularly eye-catching just before it flowers when it displays literally hundreds of wiry upright stems, each punctuated by tight flower buds. [c, i, cv, m]

Sedum
Stonecrop
Stonecrop Family (Crassulaceae)

Plant Type: Evergreen or deciduous succulent perennials.
Climate Zones: Varies by species.
Light: Sun to shade.
Soil: Well-drained.
Water: Drought tolerant to moderate.
Origin: Global.
Garden Uses: Rock, succulent, carpet and tapestry, green roof.

Angelina stonecrop.

Many of the 600 species of stonecrops are carpet-forming groundcovers—a fact that has not gone unnoticed by horticulturists in search of alternatives to the lawn. Stonecrops originate from a broad range of habitats, although many species naturally occur in well-drained sites where they face little vegetative competition. Their foliage color is highly variable, ranging from silver blue to forest green, and the fleshy leaves come in an array of shapes, from oval to lanceolate. White, pink, or yellow flowers are produced in small clusters. Infestations of aphids, followed by ants, can become problematic and may require treatment.

Common stonecrop *(S. acre)* is a creeping species 2 to 4 inches tall with bright green leaves and golden summer flowers. Hardy, durable, drought tolerant, and assertive, this plant can become weedy in some situations. Common stonecrop is frequently used on green roofs in Europe and the eastern United States. The selection 'Aureum' has gold tips on the new leaves. [all except ld]

Coppertone stonecrop, *(S. adolphii,* syn. *S. nussbaumerianum)* is a low-growing subshrub that reaches 1 foot tall and 2 feet wide. Its 1-inch-long yellow-green

leaves have a copper–red blush and are held along thick decumbent stems. In spring, flat-topped clusters of white flowers appear above the foliage. This succulent prefers partial shade in interior sites. [c, i]

White stonecrop *(S. album)* has dark green leaves that blush red in winter. Vigorous and assertive, it spreads

White stonecrop.

quickly from rooting fragments and can become a nuisance. White and sometimes pink flowers form in summer just above the 6-inch-high foliage. 'Coral Carpet' has a lower, denser habit, and its new growth turns coral red when stressed by drought or cold. 'Chloroticum' has pale yellow-green leaves and a compact habit. [all except ld]

Corsican stonecrop *(S. dasyphyllum)* forms tight mats up to 4 inches tall and 12 inches wide. In summer, white flowers tinged with pink cover the downy gray foliage. [all except ld]

Palmer's sedum *(S. palmeri)* comes from Mexico's Sierra Madre Oriental and is a good choice for hotter interior sites. Low-growing rosettes of waxy blue-green leaves form an attractive compact mound to 12 inches tall and 24 inches wide. Prolific yellow flowers cover the foliage in early spring. Use this versatile, drought-tolerant species in both sun and partial shade. [all except ld]

Christmas cheer (*Sedum × rubrotinctum*) does not bloom in December, but it does take its common name from colors that are associated with this holiday. The pulpy, jellybean-like leaves are green, with red and yellow tips, and these colors can be especially vivid in dry, sunny locations. The plant has rambling stems and reaches 6 to 8 inches high and up to 1 foot wide. Yellow summer flowers are borne on short stocks just above the foliage. 'Compacta' is a dwarf form that grows to 4 inches tall and wide. [c, i, cv]

Angelina stonecrop (*S. rupestre* 'Angelina') presents a bold presence in the garden with its narrow golden yellow leaves. The foliage is paramount, as it seldom blooms. This stonecrop has a low, trailing habit and reaches 3 to 6 inches high. In hotter interior climate zones, plants should receive partial shade to prevent burning. [all except ld]

Pacific stonecrop *(S. spathulifolium)* may appeal to native plant enthusiasts, since this species is found along the West Coast from California to British Columbia. Its tight rosettes of small silver-gray to purple leaves are held on short creeping stems. The plant can form thick mats 4 inches tall and 12 inches wide that are topped

Above: Christmas cheer.
Left: Pacific stonecrop.
DAVID FROSS

Sempervivum
HOUSELEEK, HEN-AND-CHICKENS
Stonecrop Family (Crassulaceae)

Plant Type: Succulent.
Climate Zones: All except low desert.
Light: Sun to partial shade.
Soil: Well-drained.
Water: Occasional to moderate.
Origin: Europe, Morocco, and western Asia.
Garden Uses: Rock, succulent, carpet and tapestry, green roof.

The scientific name for houseleeks literally means "live forever," so it is no surprise that these undemanding plants have been cultivated for hundreds of years. In the 8th century, Emperor Charlemagne mandated their planting on all rooftops for fire prevention. Down at ground level, houseleeks are popular rock garden plants. They also make fine small-scale groundcovers and are perfect for containers or crevices between pavers or rock walls. Houseleeks tolerate freezing temperatures and fare particularly well in colder regions. In desert areas, they need protection from the hot sun, and in all warm climates, flower production is not as reliable. When in bloom, the pretty flowers add a dash of color above the low-growing, tightly clustered rosettes. Houseleeks readily propagate from offsets, which explains their other common name, hen-and-chickens. Once a rosette flowers, it dies, leaving a hole that is eventually filled by nearby "chicks." Of the approximately 40 species of houseleek, those listed below are the most widely grown in California.

Cobweb houseleeks *(S. arachnoideum)* is named for the gossamer hairs that stretch from one leaf tip to the next, creating an intricate web across the surface of the rosette. Its leaves are actually light to medium green,

but on plants grown in full sun, the webbing makes each rosette appear white. The young offsets reach across the colony, in search of an opening in which to take root. Mature rosettes are rounded in outline and

Cobweb houseleeks and Cape Blanco Pacific stonecrop (lower left).

by yellow flowers. Plants do best in well-drained soils and prefer partial shade away from the coast. 'Cape Blanco' has a compact habit and chalky-gray foliage, while 'Purpureum' has foliage flushed with varying shades of purple. [c, i, cv, m]

Two-row stonecrop *(S. spurium)* is a colorful, trailing species to 4 inches tall. Its elliptical 1-inch-long leaves vary from green to burgundy; some even appear bicolored, with bronze-tipped margins. In summer, it produces dense clusters of red to white flowers that are held 3 to 5 inches above the foliage. 'Dragon's Blood' has dark red flowers and purple foliage. 'Tricolor' features green, cream, and pink leaves with pink flowers. In colder climate zones, this species is semi-deciduous during winter. [all except ld]

Sedum stefco features small green leaves that can turn vivid red during winter in colder areas. This dense low-growing stonecrop reaches 2 to 4 inches tall and is topped by white flowers in summer. It is both durable and drought tolerant. [all except ld]

Hen-and-chickens. SAXON HOLT

Above: Blue chalksticks.
DAVID FROSS
Left: Narrow-leaf chalksticks.

1½ to 2½ inches wide, depending upon exposure to the sun. The star-shaped flowers are dusky red and are held on 4- to 6-inch-long stalks.

Montane houseleeks *(S. montanum)* looks like cobweb houseleek, minus the cobwebs, and has similar flowers as well. Each 2- to 3-inch-wide rosette resembles a succulent green rose.

Hen-and-chickens *(S. tectorum)* has rosettes reminiscent of plump water lilies. They vary in size from 2 to 5 inches wide and are composed of oval leaves with deep red or purple tips. The purple-red 1-inch-wide flowers are borne on densely hairy stalks that measure 1 to 2 feet tall. Many cultivars have been selected over the years, varying in size and leaf coloration.

Senecio
CHALKSTICKS
Sunflower Family (Asteraceae)

Plant Type: Evergreen succulent perennials.
Climate Zones: Varies with species.
Light: Sun to partial shade.
Soil: Well-drained.
Water: Drought tolerant to occasional.
Origin: Worldwide except for Antarctica.
Garden Uses: Rock, succulent, carpet and tapestry, green roof.

These plants are all about foliage. The color and form of their succulent leaves is unlike anything else, and a mass planting of chalksticks leaves a lasting impression. Their white flowers, however, are nondescript and borne on short branched inflorescences. The following three species are at their best in coastal gardens, where excessive heat and freezing temperatures are both uncommon.

Narrow-leaf chalksticks *(S. cylindricus)* develops an erect growth habit and may reach from 1 to 3 feet tall and spread equally wide. The pale green succulent leaves are long and narrow, measuring about ¹/₈ inch thick and up to 4 inches long. Older plants will have thick succulent stems that exceed 1 inch in diameter. This plant is often sold as S. vitalis. [c, i]

Blue chalksticks *(S. mandraliscae)* may reach from 1 to 2 feet tall and will spread to 2 feet or more wide. The fingerlike succulent blue leaves are from 3 to 4 inches long. [c, i, ld]

Little blue chalksticks *(S. serpens)* is smaller in all respects than blue chalksticks. Plants may reach about 1 foot tall and are equally wide. The succulent leaves are slightly longer than 1 inch in length. This species is less tolerant of extreme heat. [c, i]

Sesleria
MOOR GRASS
Grass Family (Poaceae)

Plant Type: Evergreen, cool-season grasses.
Climate Zones: Varies with species.
Light: Sun to shade.
Soil: Adaptable.
Water: Varies with species.
Origin: Europe, western Asia, northern Africa.
Garden Uses: Greensward, meadow, rock, succulent, carpet and tapestry, green roof.

Moor grasses are noteworthy for their durable character, longevity, adaptability, and densely tufted form. They are outstanding as groundcovers, for edging, or tucked

Above: Autumn moor grass.
Left: Blue moor grass.

an excellent choice for meadow gardens and tolerates light shade, moist or dry conditions, and root competition from established trees. The common name refers to its autumn flowering season; however, plants in mild climate areas may bloom in spring and summer. [all]

Blue moor grass *(S. caerulea)* grows slowly to 1 foot tall and 1 to 2 feet wide. The handsome two-tone foliage is dark green on the upper surface and blue-glaucous below. This species does best with moderate to regular water, becoming more drought tolerant with age. In coastal gardens, it performs well in sun or shade; farther inland, it needs protection from the hot afternoon sun. Plants tolerate light foot traffic. [all except m]

Greenlee's Hybrid moor grass *(S.* 'Greenlee's Hybrid'*)* is a vigorous hybrid of unknown parentage. The foliage is similar to blue moor grass and the flowers are more closely aligned to those of autumn moor grass. Plants thrive with occasional irrigation and grow 1 foot tall and 2 or more feet wide. [all]

Solidago
GOLDENROD
Sunflower Family (Asteraceae)

Plant Type: Semi-evergreen herbaceous perennials.
Climate Zones: Varies with species.
Light: Sun to partial shade.
Soil: Adaptable.
Water: Drought tolerant to moderate.
Origin: Primarily North America; a few species in Europe, Asia, and South America.
Garden Uses: Meadow, carpet and tapestry, green roof.

The Golden State has a number of native goldenrods, yet few gardeners cultivate these undemanding and attractive perennials. Perhaps the mistaken belief that they contribute to hay fever or concern about their

Canada goldenrod.

into nooks and crannies. They send up narrow 2- to 3-inch-long inflorescences that are especially attractive when coated with creamy white stamens. Moor grasses require minimal maintenance. Prune them to ground level, as needed, to remove accumulated dead leaves.

Autumn moor grass *(S. autumnalis)* forms green to yellow-green clumps 1 to 1½ feet tall and wide. It is

rather aggressive nature keeps them from becoming more popular. They are well suited to large-scale plantings where their rhizomes can freely wander, especially in naturalistic meadows. Their bright yellow flower clusters add welcome color in summer and fall and attract a wide array of beneficial insects. Annually prune or mow goldenrods after flowering to remove the spent stalks and withering leaves.

California goldenrod *(S. californica)* has softly pubescent, slightly gray-green leaves and sends up 1- to 4-foot-tall flower stalks. The inflorescence may be slender and wandlike or more irregular. This widespread species tolerates a broad range of conditions; site it in full sun for optimal flowering and keep irrigation to a minimum to curb its spread. [all]

Canada goldenrod *(S. canadensis* ssp. *elongata)* has less hairy, more coarsely toothed foliage and a greener appearance than California goldenrod, but its inflorescence is equally variable in shape. Plants look best with occasional summer irrigation along the coast and moderate watering in inland regions. Even with supplemental water, the leaves may turn brown before plants begin to bloom; keep this in mind when placing them in the garden. [c, m]

Sphaeralcea
GLOBE MALLOW
Mallow Family (Malvaceae)

Plant Type: Evergreen to semi-evergreen perennials.
Climate Zones: Varies with species.
Light: Sun.
Soil: Well-drained.
Water: Drought tolerant to occasional.
Origin: Southwestern United States to South America, and South Africa.
Garden Uses: Meadow, rock, succulent, carpet and tapestry.

Globe mallows are prized for their numerous arching wandlike inflorescences, each carrying dozens of brightly colored flowers that resemble miniature hollyhocks. In warm, dry gardens these plants typically produce very little foliage, and the plants fade into the background when not in flower. Their foliage and stems are densely covered with stellate (starlike) hairs that make the plants appear whitish, gray, tawny, or golden. The leaves are generally fan shaped with three lobes. These are very low-maintenance plants; all that is required is to remove the spent inflorescences. The plants listed here may grow from 2 to 5 feet tall and spread from 3 to 6 feet wide when they are in full bloom. Plants flower in spring and early summer, but their bloom period can be easily extended by judicious use of supplemental water.

Above: Apricot mallow.
Left: Louis Hamilton mallow.
CAROL BORNSTEIN

Apricot mallow *(S. ambigua)* typically has bright orange flowers, but their color can vary from rich grenadine ('Louis Hamilton') to pale washed-out orange and even pink ('Papago Pink'). [all]

Pink mallow *(S. ambigua* var. *rosacea)* is only found naturally in the Santa Rosa Mountains south of Palm Springs. The flowers of this variety vary from 1 to 2 inches across and can be any shade of pink. Plants perform best in warm to hot gardens that do not experience hard freezes. [c, i, ld, hd]

Trailing mallow *(S. philippiana)* produces colorful, rosy red inch-wide flowers from spring to summer. This durable, fast-growing South American plant may reach from 1 to 2 feet tall and spread to 5 feet or more. The stems and deeply lobed leaves appear to be gray-green due to the presence of many white hairs. This plant is sometimes incorrectly sold as *S. munroana*. [c, i, cv, ld]

Sporobolus
DROPSEED
Grass Family (Poaceae)

Plant Type: Deciduous to semi-evergreen, warm-season grasses.
Climate Zones: All.
Light: Sun.
Soil: Adaptable.
Water: Drought tolerant to moderate.
Origin: North and South America, Europe, Asia, and Africa.
Garden Uses: Meadow, rock, succulent, carpet and tapestry, green roof.

When in flower, dropseeds are easily among the most beautiful bunchgrasses. Their seemingly delicate inflorescences bring graceful movement to the garden for months on end. They share a tough character and adapt well to varied soils and watering regimes. Use these handsome plants liberally in meadow gardens or tapestries, along narrow beds, or in combination with bold-textured succulents.

Alkali sacaton *(S. airoides)* was a major component of native grasslands in California's Central Valley. Although tolerant of alkaline soils, it adapts well to most soil conditions and occurs in the central and western parts of the United States and Mexico. It forms densely tufted mounds 1 to 3 feet tall and slightly wider. The gray-green foliage turns light tan in winter and can be cut back at that time, although clumps don't need annual pruning. The airy panicles are pinkish purple when they open in midsummer but eventually fade to a straw color. Alkali sacaton does best with minimal irrigation in coastal gardens and moderate water inland.

Prairie dropseed *(S. heterolepis)* has threadlike green foliage that forms fine-textured 1½-foot-tall mounds. With cold weather, it turns warm shades of orange and copper. The plumose flowers, held on slender stalks, are surprisingly fragrant, variously described as sweet

Giant sacaton.

to pungent. A slow-growing species, it is long-lived and rarely needs cutting back. Plants initially grow best with some moisture before becoming drought tolerant with age. This native of Canada and the central and northeastern United States appears on endangered and threatened species lists in several states.

Giant sacaton *(S. wrightii,* syn. *S. airiodes* var. *wrightii)* can be found in the southwestern United States and Mexico. It reaches 4 to 5 feet tall in flower and has gray-green foliage that is evergreen in coastal areas. The tan flower spikes resemble narrow bottlebrushes.

Stipa gigantea
GIANT FEATHER GRASS
Grass Family (Poaceae)

Plant Type: Cool-season perennial grass.
Climate Zones: Coastal, inland, and Central Valley.
Light: Sun to partial shade.
Soil: Adaptable, but well-drained preferred.
Water: Infrequent to moderate.
Origin: Southwestern Europe and northern Africa.
Garden Uses: Meadow, rock, succulent, green roof.

Dramatic and stately, giant feather grass is an exceptional choice for California gardens. It forms an open

Alkali sacaton. CAROL BORNSTEIN

Giant feather grass.

Top: Wall germander. Bottom: Cat thyme.

to dense mound of fine-textured basal foliage to 2 feet tall. From spring to early summer, rigid flowering stems ascend 4 to 8 feet above the foliage and hold a panicle of flowers that remains showy well after the long-awned seeds have dropped. Remove the flower stems in late season to enjoy the elegant form of the foliage throughout winter. This grass exhibits some dormancy in colder areas but is otherwise evergreen in most of California's climate zones.

Teucrium
GERMANDER
Mint Family (Lamiaceae)

Plant Type: Shrubs, subshrubs, and herbaceous perennials.
Climate Zones: Varies with species.
Light: Sun.
Soil: Well-drained.
Water: Drought tolerant to moderate.
Origin: Europe, Asia, North and South America.
Garden Uses: Meadow, rock, succulent, carpet and tapestry, green roof.

This large genus of 300-plus species includes many fine ornamentals, ranging in stature from herbs to di-

minutive or medium-sized shrubs. Most occur naturally in lean, rocky soils in relatively dry habitats. Too diverse to categorize other than by origin, the following selections all hale from the Mediterranean region.

Wall germander *(T. chamaedrys)* attracts numerous bees with its terminal spikes of small, summer-blooming magenta-pink flowers. This low-growing subshrub reaches 1 to 2 feet tall and 2 to 3 feet wide. Dark green shiny toothed leaves line the slender stems. Use this

Fruity germander.

versatile plant for edging, in small-scale groundcovers, or as a low, clipped hedge. Shear it periodically to retain a dense habit. 'Nana', 'Prostratum', and 'Compactum' are dwarf selections that grow roughly 4 to 6 inches high and spread up to 3 feet wide. [all]

Bush germander (*T. fruticans*) has a decidedly silvered appearance due to the white color of its stems and lower leaf surfaces. This handsome 4- to 8-foot-tall shrub produces showy blue-purple flowers primarily in summer, with sporadic blossoms year-round. Typically rather lanky in habit, it benefits from periodic pruning to promote better form. The cultivars 'Azureum' and 'Compactum' both have deeper blue flowers; the former grows 4 to 5 feet tall, the latter tops out at 3 feet. All are effective as topiary or informal or clipped hedges. [all]

Fruity germander (*T. majoricum*, syn. *T. cossonii* 'Majoricum') forms low mounds 4 to 8 inches tall and 2 to 3 or more feet wide. During spring and summer, or year-round in some regions, small heads of rosy purple honey-scented flowers cover the narrow silvery gray leaves. This species is an excellent choice for rock gardens, groundcovers, and dry borders, but do be careful about placement because it is a magnet for bees. [c, i, cv]

Cat thyme (*T. marum*) will definitely need protection from cats, who can love it to death. This silvery white subshrub grows 1½ feet tall and wide and bears magenta-pink to purple flowers at the tips of its upright stems. The excellent drainage of a gravel garden would suit it perfectly. [c, i, cv, m]

Thymus
THYME
Mint Family (Lamiaceae)

Plant Type: Evergreen subshrubs or herbaceous perennials.
Climate Zones: All except low desert.
Light: Sun to partial shade.
Soil: Adaptable, well-drained preferred.
Water: Infrequent to moderate.
Origin: Southern Europe to Asia.
Garden Uses: Meadow, rock, carpet and tapestry, kitchen, green roof.

Cultivated for centuries as kitchen herbs, the thymes belong to a large genus that includes a number of species of value to horticulture. These plants have small aromatic leaves—the source of their culinary appeal—and whorled clusters of diminutive pink to mauve or white flowers. In late spring and summer, their blossoms attract a continuous stream of bees. Prostrate forms work well as small-scale groundcovers, and most species are useful in kitchen gardens and gravel and rock gardens. Thymes are best in full sun and well-drained soils. An annual shearing of taller species will maintain them in a more compact form.

Lemon thyme (*T. × citriodorus*) has lemon-scented oval leaves and pale lavender flowers. The foliage, both dried and fresh, adds wonderful flavor to a variety of dishes. Growing to 12 inches high, this hybrid is suitable for a kitchen garden or in a container. A variety of cultivars are also available: 'Doone Valley' is a low-growing form with yellow-spotted leaves; 'Aureus' has

Lime thyme. SAXON HOLT

Thyme lawn.

Creeping thyme and flagstone, Seaside Gardens.

gold-flecked leaves; 'Lime' has a creeping habit with bright lime green leaves; and 'Variegatus' has silver-white foliage.

Creeping thyme, or mother of thyme *(T. praecox arcticus,* syn. *T. drucei),* features a low mat-forming habit and dark green leaves that have a delightful fragrance when crushed. The late spring to summer flowers are variable in color, typically purple to rose. 'Elfin' forms a dense carpet of gray-green foliage and seldom blooms. 'Pink Chintz' is pink-flowered with creeping stems that reach 1 inch high and spread 12 inches wide. 'Coccineum' has bright purple-red flowers on 2- to 4-inch-tall foliage.

Woolly thyme *(T. pseudolanuginosus)* derives its common name from the fine hairs that cover its gray leaves. Spreading up to 3 feet wide, it hugs the ground and forms an undulating carpet. Pink flowers are produced in modest numbers throughout summer.

Common thyme *(T. vulgaris)* is the classic culinary thyme favored for use in the kitchen. Native to the western Mediterranean Basin, it forms an erect branching subshrub to 12 inches high and wide. It flowers in summer, with blossoms that range from white to purple. A number of varieties have been selected for their foliage color: 'Argenteus' has silver-edged leaves; 'Aureus' features golden-edged leaves; 'Orange Balsam' has green leaves with a strong orange scent.

Tulbaghia violacea
SOCIETY GARLIC
Onion Family (Alliaceae)

Plant Type: Rhizomatous perennial.
Climate Zones: All except high desert and mountains.
Light: Sun to partial shade.
Soil: Adaptable.
Water: Occasional.
Origin: South Africa.
Garden Uses: Meadow, rock, succulent, carpet and tapestry, green roof.

Whenever this plant is used in quantity, its odor permeates the entire garden unless there is ample air circulation. A mass planting of society garlic should only be considered by those who are comfortable with its decidedly strong scent. Aside from that issue, this is a plant with some compelling attributes: it requires little attention, looks great with larger rocks and with gravels of all sizes, and it can be very effective in parkways and street medians. Society garlic produces numerous lax, semi-succulent, narrow blue-gray leaves. Its lavender-pink flowers are freely produced atop numerous 1- to 2-foot-tall stems from spring to early summer, though some flowers are present at nearly all times of the year. For maintenance, an annual "haircut" from either a mower or a string-line trimmer is all that is needed. In areas with warmer winters, this trimming is best accomplished during fall; in areas with colder winters, do this task in early spring, after the chance of frost has passed. 'Silver Lace' is a selection with white-margined leaves that give the clumps of foliage a pleasing gray appearance.

Verbena
VERBENA
Verbena Family (Verbenaceae)

Plant Type: Deciduous to evergreen herbaceous perennials and subshrubs.
Climate Zones: Varies with species.
Light: Sun.
Soil: Well-drained.
Water: Drought tolerant to moderate.
Origin: North and South America.
Garden Uses: Meadow, rock, succulent, carpet and tapestry, green roof.

Verbenas add dependable, vibrant color to the garden. Their dome-shaped to flat-topped inflorescences are particularly attractive to butterflies. Other than seasonal pruning, the verbenas described here are low-maintenance plants. Provide them with good air circulation to avoid powdery mildew infestations.

Purple top *(V. bonariensis)* lends a strong vertical element to meadows, narrow beds, and borders. This upright herbaceous perennial from South America reaches 3 to 6 feet tall and 2 to 3 feet wide. Its open branching creates an airy, see-through effect and makes the summer-blooming bright purple flowers appear to

Society garlic.

Purple top. SAXON HOLT

Above: De La Mina verbena.
Left: Vervain.

A stiffly upright herb, it grows to 2 feet tall, has coarsely toothed leaves, and displays light to dark purple flowers in spring and summer. This hardy perennial originates from South America and tolerates a broad range of moisture conditions. To control vervain and to keep it looking good, pull unwanted runners as needed and cut back the spent stems. [all]

Yucca
YUCCA, SPANISH BAYONET
Agave Family (Agavaceae)

Plant Type: Evergreen semi-succulent subshrubs, shrubs.
Climate Zones: Varies with species.
Light: Sun to partial shade.
Soil: Adaptable.
Water: Drought tolerant to occasional.
Origin: United States south to northern Central America.
Garden Uses: Rock, succulent, carpet and tapestry.

Thick waxy cream to white flowers in spring to summer and narrow lance-shaped leaves are hallmarks of this hardy genus. Depending on species, some yuccas

float in midair. Plants self-sow freely. Purple top is particularly prone to powdery mildew. The cultivar 'Little One' grows to 2 feet tall, has slightly smaller flowers, and is reputedly sterile. [all except m]

Goodding's verbena *(V. gooddingii)* is a sprawling, deciduous herb that measures 1 foot tall and 3 to 4 feet across. The leaves are deeply lobed and the springtime lavender to purple flowers are sweetly fragrant. This desert dweller from the southwest United States needs hot, sunny, dry conditions in order to thrive. Even under ideal circumstances, it may be short-lived. [all except m]

Cedros Island verbena *(V. lilacina)* blooms practically year-round in the central and southern parts of California. It is a wonderfully floriferous subshrub from Baja California and forms evergreen mounds 2 to 4 feet tall and 2 to 4 or more feet wide. The light purple sweetly scented flower heads hover above the dissected leaves. Lightly shear the spent blossoms off young plants or selectively prune older specimens to promote a dense habit. The cultivar 'De La Mina' has deep purple flowers; 'Paseo Rancho' is light purple. [c, i, cv, ld]

Vervain *(V. rigida)* spreads via rhizomes and pops up at random, adding an element of surprise to the garden.

Banana yucca. STEPHEN INGRAM

Soft-leaf yucca. SAXON HOLT

Above: Color Guard yucca Left: Walbristar yucca.

have thick rigid leaves with a sharp terminal spine—which lends them their common name, Spanish bayonet—while others have thin lax leaves with a soft tip. For the purposes of this book, the smaller yuccas are highly recommended.

Banana yucca *(Y. baccata* var. *baccata)* probably boasts the largest individual flowers of any member of this hardy genus. Its pendant blossoms reach up to 5 inches long and are displayed in dense showy clusters on stout stems that reach 3 to 4 feet in height. The outside of the petals is often suffused with a deep reddish brown. Banana yucca's stiff blue-green to dark green leaves are about 2 to 3 feet long and culminate in sharp tips. This yucca takes its common name from the swollen fleshy green pods that enclose its berrylike seeds. Mature plants are quite variable in size but typically form stemless clumps about 4 feet tall and 6 to 8 feet wide. [all]

Adam's needle *(Y. filamentosa)* is essentially trunkless and has moderately stiff leaves with sharp tips. Plants may reach from 2 to 3 feet in height and form expanding clumps over time. The 6-foot-tall flower stems produce a bounty of white bell-shaped flowers. 'Color Guard' has green leaves with a prominent central yellow stripe, and its leaves turn pinkish during cold winter weather. 'Bright Edge' has green leaves with thin yellow margins. [all]

Dwarf yucca *(Y. nana)* forms stemless rosettes of stiff deep green leaves with fibrous margins and sharp

tips. The smallest member of the genus, mature plants are typically 6 inches tall and vary in diameter from 1 to 2 feet. Its flower stalks may reach 3 feet high and carry numerous white bell-shaped flowers. [all]

Soft-leaf yucca *(Y. recurvifolia)* has flexible, relatively thin lax leaves that are 2 to 3 feet long and 2 to 3 inches wide. Mature plants vary in height from 3 to 6 feet tall and form expanding clumps over time. Flower stalks rise 2 to 5 feet above the foliage and bear showy bell-shaped white flowers. 'Hinvargas' (Margaritaville™/PP) has attractive creamy green variegated foliage. 'Monca' (Banana Split™/PP) has creamy yellow variegated foliage. 'Walbristar' (Bright Star PP) has strikingly golden-edged leaves that have green centers. Flower spikes are infrequently produced but are spectacular: the buds are pink while the bell-shaped blossoms are white. [all except m]

Zauschneria (syn. *Epilobium*)
CALIFORNIA FUCHSIA
Evening Primrose Family (Onagraceae)

Plant Type: Semi-evergreen subshrubs and herbaceous perennials.
Climate Zones: All.
Light: Sun to partial shade.
Soil: Adaptable, well-drained preferred.
Water: Drought tolerant to occasional.
Origin: California Oregon, Wyoming, New Mexico, and northern Mexico.
Garden Uses: Meadow, rock, succulent, carpet and tapestry, green roof.

California fuchsias are invaluable for their glorious displays of orange-red flowers. Their tubular nectar-filled blossoms attract hummingbirds, thereby bringing another colorful element to the garden. The tremendous variability found amongst California fuchsias in the wild has spawned the introduction of dozens of cultivars. Plants range in size from prostrate mat-forming ground-covers to upright 3- to 4-foot-tall perennials. Some form distinct clumps, whereas others spread aggressively by rhizomes. Plants begin flowering in late spring or summer and continue well into fall. Although the typical color is orange-red, a broad spectrum of salmons, pinks, and whites are also available. Foliage color is equally variable, with greens tinged yellow, blue, or gray, as well as coated with silvery white. Leaf size ranges from threadlike to ½ inch wide.

Once established, California fuchsias are drought tolerant. They flower best, however, with modest summer irrigation and thrive in lean soils. Except for first-year plants and those with woody stems, prune them to the ground in autumn or winter. To prevent taller plants from splaying open at flowering, stake them or pinch their tips in spring. Contain rhizomatous forms with a root barrier. Leafhopper infestations can turn their leaves brown and root mealybugs can stunt fuchsias; if damage is severe, plants may require treatment to restore healthy growth. Occasional flea beetle infestations can skeletonize the leaves almost overnight.

Botanists are still sorting out the complex taxonomy of California fuchsias. *Zauschneria californica* (syn. *Epilobium canum* ssp. *canum)* is the most widely grown species and exhibits the aforementioned variability across its vast natural range. A few of its many rewarding cultivars, and one other species, are listed below.

Catalina California fuchsia (*Z.* 'Catalina') is the largest cultivar and is capable of reaching 5 feet in height, although 2 to 4 feet is more typical. The soft silvery leaves and orange-red flowers make for a striking combination.

Everett's Choice California fuchshia (*Z.* 'Everett's Choice') is a robust, prostrate selection that spreads 3 to 5 feet wide. This profuse bloomer has scarlet flowers and fuzzy gray-green leaves covered with long, viscid hairs.

Above: California fuchsia.
Left: Catalina California fuchsia.

Hurricane Point California fuchsia (*Z.* 'Hurricane Point') is a woody selection that grows 1 to 2 feet tall and 2 to 4 feet wide and has narrow sage green leaves. The arching branches, tipped with orange-red flowers, are particularly effective where they cascade over boulders or retaining walls.

Humboldt County fuchsia *(Z. septentrionalis)* is a distinct species that occurs in northern California and forms beautiful silver-leaved mats. 'Select Mattole' is one of the best cultivars. Protect it from hot afternoon sun when planted in the Central Valley or inland southern California.

California fuchsia. DAVID FROSS

Recommended Plant Selections

Most gardeners find it useful to have a menu of choices when selecting a plant for a particular function or desirable feature. Consulting a list can make garden planning more manageable, whether you are picking a groundcover, a plant with aromatic foliage, or species that will flourish on a site that is exposed to frequent dry wind. To help with these kinds of decisions, the following lists provide recommendations of species and cultivars from this book for a variety of common landscape situations or plant attributes. These lists are not exhaustive and other plants may be appropriate. Don't be afraid to experiment, but be sure to consult the profiles for details about each plant.

The entries in each list are organized alphabetically by scientific name and accompanied by a common name. If an individual species has several forms and/or cultivars, these are not listed separately but are included in the recommendation unless noted otherwise. For example, when *Eriogonum fasciculatum* appears on a list, this infers that var. *polifolium* and the cultivars 'Dana Point', 'Theodore Payne', and 'Warriner Lytle' are all suitable choices. If a genus name is followed by the notation "(all)", this means that all of the species,

cultivars, hybrids, and varieties within the genus that are described in the book are included in the recommendation. For example, the entry *Achillea* "(all)" means that all three yarrow species as well as the numerous cultivars and hybrids in the book fit the list's description.

Fescues, sedges, foothill needlegrass, and common yarrow are blended in this meadow garden of California natives. SAXON HOLT

AGGRESSIVE

These plants have the potential to be invasive in the garden. They spread primarily vegetatively: by stolons, rhizomes and/or rooting stems.

Aggressive: Carpet geranium.

Achillea millefolium, common yarrow
Artemisia ludoviciana, western mugwort
Aster chilensis, coast aster
Carex praegracilis, clustered field sedge
C. subfusca, mountain sedge
Erigeron karvinskianus (also spreads by seed),
   Santa Barbara daisy
Geranium incanum, carpet geranium
Hypericum calycinum, creeping Saint John's wort
Lantana montevidensis, spreading lantana
Leymus triticoides, creeping wild rye
Oenothera speciosa, Mexican evening primrose
Sedum acre, common stonecrop
S. album, white stonecrop
S. stefco, stonecrop
Solidago (all), goldenrod
Verbena rigida, vervain
Zauschneria californica (some cultivars),
   California fuchsia

AROMATIC FOLIAGE

These plants have aromatic foliage. In some cases, the leaves need to be crushed or bruised to release their fragrance. The [u] indicates plants that are generally considered to have an unpleasant smell.

Achillea (all), yarrow [u]
Artemisia californica, California sagebrush
A. dracunculus, French tarragon
A. tridentata, Great Basin sagebrush
Cistus × hybridus, white rockrose
C. 'Sunset', Sunset cistus
Helleborus foetidus, bear's foot hellebore [u]
Juniperus (all), juniper

Lantana (all), lantana [u]
Lavandula (all), lavender
Nepeta (all), catmint
Origanum (all), oregano

Aromatic Foliage: Lavender.

Pelargonium (all except *peltatum*), geranium
Ribes viburnifolium, Catalina perfume
Rosmarinus officinalis, rosemary
Salvia 'Bee's Bliss', Bee's Bliss sage
S. leucophylla 'Pt. Sal Spreader', Point Sal Spreader sage
S. mellifera 'Terra Seca', Terra Seca black sage
S. spathacea, hummingbird sage
Santolina (all), santolina
Teucrium marum, cat thyme
Thymus (all), thyme
Tulbaghia violacea, society garlic [u]

ATTRACTIVE TO BEES

Native bees and honey bees find these plants especially attractive.

Achillea (all), yarrow
Aster chilensis, coast aster
Ceanothus (all), ceanothus
Cistus (all), rockrose

Attractive to Bees: Sageleaf rockrose.

Cotoneaster (all), cotoneaster
Dalea greggii, trailing indigo bush
Eriogonum (all), buckwheat
Lantana (all), lantana
Lavandula (all), lavender
Lessingia filaginifolia, California aster
Origanum (all), oregano
Phyla nodiflora, lippia
Rosmarinus officinalis, rosemary
Salvia (all), sage
Solidago (all), goldenrod
Teucrium (all), germander
Thymus (all), thyme
Verbena (all), verbena
Zauschneria (all), California fuchsia

BULLETPROOF

The following plants tolerate a wide range of garden conditions, and most gardeners consider them easy to grow.

Bulletproof: Deer grass.

Achillea (all), yarrow
Agapanthus (all), lily-of-the-Nile
Agave (all), agave
Aloe (all), aloe
Aster chilensis, coast aster
Bergenia (all), bergenia
Bouteloua (all), grama grass
Carex (all), sedge
Crassula ovata, jade plant
Erigeron karvinskianus, Santa Barbara daisy
Hesperaloe parviflora, red yucca
Hypericum calycinum, creeping Saint John's wort
Lantana (all), lantana
Leymus (all), wild rye
Muhlenbergia (all), muhly
Myoporum parvifolium, creeping myoporum
Nandina domestica, heavenly bamboo
Opuntia (all), prickly-pear

Pennisetum orientale, oriental fountain grass
Rosmarinus officinalis, rosemary
Ruscus (all), butcher's broom
Sporobolus (all), dropseed
Stipa gigantea, giant feather grass
Tulbaghia violacea, society garlic
Yucca (all), yucca

DEER RESISTANT

Deer typically do not eat the plants on this list.

Achillea (all), yarrow
Achnatherum (all), needlegrass
Agapanthus (all), lily-of-the-Nile
Agave (all), agave
Agrostis pallens, dune bent grass
Aloe (all), aloe
Aristida purpurea, purple three-awn
Artemisia (all), sagebrush
Aster chilensis, coast aster
Berberis (all), barberry
Bothriochloa barbinodis, silver beardgrass
Bougainvillea, bougainvillea
Bouteloua (all), grama grass
Buchloe dactyloides, buffalo grass
Carex (all), sedge
Cotoneaster (all), cotoneaster
Deschampsia caespitosa, tufted hair grass
Erigeron (all), fleabane
Eriogonum (all), buckwheat (except flowers on some)
Euphorbia (all), euphorbia
Festuca (all), fescue
Fragaria (all), strawberry
Gazania (all), gazania
Geranium (all), cranesbill
Helictotrichon sempervirens, blue oat grass
Helleborus (all), hellebore
Hemerocallis (all), daylily
Hypericum calycinum, creeping Saint John's wort

Deer Resistant: Sulfur buckwheat.

Iris (all), iris (except flowers on some)
Lantana (all), lantana
Lavandula (all), lavender
Leymus (all), wild rye
Muhlenbergia (all), muhly
Nandina domestica, heavenly bamboo
Nassella (all) needlegrass
Nepeta (all), catmint
Origanum (all), oregano
Pennisetum orientale, oriental fountain grass
Ribes viburnifolium, Catalina perfume
Rosmarinus officinalis, rosemary
Salvia (all), sage
Santolina (all), santolina
Sesleria (all), moor grass
Sporobolus (all), dropseed
Stipa gigantea, giant feather grass
Thymus (all), thyme
Verbena (all), verbena
Zauschneria (all), California fuchsia

DRIED ARRANGEMENTS

These plants possess flowers, fruits, or foliage that are useful in dried arrangements.

Achillea (all), yarrow
Achnatherum (all), needlegrass
Agave (all) agave
Aloe (all except *ciliaris*), aloe
Aristida purpurea, purple three-awn
Artemisia tridentata, Great Basin sagebrush
Bothriochloa barbinodis, silver beardgrass
Bouteloua (all), grama grass
Dierama pendulum, fairy wand
Eriogonum arborescens, Santa Cruz Island buckwheat
E. fasciculatum, California buckwheat
Hesperoyucca whipplei, chaparral yucca
Iris (all), iris
Juncus patens, wire grass

Lavandula (all), lavender
Leymus cinereus, Great Basin wild rye
L. condensatus, giant wild rye
Muhlenbergia (all except *dumosa*), muhly
Nassella (all), needlgrass
Pennisetum orientale, oriental fountain grass
Ruscus (all), butcher's broom
Salvia leucophylla 'Pt. Sal Spreader',
    Point Sal Spreader sage
S. mellifera 'Terra Seca', Terra Seca black sage
S. spathacea, hummingbird sage
Sporobolus (all), dropseed
Stipa gigantea, giant feather grass
Yucca (all), yucca

DRY SHADE

The plants on this list tolerate and in some regions prefer dry shade. These are sites in full to partial shade—typically beneath trees—that receive minimal or no supplemental irrigation. Those marked with an [r] generally tolerate root competition from trees especially well.

Agave attenuata, foxtail agave
Agave bracteosa, candelabrum agave
Agrostis pallens, dune bent grass
Aeonium (all), aeonium
Arctostaphylos (all except 'Emerald Carpet' and
    'John Dourley'), manzanita
Berberis (all), barberry [r]
Bergenia, bergenia
Carex (all except *flacca* and *testacea*), sedge
Ceanothus (all except *hearstiorum* and *maritimus*),
    ceanothus
Crassula multicava, fairy crassula
Dudleya virens ssp. *hassei,* Catalina Island dudleya [r]
Echeveria elegans, elegant hen and chicks
Echeveria × imbricata, hen and chicks
Festuca californica, California fescue [r]
Fragaria vesca, woodland strawberry

Dry Shade:
Dune bent grass.

Dried Arrangements: Giant feather grass.

Graptopetalum paraguayense, ghost plant [r]
Helleborus (all), hellebore [r]
Heuchera hybrids (Rancho Santa Ana hybrids),
    coral bells
Heuchera maxima, island alum root [r]
Iris douglasiana, Douglas iris [r]
Iris Pacific Coast Hybrid (some cultivars), Pacific Coast
    Hybrid iris
Iris unguicularis, winter iris
Iva hayesiana, poverty weed
Juncus patens, wire grass
Leymus condensatus, giant wild rye [r]
Leymus triticoides, creeping wild rye [r]
Nandina domestica, heavenly bamboo [r]
Nassella lepida, foothill needlegrass
Pelargonium tomentosum, peppermint geranium
Ribes viburnifolium, Catalina perfume [r]
Ruscus (all), butcher's broom [r]
Salvia spathacea, hummingbird sage [r]
Sedum rupestre 'Angelina', Angelina stonecrop
S. × *rubrotinctum,* Christmas cheer
S. spathulifolium, Pacific stonecrop [r]
Sempervivum (all), houseleek

DRY WIND
These plants tolerate low-humidity wind.

Achillea (all), yarrow
Agapanthus (all), lily-of-the-Nile
Agave (all), agave
Aloe (all), aloe
Artemisia (all except *pycnocephala*), sagebrush
Baccharis (all), coyote brush
Berberis (all), barberry
Carex (all), sedge

*Dry Wind:
Cotoneaster,
juniper..*

Cistanthe grandiflora, rock purslane
Cistus (all), rockrose
Cotoneaster (all), cotoneaster
Crassula (all), crassula
Dudleya (all), dudleya
Erigeron karvinskianus, Santa Barbara daisy
Eriogonum (all), buckwheat
Euphorbia (all), euphorbia
Festuca (all), fescue
Gaura lindheimeri, gaura
Gazania (all), gazania
Hemerocallis (all), daylily
Hesperaloe parviflora, red yucca
Juniperus (all), juniper
Lantana (all), lantana
Lavandula (all), lavender
Muhlenbergia (all), muhly
Nandina domestica, heavenly bamboo
Nassella (all), needlegrass
Oenothera (all), evening primrose
Portulacaria afra, elephant's food
Rosmarinus officinalis, rosemary
Salvia (all), sage
Santolina (all), santolina
Stipa gigantea, giant feather grass
Teucrium (all), germander
Yucca (all), yucca
Zauschneria (all), California fuchsia

FAST GROWING
The following plants have a fast rate of growth.

Achillea millefolium, common yarrow
Agapanthus (all), lily-of-the-Nile
Aloe ciliaris, climbing aloe
Arctotis (all), African daisy
Aristida purpurea, purple three-awn
Aster chilensis, coast aster
Bougainvillea, bougainvillea
Ceanothus thyrsiflorus var. *griseus,* Carmel creeper
    ceanothus
C. 'Joyce Coulter', Joyce Coulter ceanothus
Cistus (all), rockrose
Dalea greggii, trailing indigo bush
Dudleya virens ssp. *hassei,* Catalina Island dudleya
Erigeron karvinskianus, Santa Barbara daisy
Eriogonum (all except *umbellatum* and *wrightii*),
    buckwheat
Euphorbia (all except 'Tasmanian Tiger' and 'Glacier
Blue'), euphorbia
Fragaria chiloensis, beach strawberry
Gaura lindheimeri, gaura
Gazania (all), gazania
Geranium incanum, carpet geranium

Fast Growing: De La Mina verbena.

Hypericum calycinum, creeping Saint John's wort
Lantana (all), lantana
Lavandula (all), lavender
Leymus triticoides, creeping wild rye
Myoporum parvifolium, creeping myoporum
Oenothera speciosa, Mexican evening primrose
Rosmarinus officinalis, rosemary
Salvia (all), sage
Solidago (all), goldenrod
Sphaeralcea philippiana, trailing mallow
Teucrium (all), germander
Tulbaghia violacea, society garlic
Verbena (all), verbena
Zauschneria (all), California fuchsia

FROST TENDER

These plants will not tolerate freezing temperatures on a regular basis, although some will tolerate an occasional freeze if they are well established and healthy.

Aeonium (all), *aeonium*
Agave attenuata, foxtail agave
A. desmetiana, smooth agave
A. 'Joe Hoak', Joe Hoak agave

Frost Tender: Bougainvillea.

Aloe ciliaris, climbing aloe
A. plicatilis, fan aloe
Bougainvillea (all when young; established plants come back from the roots), bougainvillea
Cotyledon orbiculata, pig's ear
Dymondia margaretae, silver carpet
Dudleya (all except *pulverulenta* and *virens* ssp. *hassei*), dudleya
Echeveria derenbergii, painted lady echeveria
Echinocactus grusonii, golden barrel cactus
Kalanchoe (all), kalanchoe
Lantana (all when young; established plants come back from the roots)
Senecio (all) chalksticks
Verbena lilacina (frost tolerance not yet fully understood), Cedros Island verbena

HUMMINGBIRDS

The flowers on these plants are especially attractive to hummingbirds.

Hummingbirds: California fuchsia.

Aloe (all), aloe
Arctostaphylos (all), manzanita
Bougainvillea, bougainvillea
Cotyledon orbiculata, pig's ear
Dudlyea (all), dudleya
Echeveria (all), echeveria
Hesperaloe parviflora, red yucca
Heuchera (all), coral bells

Kalanchoe (all), kalanchoe
Lantana (all), lantana
Lavandula (all), lavender
Nepeta (all), catmint
Origanum (all), oregano
Pelargonium (all), geranium
Rosmarinus officinalis, rosemary
Salvia (all), sage
Teucrium (all), germander
Tulbaghia (all), society garlic
Verbena (all), verbena
Zauschneria (all), California fuchsia

POISONOUS/ALLERGENIC

Plants on this list come with a caution. Those followed by [a] produce allergenic pollen. Contact with plants followed by [d] may cause dermatitis. Plants marked with [p] are poisonous if ingested, and the poisonous part(s) are indicated.

Poisonous/ Allergenic: Wood spurge.

Achillea millefolium (all), yarrow [d]
Achnatherum (all), needlegrass [a]
Agapanthus (all), agapanthus [a] and [p, foliage and bulb]
Agave (all), agave [d]
Agrostis pallens, dune bent grass [a]
Aloe (all), aloe [a]
Aristida purpurea, purple three-awn [a]
Artemisia (all), sagebrush [d]
Aster chilensis, coast aster [d]
Baccharis (all), coyote brush [a]
Bellis perennis, English daisy [a]
Berberis (all), barberry [p, all parts except berries]
Bothriochloa barbinodis, silver beardgrass [a]
Bouteloua (all), grama grass [a]
Crassula arborescens, silver jade plant [p, all parts]

C. ovata, jade plant [p, all parts]
Deschampsia cespitosa, tufted hair grass [a]
Erigeron (all), fleabane [d]
Eriogonum (all), buckwheat [a, moderately allergenic]
Euphorbia (all), euphorbia [d] and [p, all parts and sap]
Festuca (all), fescue [a]
Helictotrichon sempervirens, blue oat grass [a]
Helleborus (all), hellebore [d, p, all parts]
Iva hayesiana, poverty weed [a and d]
Lantana (all), [a] and [p, leaves and berries]
Leymus cinereus, Great Basin wild rye [a]
L. condensatus, giant wild rye [a]
Muhlenbergia (all), muhly [a]
Nassella (all), needlegrass [a]
Opuntia, prickly-pear [d]
Sesleria (all), moor grass [a]
Sporobolus (all), dropseed [a]
Stipa gigantea, giant feather grass [a]

POOR DRAINAGE

These plants will tolerate poor drainage, whether it is caused by naturally heavy clay soils or by compaction due to construction or other disturbance.

Agapanthus (all), lily-of-the-Nile
Aster chilensis, coast aster
Baccharis (all), coyote brush
Berberis aquifolium 'Compacta', Compacta Oregon grape
Bergenia, bergenia
Bothriochloa barbinodis, silver beardgrass
Bouteloua (all) grama grass
Buchloe dactyloides, buffalo grass
Carex (all), sedge
Ceanothus thyrsiflorus var. *griseus,* Carmel creeper ceanothus
Cotoneaster (all), cotoneaster

Poor Drainage: Coyote brush, lily-of-the-Nile.

Deschampsia cespitosa, tufted hair grass
Erigeron glaucus, seaside daisy
E. karvinskianus, Santa Barbara daisy
Hemerocallis (all), daylily
Heuchera maxima, island alum root
Iris douglasiana, Douglas iris
I. germanica hybrids, bearded iris
Iva hayesiana, poverty weed
Juncus patens, wire grass
Lantana (all), lantana
Leymus (all), wild rye
Muhlenbergia (all), muhly
Nandina domestica, heavenly bamboo
Oenothera speciosa, Mexican evening primrose
Pennisetum orientale, oriental fountain grass
Ribes viburnifolium, Catalina perfume
Rosmarinus officianlis, rosemary
Salvia spathacea, hummingbird sage
Sesleria (all), moor grass
Solidago (all) goldenrod
Sporobolus airoides, dropseed
Tulbaghia violacea, society garlic
Zauschneria californica, California fuchsia

SEASHORE CONDITIONS

The following plants are tolerant of exposed areas adjacent to the ocean where winds and salt spray are the norm. (Many other plants—too many to list—can safely be planted in coastal areas in protected sites beyond the ocean spray.)

Achillea (all), yarrow
Aeonium arboreum 'Zwartkop', Zwartkop aeonium
A. canariensis, dinner-plate aeonium
A. haworthii, pinwheel aeonium
A. 'Tricolor', kiwi aeonium
Agapanthus (all), lily-of-the-Nile
Agave americana 'Medio Picta Alba', Medio Picta Alba
    agave
A. attenuata, foxtail agave
Aloe maculata, soap agave
A. striata, coral aloe
A. vera, aloe vera
Arctostaphylos (all), manzanita
Artemisia californica, California sagebrush
A. 'Powis Castle', Powis Castle wormwood
A. pycnocephala, sandhill sagebrush
Aster chilensis, coast aster
Baccharis (all), coyote brush
Carex divulsa, Berkeley sedge
C. praegracilis, clustered field sedge
C. testacea, orange New Zealand sedge
Ceanothus (all), ceanothus
Cistus (all), rockrose

Seashore Conditions: Sonoma Coast common yarrow.

Convolvulus (all), morning glory
Cotyledon orbiculata, pig's ear
Crassula ovata, jade plant
C. falcata, airplane plant
Dudleya (all except *densiflora*), dudleya
Erigeron glaucus, seaside daisy
E. karvinskianus, Santa Barbara daisy
Eriogonum (all except *compositum, crocatum,*
    umbellatum, and *wrightii*), buckwheat
Festuca glauca, blue fescue
F. rubra, creeping red fescue
Fragaria chiloensis, beach strawberry
Gaura lindheimeri, gaura
Gazania (all), gazania
Geranium incanum, carpet geranium
Helictotrichon sempervirens, blue oat grass
Hemerocallis (all), daylily
Heuchera maxima, island alum root
Iris douglasiana, Douglas iris
I. germanica hybrids, bearded iris
I. unguicularis, winter iris
Juncus patens, wire grass
Juniperus (all), juniper
Lantana (all), lantana
Lavandula (all), lavender
Lessingia filaginifolia 'Silver Carpet', Silver Carpet
    California aster
Leymus condensatus, giant wild rye
Muhlenbergia (all except *emersleyi* and *lindheimeri*),
    muhly
Nassella (all), needlegrass
Pelargonium (all), geranium
Pennisetum orientale, oriental fountain grass
Rosmarinus officinalis, rosemary
Salvia leucophylla 'Pt. Sal Spreader', Point Sal Spreader
    sage
S. mellifera 'Terra Seca', Terra Seca black sage
Santolina (all), santolina
Senecio (all), chalksticks
Sesleria (all), moor grass

Teucrium fruticans, germander
Yucca filamentosa, Adam's needle
Zauschneria (all), California fuchsia

SILVER, GRAY, WHITE, OR BLUE FOLIAGE

These plants have silver, gray, white, or blue foliage.
Those with a [g] have green forms as well (which may
be more common in some species). Coloration may vary
by season or geographic area.

*Silver, Gray, White,
or Blue Foliage:
Above: African daisy.
Left: Wire grass.*

Achillea clavennae, greek yarrow
A. tomentosa, woolly yarrow
Aeonium haworthii, pinwheel aeonium
Agave attenuata, foxtail agave [g]
A. deserti, desert agave
Aloe plicatilis, fan aloe
Arctostaphylos 'John Dourley', John Dourley manzanita
A. 'Pacific Mist', Pacific Mist manzanita
A. pumila, dune manzanita [g]
Arctotis (all), African daisy

Artemisia (all except *dracunculus*), sagebrush
Carex flacca, blue sedge
Cistanthe grandiflora, rock purslane
Convolvulus cneorum, ground morning glory
Cotyledon orbiculata, pig's ear
Crassula arborescens, silver jade plant
C. falcata, airplane plant
Dalea greggii, trailing indigo bush
Delosperma 'Oberg', Oberg iceplant
D. sphalmanthoides, tufted ice plant
Dudleya anthonyi, Anthony dudleya
D. brittonii, Britton dudleya [g]
D. pulverulenta, chalk dudleya
D. virens ssp. *hassei,* Catalina Island dudleya
Dymondia margaretae, silver carpet
Echeveria (all except *agavoides*), echeveria
Eriogonum arborescens, Santa Cruz Island buckwheat
E. cinereum, ashyleaf buckwheat
E. compositum, rock buckwheat
E. crocatum, saffron buckwheat
E. fasciculatum var. *polifolium,* interior California
    buckwheat
E. latifolium, coast buckwheat [g]
E. umbellatum, sulfur buckwheat [g]
Euphorbia (all except × *martinii*), euphorbia
Festuca californica, California fescue [g]
F. glauca, blue fescue
F. idahoensis, Idaho fescue [g]
F. rubra, creeping red fescue [g]
Gazania (all), gazania [g]
Graptopetalum paraguayense, ghost plant
Helictotrichon sempervirens, blue oat grass
Helleborus argutifolius, Corsican hellebore [g]
H. × *sternii,* (no common name) [g]
Hesperoyucca whipplei, chaparral yucca [g]
Juncus patens (some cultivars), wire grass [g]
Juniperus (all), juniper [g]
Kalanchoe (all), kalanchoe
Lavandula (all), lavender [g]
Lessingia filaginifolia, California aster
Leymus cinereus, Great Basin rye
L. condensatus 'Canyon Prince', Canyon Prince wild rye
L. triticoides 'Grey Dawn', Grey Dawn creeping wild rye
Muhlenbergia emersleyi, bull grass
M. lindheimeri, Lindheimer's muhly
M. pubescens, soft blue Mexican muhly
Nepeta × *faassenii,* catmint
Oenothera caespitosa, fragrant evening primrose
O. californica, California evening primrose
Opuntia basilaris, prickly-pear
Origanum dictamnus, dittany of Crete
O. rotundifolium, round-leaved oregano
Salvia 'Bee's Bliss', Bee's Bliss sage
S. chamaedryoides, germander sage
S. leucophylla 'Point Sal Spreader', Point Sal Spreader sage

Santolina chamaecyparissus, lavender cotton
Sedum dasyphyllum, Corsican stonecrop
S. palmeri, Palmer's sedum
S. spathulifolium, Pacific stonecrop
Senecio mandraliscae, blue chalksticks
S. serpens, little blue chalksticks
Sesleria caerulea, blue moor grass
Sphaeralcea ambigua, apricot mallow [g]
Teucrium (all except *chamaedrys*), germander
Thymus pseudolanuginosus, woolly thyme
Yucca baccata var. *baccata,* banana yucca [g]
Zauschneria californica, California fuchsia [g]
Z. septentrionalis, Humboldt County fuchsia

SLOW GROWING
These plants have a slow rate of growth.

Agave victoria-reginae, Queen Victoria agave
Aloe plicatilis, fan aloe
Berberis nervosa, longleaf barberry
Berberis repens, creeping barberry
Crassula arborescens, silver jade plant
Crassula ovata, jade plant
Hesperoyucca whipplei, chaparral yucca
Iris Pacific Coast Hybrids (some cultivars), Pacific Coast Hybrid iris
Ribes viburnifolium (sometimes), Catalina perfume
Ruscus (all), butcher's broom
Yucca baccata var. *baccata,* banana yucca

SPINY OR PRICKLY
The plants on this list have spines or prickles.

Agave americana 'Medio Picta Alba', Medio Picta Alba agave
Agave deserti, desert agave
Agave desmettiana, smooth agave
Agave 'Joe Hoak', Joe Hoak agave
Agave parryi, artichoke agave
Agave victoria-reginae (somewhat), Queen Victoria agave
Aloe × *nobilis,* gold tooth aloe
Aloe maculata (somewhat), soap aloe
Aloe vera (somewhat), aloe vera
Berberis aquifolium 'Compacta', Compacta Oregon grape
Berberis nervosa, longleaf barberry
Berberis repens (somewhat), creeping barberry
Bougainvillea, bougainvillea
Echeveria agavoides (somewhat), agave echeveria
Echinocactus grusonii, golden barrel cactus
Hesperoyucca whipplei, chaparral yucca
Juniperus chinensis (some cultivars), Chinese juniper
Juniperus procumbens 'Nana', Nana Japanese garden juniper
Juniperus sabina (some cultivars, Savin juniper)
Opuntia (all), prickly-pear
Ruscus aculeatus, common butcher's broom
Yucca baccata var. *baccata* (somewhat), banana yucca
Yucca nana, dwarf yucca

Slow Growing: Silver jade plant hybrid.

Spiny or Prickly: Gold tooth aloe.

Sunset Zones for Profiled Plants

The following list of *Sunset* climate zones covers the plants profiled in this book and was compiled to aid readers who are accustomed to the *Sunset* climate zone system. These recommendations do not always match the ones contained in *Sunset Western Garden Book* and only include zones found in California. Where a genus name is followed by "(all)," the recommended *Sunset* zones apply to all the species and cultivars in the book from that genus.

Latin Name / Common Name / *SUNSET* ZONES

Achillea (all); yarrow; 1A-3A, 7-11, 13-24

Achnatherum hymenoides; Indian rice grass; 7-11, 14-16, 18-24

A. speciosum; desert needlegrass; 7-11, 14-24

Aeonium (all); aeonium; 15-24

Agapanthus (all); lily-of-the-Nile; 7-9, 14-24

Agave americana 'Medio Picta Alba'; Medio Picta Alba agave; 10, 13-24

A. attenuata; foxtail agave; 18-24

A. bracteosa; candelabrum agave; 13-24

A. deserti; desert agave; 13, 15, 18-24

A. desmettiana; smooth agave; 18-24

A. geminiflora; twin-flowered agave; 13, 20-24

A. 'Joe Hoak'; Joe Hoak agave; 18-24

A. parryi; artichoke agave; 2B, 3, 7-11, 13-24

A. victoria-reginae; Queen Victoria agave; 10, 13, 15-17, 21-24

A. vilmoriniana; octopus agave; 13-24

Agrostis pallens; dune bent grass; 14-24

Aloe aristata; torch plant; 8, 9, 13-24

A. ciliaris; climbing aloe; 8, 9, 13-24

A. maculata; soap aloe; 8, 9, 13-24

A. × *nobilis;* gold tooth aloe; 8, 9, 13-24

A. plicatilis; fan aloe; 18-24

A. 'Rooikappie'; red riding hood aloe; 13, 16-24

A. sinkatana; reblooming aloe; 13, 16-24

A. striata; coral aloe; 8, 9, 13-24

A. vera; aloe vera; 8, 9, 13-24

Arctostaphylos edmundsii; Edmunds manzanita; 7-9, 14-24

A. 'Emerald Carpet'; Emerald Carpet manzanita; 7-9, 14-24

A. hookeri; Hooker manzanita; 7-9, 14-24

A. 'John Dourley'; John Dourley manzanita; 7-9, 14-24

A. × *media;* media manzanita; 4, 7-9, 14-24

A. 'Pacific Mist'; Pacific Mist manzanita; 7-9, 14-24

A. pumila; dune manzanita; 14-24

A. uva-ursi; kinnikinnick; 1A-4, 7-9, 14-24

Arctotis; African daisies; 7 9, 14 24

Aristida purpurea; purple three-awn; 1A-4, 7-11, 13-24

Artemisia arborescens; large wormwood; 7-9, 14-24

A. californica; California sagebrush; 7-9, 14-24

A. dracunculus; French tarragon; 2B, 3A, 7-11, 14-24

A. ludoviciana; western mugwort; 1A, 2A, 3A, 7-11, 13-24

A. 'Powis Castle'; Powis Castle wormwood; 2B, 3A, 7-11, 13, 14-24

A. pycnocephala; sandhill sagebrush; 7, 14-17, 19-24

A. tridentata; Great Basin sagebrush; 1A, 2A, 3A, 7-11, 14-24

A. versicolor 'Sea Foam'; Sea Foam artemisia; 1A-3A, 9-11, 14-24

Aster chilensis; coast aster; 7-9, 14-24

Baccharis 'Centennial'; Centennial coyote brush; 7-11, 13-24

B. pilularis; coyote brush; 7-11, 14-24

B. 'Starn'; Starn coyote brush; 10, 11, 13

Bellis perennis; English daisy; 1A, 2A, 3A, 7-11, 14-24

Berberis aquifolium 'Compacta'; Compacta Oregon grape; 2A, 2B, 3A, 4, 7-9, 14-24

B. nervosa; longleaf barberry; 2B, 3A, 4, 7-9, 14-24

B. repens; creeping barberry; 2B, 3A, 3B, 4, 7-11, 14-24

Bergenia; bergenia; 1A-4, 7-9, 14-24

Bothriochloa barbinodis; silver beardgrass; 7-9, 14-16, 18-24

Bougainvillea; bougainvillea; 13-24

Bouteloua curtipendula; side-oats grama; 1A, 2A, 3A, 7-11, 13-24

B. gracilis; blue grama; 1A, 2A, 3A, 7-11, 13-24

Buchloe dactyloides; buffalo grass; 1A, 2A, 3A, 8-11, 13-16, 18-22

Carex divulsa; Berkeley sedge; 1A-4, 7-9, 14-24

C. flacca; blue sedge, carnation grass; 3A, 7-9, 14-24

C. pansa; dune sedge; 7-9, 14-24

C. praegracilis; field sedge; 1A-4, 7-9, 11-24

C. subfusca; mountain sedge; 1A-4, 7-9, 11, 13-24

C. testacea; orange New Zealand sedge; 7-9, 14-24

C. texensis; Catlin sedge; 7-9, 14-24

Ceanothus (all); ceanothus; 7-9, 14-24

Cistanthe grandiflora; rock purslane; 7-10, 13-24

Cistus (all); rockrose; 7-9, 14-24

Convolvulus cneorum; bush morning glory; 7-9, 13-24

C. sabatius; ground morning glory; 4, 7-9, 13-24

Cotoneaster dammeri; bearberry cotoneaster; 7-11, 14-24

C. horizontalis; rock cotoneaster; 7-11, 14-24

C. microphyllus; rockspray cotoneaster; 7-9, 14-24

C. salicifolius 'Repens'; willowleaf cotoneaster; 3B-24

Cotyledon orbiculata; pig's ear; 13, 16, 17, 21-24

Crassula arborescens; silver jade plant; 8, 9, 13-24

C. capitella 'Campfire'; Campfire crassula; 8, 9, 14-24

C. perfoliata var. *falcata;* airplane plant; 8, 9, 14-24

C. multicava; fairy crassula; 8, 9, 13-24

C. ovata; jade plant; 8, 9, 14-24

C. schmidtii; no common name; 8, 9, 14-24

Dalea greggii; trailing indigo bush; 7, 10-16, 18-23

Delosperma astoni 'Blut'; Blut ice plant; 7-11, 14-24

D. congestum 'Gold Nugget'; Gold Nugget ice plant; 7-11, 14-24

D. 'Mesa Verde'; Mesa Verde ice plant; 1A, 2A, 3A, 7-11, 13-24

D. 'Oberg'; Oberg ice plant; 7-11, 14-24

D. sphalmanthoides; tufted ice plant; 2A, 3A, 7-11, 14-24

Deschampsia cespitosa; tufted hair grass; 2A, 3A, 7-9, 14-24

Dierama pendulum; fairy wand; 4, 7-9, 14-17, 20-24

Dudleya anthonyi; Anthony dudleya; 16-24

D. brittonii; Britton dudleya; 16-24

D. densiflora; Fish Canyon dudleya; 16-24

D. edulis; ladies' fingers dudleya; 16-24

D. farinosa; coast dudleya; 7, 14-17, 19-24

D. pulverulenta; chalk dudleya; 16-24

D. virens ssp. *hassei;* Catalina Island dudleya; 16-24

Dymondia margaretae; silver carpet; 8-9, 15-24

Echeveria agavoides; agave echeveria; 8, 9, 14-24

E. derenbergii; painted lady echeveria; 15-24

E. elegans; elegant hen and chicks; 8, 9, 14-24

E. × *imbricata;* hen and chicks; 8, 9, 14-24

Echinocactus grusonii; golden barrel cactus; 13, 15-24

Erigeron glaucus; seaside daisy; 14-17, 22-24

E. karvinskianus; Santa Barbara daisy; 8, 9, 13-24

E. scopulinus; mat daisy; 2A, 3A, 7-11, 13-24

Eriogonum arborescens; Santa Cruz Island buckwheat; 7-9, 14-24

E. cinereum; ashyleaf buckwheat; 14-17, 19-24

E. compositum; rock buckwheat; 1A-3A, 7-9, 14-22

E. crocatum; saffron buckwheat; 14-24

E. fasciculatum; California buckwheat; 7-9, 13-24

E. fasciculatum var. *polifolium;* interior California buckwheat; 11, 13

E. grande var. *rubescens;* red-flowered buckwheat; 14-24

E. latifolium; coast buckwheat; 15-17, 22-24

E. umbellatum var. *polyanthum;* sulfur buckwheat; 1A-3A, 4, 7-9, 14-24

E. wrightii; Wright's buckwheat; 7-11, 14-24

Euphorbia characias; wood spurge; 14-17, 20-24

E. cyparissias; cypress spurge; 2A, 3A, 7-11, 14-24

E. × *martinii;* martin spurge; 3A, 7-11, 14-24

E. myrsinites; myrtle spurge; 2A, 3A, 7-11, 14-24

E. rigida; silver spurge; 7-11, 14-24

E. seguieriana ssp. *niciciana;* 7-11, 14-24

Festuca californica; California fescue; 1A-4, 7-9, 14-24

F. glauca; blue fescue; 1A, 2A, 3A, 7-11, 14-24

F. idahoensis; Idaho fescue; 1A, 2A, 3A, 7-10, 14-24

F. mairei; Maire's fescue; 2A, 3A, 7-11, 14-24

F. rubra; creeping red fescue; 1A, 2A, 3A, 7-10, 14-24

Fragaria chiloensis; beach strawberry; 7-9, 14-24

F. vesca; woodland stawberry; 3A, 7-9, 14-24

Gaura lindheimeri; gaura, butterfly gaura; 4, 7-11, 13-24

Gazania; gazania; 8-11, 13-24

Geranium 'Frances Grate'; Frances Grate cranesbill; 14-24

G. incanum; carpet geranium; 14-24

G. paraguayense; ghost plant; 13, 17, 19-24

Helictotrichon sempervirens; blue oat grass; 1A, 2A, 3A, 7-9, 14-24

Helleborus argutifolius; Corsican hellebore; 4, 7-9, 14-24

H. foetidus; bear's foot hellebore; 2B-4, 7-9, 14-24

H. orientalis; Lenten rose; 2B-4, 7-10, 14-24

H. × *sternii;* no common name; 4, 7-9, 14-24

Hemerocallis; daylily; 1A-3A, 4, 7-11, 13-24

Hesperaloe parviflora; red yucca; 2B, 3, 7-11, 13-16, 18-24

Hesperoyucca whipplei; chaparral yucca; 2A, 2B, 3A, 4, 7-11, 13-24

Heuchera elegans; elegant coral bells; 2A, 2B, 3A, 7-9, 14-24

H. hybrids; Rancho Santa Ana hybrids; 14-24

H. hybrids; Canyon series coral bells; 2A, 2B, 3A, 4-9, 14-24

H. maxima; island alum root; 15-24

Hypericum calycinum; creeping St. John's wort; 2-4, 7-9, 11, 13-24

H. coris; yellow coris; 4, 7-9, 14-24

Iris arilbred hybrids; arilbred iris; 1A-3A, 4, 7-11, 13-24

I. douglasiana; Douglas iris; 4, 7-9, 14-24

I. germanica hybrids; bearded iris; 1A-3A, 4, 7-11, 13-24

I. Pacific Coast Hybrid; Pacific Coast Hybrid iris; 4, 7-9, 14-24

I. spuria; butterfly iris; 2A, 2B, 3A, 4, 7-11, 13-24

I. unguicularis; winter iris; 4, 7-9, 14-24

Iva hayesiana; poverty weed; 7-9, 14-24

Juncus patens; wire grass, California gray rush; 4-9, 14-24

Juniperus (all); juniper; 1A-4, 7-11, 13-24

Kalanchoe beharensis; feltbush; 13, 21-24

Kalanchoe fedtschenkoi; rainbow scallops; 19-24

K. grandiflora; no common name; 19-24

K. luciae; paddle plant; 20-24

K. orgyalis; copper spoons; 20-24

K. pumila; flower dust plant; 20-24

K. thyrsiflora; kalanchoe; 20-24

K. tomentosa; panda plant; 13, 23, 24

Lantana (all); lantana; 8, 9, 13-24

Lavandula angustifolia; English lavender; 2A, 2B, 3A, 4, 7-11, 13-24

L. dentata; French lavender; 8, 9, 13-24

L. × *intermedia;* lavandin; 4, 7-11, 13-24

L. latifolia; spike lavender; 8, 9, 13-24

L. stoechas; Spanish lavender; 4, 7-11, 13-24

Lessingia filaginifolia; California aster; 7-9, 14-24

Leymus cinereus; Great Basin wild rye; 4, 7-11, 13-24

L. condensatus; giant wild rye; 7, 8, 14-24

L. triticoides; creeping wild rye; 1A-4, 7-11, 14-24

Muhlenbergia capillaris; pink muhly; 4, 7-11, 13-24

M. dumosa; bamboo muhly; 8-11, 13-24

M. emersleyi; bull grass; 2A, 2B, 3A, 4, 7-11, 13-24

M. lindheimeri; Lindheimer's muhly; 7-11, 13-24

M. pubescens; soft blue Mexican muhly; 8-11, 13-24

M. rigens; deer grass; 4, 7-11, 13-24

Myoporum parvifolium; creeping myoporum; 8, 9, 13-24

Nandina domestica and cultivars; heavenly bamboo; 3A, 4, 7-11, 13-24

Nassella (all); needlegrass; 7-9, 11, 14-24

Nepeta (all); catmint; 1A-4, 7-11, 13-24

Oenothera caespitosa; fragrant evening primrose; 1A-3A, 7-14, 18-21

O. californica; California evening primrose; 1A-3A, 7-14, 18-21

O. missouriensis; Ozark suncups; 1A-4, 7-11, 13-24

O. speciosa; Mexican evening primrose; 2B, 3A, 4, 7-11, 13-24

Opuntia (all); prickly-pear; 2A, 2B, 3A, 7-16, 18-23

Origanum dictamnus; dittany of Crete; 8,9 13-24

O. laevigatum; oregano; 2, 3A, 4, 7-11, 13-24

O. majorana; sweet majoram; 8-11, 13-24

O. rotundifolium; round-leaved oregano; 2B, 3A, 4, 7-11, 13-24

O. vulgare; wild majoram, oregano; 1A-4, 7-11, 13-24

Pelargonium (all); geranium; 8, 9, 14-24

Pennisetum orientale; oriental fountain grass; 3A, 4, 7-9, 14-24

Phyla nodiflora; lippia; 8-11, 13-24

Portulacaria afra; elephant food; 8, 9, 14, 15, 18-24

Ribes viburnifolium; Catalina perfume, evergreen currant; 7-9, 14-17, 19-24

Rosmarinus officinalis and cultivars; rosemary; 7-11, 13-24

Ruscus aculeatus; common butcher's broom; 4, 7-11, 13-24

R. hypoglossum; poet's laurel; 4, 7-11, 13-24

Salvia 'Bee's Bliss'; Bee's Bliss sage; 7-9, 14-24

S. chamaedryoides; germander sage; 8, 9, 14-24

S. greggii; autumn sage; 8-11, 13-24

S. leucantha; Mexican sage; 13-24

S. leucophylla 'Pt. Sal Spreader'; Point Sal Spreader sage; 8, 9, 14-24

S. mellifera; 'Terra Seca'; Terra Seca black sage; 7-9, 14-24

S. microphylla; red canyon sage; 7-11, 13-24

S. spathacea; hummingbird sage; 7-9, 14-24

Santolina chamaecyparissus; lavender cotton; 2-4, 7-11, 13-24

S. 'Lemon Queen'; Lemon Queen santolina; 2, 3A, 4, 7-11, 13-24

S. 'Little Nicky'; Little Nicky santolina; 2, 3A, 4, 7-11, 13-24

S. rosmarinifolia; green santolina; 3A, 4, 7-9, 14-24

Sedum acre; common stonecrop; 1A-3A, 7-11, 14-24

S. album; white stonecrop; 1A-3A, 7-11, 14-24

S. adolphii; coppertone sedum; 14-24

S. dasyphyllum; Corsican stonecrop; 2A, 2B, 3A, 7-11, 14-24

S. palmeri; Palmer's sedum; 2A, 2B, 3A, 7-11, 14-24

S. × rubrotinctum; Christmas cheer; 8, 9, 14-24

S. rupestre 'Angelina'; Angelina stonecrop; 2A, 2B, 3A, 7-11, 14-24

S. spathulifolium; Pacific stonecrop; 2A, 2B, 3A, 7-9, 14-24

S. spurium; two-row stonecrop; 1A-3A, 7-10, 14-24

S. stefco; stonecrop; 1A-3A, 7-11, 14-24

Sempervivum (all); houseleek; 2, 3A, 4, 7-11, 14-24

Senecio cylindricus; narrow-leaf chalksticks; 16, 17, 21, 24

S. mandraliscae; blue chalksticks; 13, 16, 17, 21, 24

S. serpens; little blue chalksticks; 16, 17, 21, 24

Sesleria 'Greenlee's Hybrid'; Greenlee's Hybrid moor grass; 4, 7-11, 13-24

S. autumnalis; autumn moor grass; 4, 7-11, 13-24

S. caerulea; blue moor grass; 7-11, 13-24

S. californica; California goldenrod; 1A-4, 7-11, 13-24

S. canadensis ssp. *elongata;* Canada goldenrod; 1A-4, 7-11, 13-24

Sphaeralcea ambigua; apricot mallow; 3A, 7-11, 13-24

S. ambigua var. *rosacea;* pink mallow; 10, 11, 13, 18-24

S. philippiana; trailing mallow; 7-9, 13-24

Sporobolus (all); dropseed; 1A-4, 7-11, 13-24

Stipa gigantea; giant feather grass; 7-9, 14-24

Teucrium chamaedrys; wall germander; 2, 3A, 4, 7-11, 13-24

T. fruticans; bush germander; 4, 7-11, 13-24

T. majoricum; fruity germander; 7-9, 14-24

T. marum; cat thyme; 3A, 4, 7-9, 14-24

Thymus (all); thyme; 1A-3A, 7-11, 14-24

Tulbaghia violacea; society garlic; 13-24

Verbena bonariensis; purple top; 8-11, 13-24

V. gooddingii; Goodding's verbena; 7-11, 13-24

V. lilacina; Cedros Island verbena; 13-24

V. rigida; vervain; 3A, 4, 7-11, 13-24

Yucca baccata var. *baccata;* banana yucca; 1A-3A, 7, 9-11, 13-14, 18-24

Y. filamentosa; Adam's needle; 1A-3A, 4, 7-11, 13-24

Y. nana; dwarf yucca; 1A-3A, 4, 7-11, 13-24

Y. recurvifolia; soft-leaf yucca; 7-10, 13-24

Zauschneria (all); California fuchsia; 4, 7-11, 13-24

References and Suggested Readings

The following references and suggested readings are grouped into categories to aid readers in finding additional information. Resources included under General California Gardening apply to many sections of the book. Some of the following titles were used in researching more than one section of the book, but each reference is only listed once.

GENERAL CALIFORNIA GARDENING

Asakawa, Bruce, Sharon Asakawa, and Eric Asakawa. 2005. *California Gardening Rhythms: What to do each season to have a beautiful garden all year.* Nashville, TN: Cool Springs Press.

Bornstein, Carol, David Fross, and Bart O'Brien. 2005. *California Native Plants for the Garden.* Los Olivos, CA: Cachuma Press.

Brenzel, Kathleen Norris, ed. 2001. *Sunset Western Garden Book,* 8th ed. Menlo Park, CA: Sunset Publishing.

Chatto, Beth. 1988, rev. ed. *The Dry Garden.* London: Orion

Dell, Owen. 2009. *Sustainable Landscaping for Dummies.* Hoboken, NJ: Wiley Publishing.

Filippi, Olivier. 2008. *The Dry Garden Handbook: Plants and Practices for a Changing Climate.* New York: Thames & Hudson.

Gildemeister, Heidi. 2004. *Gardening the Mediterranean Way: Practical Solutions for Summer Dry Climates.* New York: Thames and Hudson.

Keator, Glenn and Alrie Middlebrook. 2007. *Designing California Native Gardens.* Berkeley and Los Angeles: University of California Press.

Perry, Robert C. 2010. *Landscape Plants for California Gardens.* Claremont, CA: Land Design Publishing.

Pittenger, Dennis R., ed. 2002. *California Master Gardener Handbook.* University of California, Agriculture and Natural Resources, Publication #3382.

Smaus, Robert. 1996. *52 Weeks in the California Garden.* Los Angeles: Los Angeles Times Syndicate.

Smith, M. Nevin. 2006. *Native Treasures: Gardening with the Plants of California.* Berkeley and Los Angeles: University of California Press.

Welsh, Pat. 1992. *Pat Welsh's Southern California Gardening: A Month-by-Month Guide.* San Francisco: Chronicle Books.

INTRODUCTION

Carson, Rachel. 1962. *Silent Spring.* New York: Houghton Mifflin.

Downing, Andrew Jackson. 1841. *Treatise on the Theory and Practice of Landscape Gardening.* New York: G.P. Putnam, London: Longman, Brown, Green & Longmans.

Pollan, Michael. 1991. *Second Nature: A Gardener's Education.* New York: Atlantic Monthly Press.

Reisner, Marc. 1986. *Cadillac Desert: The American West and Its Disappearing Water.* New York: Viking.

Scott, Frank J. 1870. *The Art of Beautifying Suburban Home Grounds.* New York: John B. Alden.

Steinberg, Ted. 2006. American Green: *The Obsessive Quest for the Perfect Lawn.* New York: W.W. Norton.

UC Irvine Today. 2010. Urban 'green' spaces may contribute to global warming, UCI study finds. January 19. http://www.today.uci.edu/news/2010/01/nr_turfgrass_100119.html

Chapter One
GARDEN DESIGNS FOR LAWN REPLACEMENT

Greenswards

Bormann, F. Herbert, Diana Balmori, and Gordon T. Geballe. 2001. *Redesigning the American Lawn: A Search for Environmental Harmony,* 2nd ed. New Haven and London: Yale University Press.

California Native Grasslands Association website. www.cnga.org

Green, Robert L., Brent D. Barnes, James H. Baird, Adam Lukaszewski, and Steven B. Ries. 2009. Evaluation of Cool-season Turfgrasses under Deficit Irrigation. Paper presented at the UC Riverside regional seminar, September 17, 2009.

Meadow Gardens

Bachrach, Julia Sniderman. Jens Jensen: Friend of the Native Landscape, *Chicago Wilderness Magazine.* Spring 2001. http://chicagowildernessmag.org/issues/spring2001/jensjensen.html

Darke, Rick. 2007. *The Encyclopedia of Grasses for Livable Landscapes.* Portland, OR: Timber Press.

Daniels, Stevie, guest editor. 1999. *Easy Lawns – Low Maintenance Native Grasses for Gardeners Everywhere.* Brooklyn Botanic Garden Handbook #160.

Daniels, Stevie. 1995. *The Wild Lawn Handbook: Alternatives to the Traditional Front Lawn.* New York: Macmillan.

Greenlee, John. 2009. *The American Meadow Garden.* Portland, OR: Timber Press.

Kingsbury, Noel. 2003. *Natural Gardening in Small Spaces.* Portland, OR: Timber Press.

Martin, Laura. 1990. *The Wildflower Meadow Book,* 2nd ed. Chester, CT: Globe Pequot Press.

Phillips, Judith. 1995. *Natural by Design: Beauty and Balance in Southwest Gardens.* Santa Fe: Museum of New Mexico Press.

Rock Gardens

Beckett, Kenneth, ed. 1993. *Alpine Garden Society Encyclopaedia of Alpines.* Two volumes. Pershore, Worcestershire, UK: AGS Publications Limited.

Chatto, Beth. 2000. *Beth Chatto's Gravel Garden: Drought-resistant Planting Through the Year.* New York: Viking Studio.

McGary, Jane, ed. 1996. *Rock Garden Plants of North America: An Anthology from the Bulletin of the North American Rock Garden Society.* Portland, OR: Timber Press, in association with the North American Rock Garden Society.

McGary, Jane, ed. 2001. *Bulbs of North America.* Portland, OR: Timber Press, in association with the North American Rock Garden Society.

McGary, Jane, ed. 2003. *Rock Garden Design and Construction.* Portland, OR: Timber Press, in association with the North American Rock Garden Society.

Schenk, George. 1964. *How to Plan, Establish, and Maintain Rock Gardens.* Menlo Park, CA: Sunset Books, Lane Book Company,

Symons-Jeune, B. H. B. 1936. *Natural Rock Gardening,* 2nd ed. New York: Charles Scribner's Sons; London: Country Life Ltd.

Thomas, Graham Stuart. 1989. *The Rock Garden and its Plants: From Grotto to Alpine House.* Portland, OR: Saga Press/Timber Press.

Succulent Gardens

Baldwin, Debra Lee. 2007. *Designing with Succulents.* Portland, OR: Timber Press.

Cactus and Succulent Society of America, Inc. 1927 to date. *Cactus and Succulent Journal.* Pahrump, NV: Cactus and Succulent Society of America, Inc.

Eggli, Urs, ed. 2003. *Illustrated Handbook of Succulent Plants: Crassulaceae.* New York: Springer.

Folsom, Debra Brown, John N. Trager, James Folsom, Joe Clements, and Nancy Scott. 1995. *Dry Climate Gardening with Succulents.* New York: Knopf Publishing Group, Pantheon Books.

Gentry, Howard Scott. 1982. *Agaves of Continental North America.* Tucson: University of Arizona Press.

Ingram, Stephen. 2008. *Cacti, Agaves, and Yuccas of California and Nevada.* Los Olivos, CA: Cachuma Press.

Irish, Mary and Gary Irish. 2000. *Agaves, Yuccas and Related Plants, a Gardener's Guide.* Portland, OR: Timber Press.

Kelaidis, Gwen Moore. 2008. *Hardy Succulents: Tough Plants for Every Climate.* North Adams, MA: Storey Publishing.

Rowley, Gordon. 2003. *Crassula: A Grower's Guide.* Italy: Cactus & Co.

Schulz, Lorraine and Attila Kapitany. 2005. *Echeveria Cultivars.* Teesdale, Victoria, Australia: Schulz Publishing.

Schulz, Rudolf. 2007. *Aeonium in Habitat and Cultivation.* San Bruno, CA: Schulz Publishing.

Walther, Eric. 1972. *Echeveria.* San Francisco: California Academy of Sciences.

Carpet and Tapestry Gardens

Beck, Beatrice M. 1990. *Drought Tolerant Planting Bibliography.* Technical Report #6. Claremont, CA: Rancho Santa Ana Botanic Garden.

Citron, Joan, ed. 2000. *Selected Plants for Southern California Gardens.* Los Angeles: Southern California Horticultural Society.

Dallman, Peter R. 1998. *Plant Life in the World's Mediterranean Climates: California, Chile, South Africa, Australia, and the Mediterranean Basin.* Sacramento: California Native Plant Society, Berkeley and Los Angeles: University of California Press.

Duffield, Mary Rose, and Warren Jones. 2001. *Plants for Dry Climates: How to Select, Grow, and Enjoy.* Cambridge, MA: Perseus Books Group.

Harlow, Nora, ed. 2004. *Plants and Landscapes for Summer-Dry Climates of the San Francisco Bay Region.* Oakland, CA: East Bay Municipal Utility District.

Hoyt, Roland Stewart. 1978. *Ornamental Plants for Subtropical Regions.* Anaheim, CA: Livingston Press.

Jones, Warren, and Charles Sacamano. 2000. *Landscape Plants for Dry Regions.* Tucson, AZ: Fisher Books.

Riedel, Peter. 1957. *Plants for Extra-Tropical Regions.* Arcadia, CA: California Arboretum Foundation.

Kitchen Gardens

Bowe, Patrick. 1996. *The Complete Kitchen Garden.* New York: Macmillan.

California Department of Housing and Community Development. 2009. Nonpotable Water Reuse Systems. www.hcd.ca.gov/codes/shl/Preface_ET_Emergency_Graywater.pdf

Creasy, Rosalind. 1982. *The Complete Book of Edible Landscaping.* San Francisco: Sierra Club.

Flores, Heather C. 2006. *Food Not Lawns.* White River Junction, VT: Chelsea Green Publishing Company.

Haeg, Fritz. 2008. *Edible Estates: Attack on the Front Lawn.* New York: Metropolis Books.

Schinz, Marina. 1985. *Visions of Paradise: Themes and Variations on the Garden.* New York: Steward, Tabori and Chang.

Green Roofs

Beattie, D. 2003. Native and ornamental plant survival research. In *Greening Rooftops for Sustainable Communities,* Proceedings of the First North American Green Roofs Conference, Chicago, May 2003.

Toronto: The Cardinal Group.

Dunnett, N. and N. Kingsbury. 2004. *Planting Green Roofs and Living Walls.* Portland, OR: Timber Press.

Green Roofs for Healthy Cities. 2004. Participant Manual for Green Roof Design 101, Introductory Course. Toronto: The Cardinal Group.

Osmundson, Theodore. 1999. *Roof Gardens: History, Design, and Construction.* New York: W.W. Norton and Company.

Snodgrass, Edmund and Lucie. 2006. *Green Roof Plants.* Portland, OR: Timber Press.

Stephenson, R. 1994. *Sedum: Cultivated Stonecrops.* Portland, OR: Timber Press.

Werthmann, Christian. 2007. *Green Roof – A Case Study.* New York: Princeton Architectural Press.

Chapter Two
HOW TO MANAGE, REDUCE, OR REMOVE YOUR LAWN

Bio-Integral Resource Center. 1987. Least-toxic Lawn Management; a BIRC reprint. Berkeley: Bio-Integral Resource Center.

Brookes, John. 1984. *The Garden Book.* New York: Crown Publishers.

Dickey, Phillip. Removing a Lawn Without Herbicides. PDF accessed at http://watoxics.org Seattle: Washington Toxics Coalition.

Duhigg, Charles. Debating How Much Weed Killer is Safe in Your Water Glass. New York Times, August 23, 2009. http://www.nytimes.com/2009/08/us/23water.html

Ellis, Barbara, W. 2007. *Covering Ground.* North Adams, MA: Storey Publishing

Environmental Protection Agency. 2004. Healthy Lawn, Healthy Environment. Washington, D.C.: U.S. Environmental Protection Agency. http://www.epa.gov/oppfead1/Publications/lawncare.pdf

Hagen, Bruce W., Barrie D. Coate, and Keith Oldham.

1991. *Compatible Plants Under and Around Oaks.* Oakland: California Oak Foundation.

Johnson, Hugh. 1979. *Principles of Gardening.* New York: Simon and Shuster.

Lanza, Patricia. 1998. *Lasagna Gardening: A New Layering System for Bountiful Gardens: No Digging, No Tilling, No Weeding, No Kidding!* Emmaus, PA: Rodale Books.

Lanza, Patricia. 2002. *Lasagna Gardening for Small Spaces: A Layering System for Big Results in Small Gardens and Containers.* Emmaus, PA: Rodale Books.

Lanza, Patricia. 2004. *Lasagna Gardening with Herbs: Enjoy Fresh Flavor, Fragrance, and Beauty with No Digging, No Tilling, No Weeding, No Kidding!* Emmaus, PA: Rodale Books.

Lawn Reform Coalition. http://www.lawnreform.org

Mine-Engineer.Com. Cement, How It is Produced. http://www.mine-engineer.com/mining/cement.htm

Power, Nancy G. 1995. *The Gardens of California: Four Centuries of Design from Mission to Modern.* New York: Clarkson N. Potter.

SafeLawns.org website. www.safelawns.org

Schmetterling, David. How to Remove a Lawn. Montana Wildlife Gardener, February 5, 2009. http://montanawildlifegardener.blogspot.com/2009/02/how-to-remove-lawn.html

Thompson, J. William and Kim Sorvig. 2000. *Sustainable Landscape Construction.* Washington, D.C.: Island Press.

Tukey, Paul. 2007. *The Organic Lawn Care Manual: A Natural, Low-Maintenance System for a Beautiful, Safe Lawn.* North Adams, MA: Storey Publishing.

Chapter Three
PLANT PROFILES

See references and suggested readings for General California Gardening and Chapter One: Garden Designs for Lawn Replacement.

SCIENTIFIC NAMES FOR NON-FEATURED PLANTS

annual rye grass, *Poa annua*
'Bella' bluegrass, *Poa pretensis*
Bermuda buttercup, *Oxalis pes-caprae*
Bermuda grass, *Cynodon dactylon*
bindweed, *Convolvulus arvensis*
bluebeard, *Caryopteris × clandonensis*
bur clover, *Medicago polymorpha*
elegant clarkia, *Clarkia unguiculata*
Flora Dwarf Bermuda grass, *Cynodon* 'Flora Dwarf'
Kentucky bluegrass, *Poa pratensis*

Kikuyu grass, *Pennisetum clandestinum*
lemonade berry, *Rhus integrifolia*
Mini Verde Bermuda grass, *Cynodon* 'Mini Verde'
nutsedges, *Cyperus esculentus, C. rotundus*
shrubby monkeyflower, *Mimulus aurantiacus*
St. Augustine grass, *Stenotaphrum secundatum*
sweetclover, *Melilotus* species
tall fescue, *Festuca arundinacea*
thread-leaf agave, *Agave filifera*
vetch, *Vicia* species

Index to Common and Scientific Plant Names

Garden Design Credits

Most gardens are the products of collaboration. A variety of professionals, including landscape architects and contractors, garden designers, nursery owners, and other consultants, may play a key role in helping a homeowner or renter create and install a garden. While the gardens shown in this book reflect the work of many individuals, designs that are principally the creation of a homeowner or renter are not included among these credits. The following list attempts to provide the names of those professionals whose work was crucial to the *design* of a particular landscape. You may see a garden in this book that should have been credited to a particular professional or firm. If so, please let us know, and we will, with permission, add their name to the following list in a future printing of *Reimagining the California Lawn.* In addition to the designers who are listed here, we appreciate all the gardeners who have already reimagined their lawns by planting beautiful, water-efficient landscapes.

—John Evarts and Marjorie Popper

Michael Barry: vi; 113 upper right
Bent Grass Landscape Architecture: 65 left
Joan S. Bolton/Santa Barbara Garden Designs: 49 bottom right; 53 bottom
Carol Bornstein: 7 top right; 12 right
Gudrun Bortman: 126 left; 127 bottom
Jessica Bortman: 59 bottom
Jennifer Carlson: 38
Andrea Cochran Landscape Architecture: 40 bottom
Rosalind Creasy: 9 top right; 35 (both); 39
Stephanie Curtis/Curtis Horticulture, Inc.: 12 bottom left
Owen Dell and Associates: 125 top right
Designs With Nature: 20 right
Greg Donovan: 15 top left; 31 top; 46 right; 79 upper right; 106 bottom left and right; 108 top right; 135 left
Puck Erickson/Arcadia Studio: 4; 25 top and bottom; 48 top; 50; 58 bottom right; 64 right; 101 top left
Virginia Feibusch: 27 top
Jenny Fleming: 16 left
Gary Fredricks Landscape Design: 36 right
David and Rainie Fross: front cover, upper right; ii; 16 right; 42 bottom; 68 right
Katherine Greenberg: 32 bottom left; 49 upper right

Isabelle Greene: 20 left; 67 upper left; 69 right; 77 left
John Greenlee: 10 top; 13; 15 right
Dan Horgan: 19 bottom; 21 right; 58 left
Jack Miles Kiesel: 33 top right
Landscapes by Davids: 56
Lutsko Associates: 12 right; 14 both; 17 bottom right; 132
Sherry Merciari Design: 27 bottom
Donald Ramsey: 59 bottom
Mary Reid: front cover, lower right; 154 (same photo)
Robin Sherill Landscape Architect: 51 top
Diana Stratton: 37 (both)
Chuck Stophcard: 17 left; 44
Suding Design: 7 bottom right; 29; 77 right
SWA Group: 41
Cynthia Tanyan: 40 top
Bernard Trainor and Associates: 22 left
Susan Van Atta: 42 top
Christopher and Barbara Warnock: 36 bottom left
Wynne Wilson/Terra Design: 32 right; 55 bottom
Gabriela Yariv Landscape Design: 19 top; 23 left; 28 bottom
Zaragoza Landscape Management: 6 right

ACKNOWLEDGMENTS

We could not have completed *Reimagining the California Lawn* without the generous support and counsel of numerous friends and colleagues. They shared many valuable ideas, created a number of the gardens found in the book, and spurred us to the finish line with their all too common question, "When will the lawn book be published?"

We thank John Evarts and Marjorie Popper for taking another plunge into the risky world of publishing and for shepherding the project to completion. We would also like to thank Katey O'Neill, who designed this book, and Sue Irwin and Marjorie Lakin Erickson, who proofread the manuscript.

We are indebted to the following people whose thoughtful reviews improved our manuscript: Randy Baldwin, Rainie Fross, Rob Lane, M. Nevin Smith, John Trager, and Don Walker.

The insights and expertise of many individuals helped this book take shape and made it easier to write: David Akers, Joan Ariel, Fred Ballerini, Michael Barry, Michael Benedict, Lilla Burgess, Susan Chamberlin, Betsy Clebsch, Cort Conley, Mike Curto, Rick Darke, Owen Dell, Barbara Eisenstein, Tom Eltzroth, Olivier Filippi, Blair Fross, Tim Fross, Lorrae Fuentes, Billy Goodnick, John Greenlee, Richard Hayden, Virginia Hayes, Susan Jett, Robert Keeffe, Sandra Landers, Neil Lucas, Roger Raiche, Bernard Trainor, Maury Treman, Richard Turner, and Ellen Zagory. Additional thanks go to the staff of Native Sons Wholesale Nursery and the horticulture staff at Rancho Santa Ana Botanic Garden and Santa Barbara Botanic Garden.

Finally, we thank the gardeners, horticulturists, landscape contractors, designers, and property owners who are working to make California gardens and landscapes responsibly connected to the land.

—Carol Bornstein, David Fross, Bart O'Brien